MORTAL CHOICES

MORTAL CHOICES

Bioethics in Today's World

RUTH MACKLIN

PANTHEON BOOKS NEW YORK

All rights reserved under International and Pan-American Copyright Conventions. Published in the United States by Pantheon Books, a division of Random House, Inc., New York, and simultaneously in Canada by Random House of Canada Limited, Toronto.

Grateful acknowledgment is made to the following for permission to reprint or adapt from previously published material: The Hastings Center: Excerpt from *Who Speaks for the Child*, edited by Willard Gaylin and Ruth Macklin. Reprinted by permission of the Hastings Center. Humana Press: Adaptation of portions of the essay, "Ethical Theory and Applied Ethics: A Reply to the Skeptics," by Ruth Macklin, to appear in *Clinical Ethics: The Nature of Applied Ethics in Medicine*, edited by Hoffmaster, Friedman, and Fraser, forthcoming. Reprinted by permission of Humana Press, Inc. Prentice-Hall: Adaptation of excerpts from *Moral Problems in Medicine*, 2/E, by Gorovitz, Macklin, Janeton, O'Connor, and Sherwin. Reprinted by permission of Prentice-Hall, Inc.

Library of Congress Cataloging-in-Publication Data
Macklin, Ruth, 1938–
Mortal choices.
Bibliography: p.
1. Medical ethics.   2. Bioethics.   I. Title.
[DNLM: 1. Bioethics.   2. Ethics, Medical.   W 50 MI58m]
R724.MI614   1987   174'.2   86-42970
ISBN 0-394-55902-9

Manufactured in the United States of America
FIRST EDITION

BOOK DESIGN BY QUINN HALL

For Jerome

Contents

Acknowledgments

THIS BOOK IS AN OUTGROWTH of my work in clinical ethics at Albert Einstein College of Medicine and its affiliated hospitals. Over the years, I have learned a great deal from my colleagues at the medical center—physicians, nurses, social workers, and other health professionals who shared their experiences and openly discussed their thoughts and feelings at our many conferences and consultations. The medical students whom I've had the good fortune to teach provided a rich source of material that helped shape my thinking about the issues addressed in the book. I owe a debt of gratitude to these colleagues and students, as well as to others outside my own medical center from whom I've profited in professional encounters and informal discussions.

My work in the hospital rarely brings me into direct contact with patients. Yet it is evident that I could not have written this book without an indirect knowledge of patients gained through my various activities in the clinical setting. Although all material is taken from actual cases, I have altered some characteristics of patients in order to protect their identity.

Some material in this book is adapted from articles previously published in *The Einstein Quarterly: Journal of Biology and Medicine*, the philosophy journal *Synthese*, the journal *Social Research*, and the *Bulletin of the American College of Surgeons*. I thank the editors of these journals for giving me the opportunity to explore some of the issues that are treated in this book. Several paragraphs in chapter 4 are adapted from my introduction to chapter 1 of *Moral Problems in Medicine*, second edition, edited by Samuel Gorovitz et al. (Englewood Cliffs, N.J.: Prentice-Hall, Inc., 1983). Part of chapter 8 appeared in "Return to the Best Interests of the Child," the final chapter of *Who Speaks for the Child?* edited by Willard Gaylin and Ruth Macklin (New York: Plenum Press, 1982), a book that was the product of a two-year project conducted at the Hastings Center while I was on the staff there. Portions of chapter 14 are taken from an essay entitled "Ethical Theory and Applied Ethics: A Reply to the Skeptics," to appear in *Clinical Ethics: The Nature of Applied Ethics in Medicine,* edited by Barry Hoffmaster, Benjamin Freedman, and Gwen Fraser (Clifton, N.J.: Humana Press, forthcoming). I am grateful to the publishers of these books for permission to use the material.

Special thanks go to those who made helpful comments and criticisms on earlier drafts of the manuscript: Frieda Chimacoff, Harry H. Gordon, Saul V. Moroff, Nancy Rhoden, and Jerome Washington. For her encouragement and enthusiastic support, which began before I had even started to write, I am grateful to Gail Hochman. The skills and insights of Wendy Goldwyn, my editor at Pantheon, were a great asset and I thank her for all her efforts. My thanks also to David Frederickson at Pantheon for his careful editorial work on the final version of the manuscript.

It is impossible to name or even to identify everyone whose ideas found their way into my thinking about the topics in this book. I express my gratitude to all of them for their contributions to bioethics in today's world.

—R.M.

MORTAL CHOICES

Ethical Dilemmas
in Medicine

A N EIGHTY-ONE-YEAR-OLD woman is admitted to the emergency room of City Hospital in distress. Her breathing is labored and the doctors diagnose bilateral pneumonia. While in the emergency room, she has a cardiac arrest. Physicians rush to resuscitate the patient, pounding on her chest, inserting lines and tubes, and begin an extensive course of antibiotic treatment. They transfer the woman to the intensive-care unit (ICU), where she remains for a month. She has a stormy history: placed on a respirator, then taken off, she remains stable for a while but soon suffers another cardiac arrest. After she is resuscitated, her condition begins to deteriorate, and after a month in the ICU it becomes clear that she has a bleak prognosis. Her pneumonia is not responding to therapy. She shows signs of malnutrition. She is suffering from heart failure as a result of her respiratory disease, and the malnutrition contributes to a worsening of her overall condition.

This case poses a dilemma of a sort that has grown common in today's practice of medicine: Who should make the critical decisions surrounding this patient's medical treatment plan? And how aggressively should she be treated—that is, how vigorously should medical procedures, drugs, and devices be applied? Family members brought the woman to the hospital emergency room, although she had been living alone and caring for herself in her own apartment. Doctors decide to transfer the patient from the ICU to the medical floor, believing that she would receive adequate care there. But nursing care on the medical floor is less intensive than in special-care units, and cardiac monitors are available only in the ICU. Everyone agrees that the patient is not getting as good care on the medical floor as she was receiving in the special-care unit, and physicians who have examined her agree that she probably won't survive this hospital stay.

As hard as it is to determine what is in this elderly patient's best interest, another factor complicates the decision-making problem: beds in the ICU are always scarce, and other patients in need of intensive care are awaiting transfer. Is it fair to remove patients already receiving intensive care to make way for others? Is it fair to others with greater need to be forced to wait for an available bed? How should the conflict be resolved between the medical needs of this patient, already in the ICU, and the equal or perhaps greater needs of other patients?

ANOTHER PATIENT, a twenty-eight-year-old man diagnosed as having chronic schizophrenia, is transferred to City Hospital from one of the state mental facilities. His family cannot be located. The patient is suffering from kidney failure, and the physicians recommend treatment with the artificial kidney, or dialysis machine, which cleanses the blood in a manner similar to biological kidneys. The patient refuses dialysis. Perhaps because of his mental illness he does not fully comprehend the extent of his medical condition and the need for treatment, and the physicians are left to deliberate about what to do.

Patients have a right to *refuse* medical treatments if they have the mental capacity to grant informed *consent*—permission for medical personnel to perform procedures—but does a schizophrenic person possess that mental capacity? Is it acceptable to coerce a person— whether he is mentally ill or not—into accepting a life-preserving therapy? Physicians decide to act on the side of life, and obtain a court order to perform the procedure in spite of the patient's objection. The man is admitted to the medical service of the hospital, where he becomes disruptive. He pulls out intravenous lines, threatens and then assaults an intern, verbally abuses the nurses and other patients, and requires heavy sedation before dialysis can be performed. Even once the regular treatments are begun, the man remains belligerent, disruptive, and uncooperative. Dialysis patients must adhere to a strict diet, but this patient sneaks down to the hospital lobby and begs for change, with which he buys potato chips and soft drinks from vending machines.

The dilemma in this case: Should this patient continue to be treated despite his resistance to dialysis and his disruptive, violent behavior? Does he have a right to treatment, in spite of his behavior, because he lacks the mental capacity to decide for himself and to behave appropriately in the hospital? Who ought to make decisions about his medical care? How can his "best interest" be determined?

THE TRAGEDY OF GIVING BIRTH to a baby with mental or physical defects is feared by most prospective parents. In earlier eras, many such tragedies would have been played out in nature's way: unable to survive, infants born very prematurely and newborns with severe, life-threatening birth defects died an early, natural death, and were mourned by their grieving parents. Today, however, infants with multiple handicaps and those with very low birthweight can often be saved, a consequence of dramatic advances in the newly developed pediatric specialty of neonatology, devoted to the care and treatment of newborns. But saving the lives of such infants does not ensure that they will be physically and mentally normal. Decisions need to be made about when—if ever—an infant's future quality of life will be so low as to warrant not taking aggressive measures to preserve its life at this early stage. The burden of making those decisions falls on medical caregivers, as well as on the baby's parents.

An infant with spina bifida, a condition of the spinal cord resulting from faulty embryological development, is born at a community hospital and rushed to the neonatal intensive-care unit of University Hospital as soon as its medical condition is diagnosed. There the baby is placed on a ventilator, hooked up to tubes and monitors, and observed carefully by skilled nurses in the unit, while awaiting the critical decisions by physicians and family about how vigorously to treat. This baby's condition is characterized by a protruding sac filled with cerebrospinal fluid and containing a defective spinal cord, called a meningomyelocele. Children with this birth defect are paralyzed below the level on the back where the lesion is located, and cannot control bladder or bowels. A common complication is an accumulation of excess fluid in the brain (hydrocephalus), since cerebrospinal fluid cannot circulate normally. Mental retardation can be avoided or lessened in some cases by inserting a shunt at the base of the skull to drain off the fluid that is exerting pressure on the brain.

This infant has one of the more severe cases of spina bifida. The lesion is high up on the spinal cord, so paraplegia is certain. The child will never be able to walk. Hydrocephalus is also present, so a decision must be made about treatment. The neonatologist is a specially trained pediatrician, dedicated to saving the lives of infants but sensitive to the concerns expressed by the parents of imperiled newborns. She recommends two therapeutic procedures: inserting the shunt to drain the fluid and lessen the chance of further brain damage; and closing the spinal defect in order to prevent infection and additional rapid loss of neurologic function. The parents, distraught and angry at the birth of a severely damaged baby, refuse both procedures. They expected a normal infant. They feel they can't cope with a mentally retarded child. The wife is employed, partly for financial reasons, but also because she has chosen to pursue a career as well as motherhood. The couple say they cannot afford the medical treatments that would continue to be necessary for a child afflicted with the most severe form of spina bifida: repeated efforts to correct orthopedic problems, revisions of the shunt, treatment of possible kidney problems, and other procedures.

The neonatologist faces a dilemma. Should she respect the parents' wishes—which seem to her rather selfish—and omit these surgical procedures, making the infant comfortable but not undertaking aggressive means to preserve its life? Should she attempt to override the parental refusal of treatment by seeking a court order to proceed with therapy despite the parents' objection? What is in this baby's best interest—a life compromised by severe physical and mental handicaps, or an early, painless death? Is this one of those cases where the quality of life is so poor as not to warrant medical treatment? Or is a life of any quality preferable to death when a patient is unable to participate in decisions about treatment? Who should speak for those incapable of speaking for themselves?

THESE CASES ARE NOT UNUSUAL in the hospitals where I work. They are brought up for discussion in "rounds," or teaching conferences with medical students and postgraduate trainees, in sessions where an ethics consultation has been requested, and at meetings of hospital ethics committees. Although physicians and others on the medical team have always discussed problematic cases, especially in teaching hospitals, what is new and different is my role in this process. I am not a doctor, nurse, social worker, psychiatrist, or member of the clergy—the traditional figures in the medical setting. I am a philosopher specializing in bioethics, an interdisciplinary field that has come into existence only in the past two decades.

The ethical questions raised by the three cases just described are typical of those addressed in bioethics: Is choosing continued life over certain death always the morally best decision? Should quality-of-life considerations be allowed to enter the picture, and if so, which standards should prevail and who should determine them? Who has the right to decide when patients or families and physicians disagree? And when should the law be brought in to override or circumvent decisions by patients or their families? Most cases in which these and other difficult ethical questions arise are problematic because they pose dilemmas—situations in which there is no clear right or wrong answer, but in which there is something to be said for both sides of the issue.

The cases just described might be termed "big ethics." The situations are dramatic, involving life-and-death decisions. They sometimes lead to the intrusion of the law, often in the form of precedent-setting court decisions. They attract media attention and, as a result, are now being discussed by an increasingly sophisticated public, more eager than in the past to participate in decisions about their own health care.

The cases in which I become involved do not often involve blatant wrongdoing or malevolent actions by physicians, nurses, or other health-care workers, though such episodes are not entirely unknown. But if no clear right or wrong answer can be found in response to ethical dilemmas in medical practice, how can a philosopher help? Just what is the role of the bioethicist—a metaphysician among physicians —in the day-to-day life of a busy academic medical center? I was surprised to discover just how often moral problems arise, confronting health-care workers who are ill prepared to deal with them. One contribution a philosopher can make is to identify the values that come into conflict, giving rise to ethical dilemmas, and to demonstrate what ethical principles are at play.

When medical decisions involve matters of life and death, the ethical considerations are obvious. But although it is apparent that such cases have significant moral dimensions, it is far from clear what the "right answer" is—or whether there even is a single right answer. In earlier eras, when medicine was about as likely to harm patients as to cure them or improve their condition, doctors rarely were confronted with life-and-death decisions. To be sure, the question of whether a physician should ever take steps to hasten a patient's death, in order to relieve intractable pain and lessen the agony of dying, probably goes back as far as does the practice of medicine. But it is only recently that scientific and technological advances have produced the remarkable medical capabilities we know today.

These advances have been a mixed blessing. The use of medical technology in all its forms causes undesired side effects and untoward consequences. These iatrogenic, or physician-caused, ailments are part of the price that must be paid for the larger number of beneficial consequences modern medicine brings to the sick or injured. The other price—no doubt unforeseen—is the creation of ethical dilemmas rarely if ever confronted in the past.

In most medical practice, few cases are of the "big ethics" sort, although they do occur regularly in acute-care hospitals. But ordinary, day-to-day situations in the hospital are also laden with ethical aspects. Because they are so pervasive, they may pass unnoticed. Because they are not life-and-death situations, they may be ignored. Not to belittle their importance, but to contrast them with the bigger, dramatic situations usually considered to be the province of bioethics and health law, non-life-and-death cases can be called "little ethics."

What sorts of cases fall under this heading? Probably the most common are those having to do with informing patients about their condition and gaining their consent for treatment. A classic example is a physician's decision not to tell a patient about the risks of a recommended procedure, lest the patient refuse the procedure. Withholding a diagnosis of terminal illness from a patient also involves disclosure— a recurrent theme in the area of "little ethics." This area deals with such behavior as withholding information from patients, as well as outright deception, which physicians often justify by appealing to the patient's own good or best interest. When a particular medical problem could be treated in more ways than one, many physicians choose the one they believe to be in the patient's best interest without consulting the patient. But who is the best judge of what is in a patient's interest?

No clear line separates "big ethics" from "little ethics." There is a continuum, a gradual shading from everyday moral problems of a non-life-and-death nature to the most dramatic occurrences that make headlines. But whether medical situations fall under one of the extremes or somewhere in between, all of us are likely to be involved at one time or another. A family lucky enough to escape having a baby with birth defects, with all the ethical decisions entailed by that tragedy, may still confront an agonizing situation at the other end of the life spectrum: the problem of making decisions on behalf of an elderly parent who can no longer decide for herself. What values—whose ethics—come into play? How can moral disagreement be resolved when parties to a dispute cannot come together?

Traditionally, doctors have considered medical decisions to be their prerogative, but much has happened in recent years to change their unquestioned authority. Change remains slow, however—and no wonder, given the centuries of medical practice in the Hippocratic tradition. Hippocrates is sometimes thought of as the father of medical ethics, and a paternalistic father he was indeed. He admonished physicians to perform their duties

> calmly and adroitly, concealing most things from the patient while you are attending to him. Give necessary orders with cheerfulness and sincerity, turning his attention away from what is being done to him; sometimes reprove sharply and emphatically, and sometimes comfort with solicitude and attention, revealing nothing of the patient's future or present condition.[1]

Hardly a prescription for honesty and openness in the physician-patient relationship!

No easy answers can be given to questions of values and ethics, nor can moral disputes be easily resolved. Some may think it best to leave such dilemmas to the law, allowing courts, or ultimately our legislatures, to decide them. But it is often remarked that the law is a blunt instrument, not very well suited to resolving such problems. What makes legal solutions better than ethical answers not derived from law? Whether laws are made by state legislatures or by Congress, the lawmakers are people, just like members of the public, drawing on their personal ethical views or their chosen religious perspectives. If the legal solutions are fashioned by courts, is their moral expertise any greater? Judges, after all, despite their legal knowledge of statutes and of precedents in the common law, are no wiser morally than the rest of us.

Courts have traditionally become involved when physicians seek to treat and a patient refuses the recommended therapy, or when parents refuse it for their child. Typically, the physician seeks a court order to authorize the treatment. But in the past decade or so, a new kind of situation has arisen. Patients who are being kept alive on respirators or other life-support mechanisms have expressed their desire to have the machinery withdrawn, but doctors or hospitals have been reluctant to do so. In some instances physicians are willing to comply with the patient's wish, or in the case of patients in a coma, with that of the family. But fearing a lawsuit by some other family member—or even worse, a charge of homicide brought by a zealous prosecutor—physicians have sought judicial solutions to their ethical quandaries.

A long line of cases involving the refusal of Jehovah's Witnesses to permit blood transfusions illustrates why doctors have traditionally gone to court. When death was the likely outcome if the patients didn't receive blood, judges have been reluctant to grant them the right to refuse. In a 1964 decision in Washington, D.C., a judge in the court of appeals, J. Skelly Wright, wrote that

> neither the principle that life and liberty are inalienable rights, nor the principle of liberty of religion, provides an easy answer to the question whether the state can prevent martyrdom. . . . The final, and compelling, reason for granting the emergency writ [to transfuse blood] was that a life hung in the balance. . . . I determined to act on the side of life.[2]

But another judge, in Chicago, came to quite the opposite conclusion in a 1965 Jehovah's Witness case:

> Even though we may consider appellant's beliefs unwise, foolish or ridiculous, in the absence of an overriding danger to society we may not permit interference . . . in the waning hours of her life for the sole purpose of compelling her to accept medical treatment forbidden by her religious principles and previously refused by her with full knowledge of the probable consequences. In the final analysis, what has happened here involves a judicial attempt to decide what course of action is best for a particular individual, notwithstanding that individual's contrary views based upon religious convictions. Such action cannot be constitutionally countenanced.[3]

Here, then, are the opinions of two judges, apparently in direct contradiction. It is tempting to conclude that the law can give little moral guidance in these matters, despite the importance of the judicial system in arriving at precedents in the common law. Both cases were decided at about the same time—a time when, both legally and ethically, changes were taking place in the way patients' rights were understood and officially recognized. Perhaps, then, since societal values were in transition, that uncertainty led to contradictory opinions by judges, whose decisions often reflect current social and moral values as well as preexisting legal precedents.

The contradiction may be only apparent, however. There is a subtle but significant difference between these two cases. In the second case, in which the patient's right to refuse transfusions was upheld, she had repeatedly informed her physician over a two-year period that her religious and medical convictions precluded her from receiving blood transfusions. Furthermore, both the patient and her husband had signed a document releasing the physician and the hospital from all civil liability that might result from failure to administer the recommended blood transfusions.

In the first case, by contrast, the patient was brought to the hospital by her husband for emergency care after losing two thirds of her body's blood supply from a ruptured ulcer. Judge Wright went to the patient's bedside and tried to communicate with her. The judge wrote: "The only audible reply I could hear was 'Against my will.' It was obvious that the woman was not in a mental condition to make a decision."[4] In his written opinion, Judge Wright also noted that if the hospital doctors let the patient die in the hospital bed, they would be exposing themselves and the hospital to the risk of civil and criminal liability.

Fear of legal liability frequently drives medical decision-making, thus contaminating the process by introducing considerations that are not patient-centered. Those worries may well have been justified in the case decided by Judge Wright, while no basis for such fears existed in the other case, because of the release signed by the patient and her husband. But these concerns have little to do with the ethical issues, or with the subtle but significant difference between these two cases.

That difference lies in the mental capacity of the two patients at the time they refused treatment. In the Chicago episode, the judge noted that "we find a competent adult who has steadfastly maintained her belief that acceptance of a blood transfusion is a violation of the law of God. Knowing full well the hazards involved, she has firmly opposed acceptance of such transfusions, notifying the doctor and hospital of her convictions and desires."[5] Judge Wright, however, took it to be obvious that the patient in his case was not in a mental condition to make a decision. To respect the autonomy of a competent patient is a moral requirement in the physician-patient relationship, a requirement only recently acknowledged and accepted by many doctors. However, the principle of autonomy has an important corollary: patients with diminished autonomy stand in need of protection. Such patients suffer an impairment in their capacity for self-rule, yet that capacity is not entirely lacking, as it would be in patients who are comatose. It would be unsound to accept at face value the initial treatment refusals of patients with diminished autonomy.

In both cases, physicians sought a court order to transfuse their Jehovah's Witness patients. In one case the judge authorized the transfusion, while the judge in the second case upheld the patient's right to refuse based on the constitutional guarantee of freedom of religion. This constitutional basis could be brought in only because the treatment refusal rested on the patient's religious convictions. A much more appropriate basis in law for treatment refusals is the doctrine of informed consent, a legal and ethical foundation for granting patients the right to full information and participation in decisions about their own treatment. Since the mid-1960s, when a religious basis for treatment refusals seemed to supply the only solid justification for allowing patients to decide to forgo a life-preserving treatment, a wider acknowledgement of patients' rights has emerged both in the common law and in legislative enactments. The right to refuse medical treatment is now recognized under the constitutional "right to privacy."

Yet the doctrine of informed consent, by now well entrenched in law and ethics, does not eliminate the moral problems inherent in decision-making. If anything, the need to disclose information to patients and obtain their voluntary, informed consent to treatment makes matters more complex and difficult. Among the most troubling features is the one that arose in the case decided by Judge Wright: what to do about patients of uncertain mental capacity, those who suffer from diminished autonomy.

While parents are presumed to act in their children's best interest, they do not always do so. It is true, of course, that Jehovah's Witness parents hold a view about what is in their child's best interest that is different from the view of those who do not accept the tenets of that religion. In general, the difficulty of arriving at objective criteria for determining what is in the best interest of anyone other than oneself is formidable. Yet for those who do not share the conviction of Jehovah's Witnesses that acceptance of blood transfusions results in eternal damnation, it is a simple matter to balance the risks and benefits of that medical procedure, and to conclude that the benefits of continued life and health far outweigh the minimal risks associated with blood transfusions.

In this clash of values—the conflict between respecting family autonomy and acting in the best medical interest of the child who is a patient—the moral weight lies on the side of preserving life and health. In other instances, where the risks of medical treatment are greater and the benefits less certain, that moral conclusion would not be so compelling. There are no absolute values, either in medicine or anywhere else in human activities. It is that feature of our moral life that makes dilemmas so frequent and so difficult to resolve. The situation of the Jehovah's Witness and blood transfusions poses a conflict of values both for the patient and for the physician.

For the patient the conflict is between prolonging life here on earth by accepting a blood transfusion, and choosing eternal life after death without damnation. Jehovah's Witnesses rest their belief on passages in the Old and New Testaments that prohibit the "eating" of blood. The religion interprets transfusions as an instance of "eating" blood, a position that rests on the medical definition of blood transfusions as a form of alimentation, formulated when the technique was first developed early in this century. Witnesses who accept blood transfusions suffer the consequence of being "cut off." Although they cherish life here on earth, they believe they are just passing through, and place a higher value on eternal life. Even those of us who do not share the belief in those metaphysical facts should be able to weigh the values in conflict from the Jehovah's Witness perspective: a choice between the remaining years of mortal life versus an eternity of afterlife without damnation.

For the physician the conflict is between respecting the patient's autonomy, the right to refuse a recommended medical treatment, and striving to promote the patient's best (medical) interest. Everything in a physician's training propels him in the direction of prolonging life, curing disease, and bringing about the best possible outcome for the patient. But in these Jehovah's Witness cases, the "best outcome" is viewed quite differently by doctor and patient. The best medical outcome is not always the same as the outcome the patient prefers—a variance that underlies numerous conflicts between physician and patient.

Ironically, despite the increased attention given to ethics in medicine, the issues are growing more complex rather than less so—in part because these issues are now being debated openly before the public in our pluralistic society and thereby being transformed from largely private matters into concerns of public policy. Nowhere is this more evident than in the care and treatment of newborns with congenital anomalies, or birth defects. Spina bifida, with its accompanying problems, is one such anomaly, and Down's syndrome, which always includes mental retardation, is another.

Professional and growing public attention to the dilemmas inherent in making treatment decisions for imperiled newborns reached its peak in the early 1980s, with the birth of two infants with congenital defects who received nationwide attention in the news media. The first of these infants, who became known as "Baby Doe," was born in 1982 in Bloomington, Indiana, with Down's syndrome and a defect in the intestinal tract. The baby's parents refused to grant consent for surgery to repair the intestinal tract, and the Indiana courts upheld their right to make that decision. The second infant, called "Baby Jane Doe," was born in 1983 on Long Island, with spina bifida and other associated birth defects. After consultation with numerous health-care professionals and with their priest, the parents decided against an aggressive treatment plan for their infant. That decision was eventually upheld by the New York State courts. When the Reagan administration decided to intervene in what had traditionally been a private matter between physicians and families, by publishing federal regulations that established a hot line for reporting episodes of nontreatment of handicapped infants, a series of unprecedented legal and policy developments transformed the moral dilemma of how to treat infants with birth defects into a major public debate. The transformation of issues that were once handled in the privacy of the doctor-patient relationship into matters of public policy has been one of the hallmarks of the developing field of bioethics.

WHEN I REFLECT on how I came to work in this field, I can only conclude that it resulted from a happy coincidence of my personal commitment to moral matters, developments taking place in academic philosophy, and increasing public attention paid to ethical issues in medicine and the other professions. Initially, I did not choose to make a career in "applied ethics" in general, or bioethics in particular. No such fields existed either in name or in practice within "respectable" academic departments of philosophy, at least not in the late 1960s, when I received my Ph.D. degree. In fact, my areas of specialization in philosophy did not include ethics—even the theoretical variety— but focused on the philosophy of science, the philosophy of mind, and the theory of knowledge, or epistemology.

In the early 1970s, along with several colleagues in the Department of Philosophy at Case Western Reserve University in Cleveland, I became involved with a program to develop a curriculum in medical ethics, as we called it then. This was a pioneering effort, since "applied ethics" was virtually unknown at the time within mainstream philosophy departments. We received support from the National Endowment for the Humanities, which launched a three-year study called Moral Problems in Medicine. This program was directed at teaching undergraduate premedical and nursing students, as well as students in the medical and other professional schools of the university. But before long, the project expanded to include consultations and case conferences with physicians and other health-care workers.

It was with some apprehension that I accepted the first invitation to enter the hospital to discuss an ethical problem. A pediatrician, involved in a case in which Jehovah's Witness parents refused recommended blood transfusions for their child, asked me to join a panel and make a brief presentation to an assembled group of hospital staff. I knew little about the Jehovah's Witness religion, and nothing about the reasons for their refusal of blood transfusions. More worrisome than my ignorance of these facts, which could be rectified, was the likely reaction of physicians to an outsider intruding into their domain: what could an "ethicist" contribute when morally concerned physicians were in a quandary?

I balked at the use of the term "ethicist" in those early days, but have come to accept it in its new meaning, a meaning that conveys the role the professional bioethicist actually plays in the medical setting rather than the older sense of the term, denoting one who knows the morally right thing to do in every situation.

Other participants in this conference were the professor of pediatrics who had arranged the session, a law professor, and an elder from the Jehovah's Witness church. Having done the necessary research on the religion and its grounds for rejecting blood transfusions, in addition to studying the more general legal and ethical situation pertaining to treatment refusals by patients and families, I was able to mount an argument in support of physicians seeking to override the parents' refusal of life-preserving blood transfusions for their child. Yet I was uneasy with my conclusion.

That uneasiness stemmed from several factors. First was a reluctance to appear as a moral authority on an issue profoundly affecting the lives of others, and on matters on which reasonable people disagree. This, I came to realize, was an occupational hazard of my newly acquired role as a bioethicist. It would arise again and again. More and more, we who had ventured into the medical world were called upon to give advice and to construct moral arguments for or against treatment decisions.

A more worrisome consideration, one that continues to plague me when I'm called upon for consultations concerning treatment refusals, is that the moral conclusion I arrived at appeared to violate a presumption favoring the right of patients and families to self-determination in the medical setting. One of the several factors that contributed to the emergence of the field of bioethics in the first place was the recognition that physicians often left patients and families out of the decision-making process. The notion that doctors, with their medical expertise, know what is best for their patients has been the prevailing idea not only within the medical profession, but also among many patients. A philosophical concept introduced early in the bioethics conversation is *autonomy*, which can be defined rather simplistically as "self-rule." The term is usually intended to refer to the patient, but is often extended to cover the family in situations where patients are incapable of participating in their own treatment decisions. Such patients can be described as lacking the capacity for "self-rule," temporarily or permanently. Since one of the driving forces behind the bioethics movement has been the attempt to give patients a greater voice in their own medical care, I was troubled to find myself advocating a course of action in which physicians could override patient or family autonomy. As I soon realized, however, an important moral distinction exists between respecting the autonomy of patients who wish to refuse treatment for themselves, and recognizing the authority of family members to make treatment refusals on behalf of their child or another relative.

Another consideration that troubled me in that first hospital consultation was that the family's refusal of blood transfusions for their child was based on religious reasons. Toleration of religious preferences is one of the most cherished values in a free society, however much some individuals may criticize the religious precepts of their neighbors. Surely the freedom to practice one's chosen religion without interference by the government or other agencies should be a right granted to patients in the medical setting, or so it would seem.

What made it rather straightforward, in the end, for me to argue that physicians should seek a court order to override parental refusal of a blood transfusion for their child was the vulnerability of the patient. He was a minor, incapable of deciding for himself. I argued that the child of Jehovah's Witness parents should be given a chance to grow to adulthood, at which time he may then decide for himself whether to adopt the religion of his parents and refuse blood transfusions.

The dilemma posed by the Jehovah's Witness patient who refuses life-preserving blood transfusions has not diminished in the years since I began working in the field. Shortly after that first clinical case conference, I was invited to contribute to the *Encyclopedia of Bioethics,* a reference work then in preparation. One of the entries I contributed was an article entitled "Rights in Bioethics." As an illustration of the legal and moral right of the competent, adult patient to refuse treatment, I chose the Jehovah's Witness example. One prepublication reviewer of the encyclopedia, a philosopher who was highly regarded but knew little about the emerging field of bioethics, made a critical comment on my draft in the margin next to the Jehovah's Witness example: "A dubious sect," the reviewer wrote. Despite his expertise in traditional philosophy, including ethics, the reviewer was woefully ignorant of some crucial facts that give rise to ethical dilemmas in the medical context.

After my first hospital consultation on blood transfusions and Jehovah's Witnesses, I began to see what role a philosopher might play. I was cautious at first—after all, thoughtful, concerned medical practitioners were baffled by the dilemmas they confronted, so how could I give answers when they were in a quandary? But I realized that as a philosopher I could make a unique contribution: I could identify the ethical principles available to help reach a resolution, and I could show how those principles might provide a satisfactory conclusion when reasonable people disagree. I could also demonstrate how that approach might fail, and delineate the reasons for the failure of exalted ethical principles to settle a moral dilemma. I could formulate questions on the metalevel of analysis: Are there any "right answers," or is everything in this arena a matter for individual decisions and subjective moral viewpoints? How can a resolution be reached when moral principles themselves come into conflict? How can the choice of one principle over another be defended?

The role of the philosopher is to provide an ethical analysis. Even when no clear solution to a dilemma can be reached, the task of providing an ethical analysis remains important. It supplies a deeper understanding of the nature of moral conflict, and offers an objective frame of reference for those who must arrive at a decision in the face of uncertainty or disagreement. It may provide "ethical comfort" for physicians or others in a position of responsibility, since a well-constructed analysis shows that moral decisions are not mere matters of taste, like a preference for ice-cream flavors, nor should they be arbitrary choices, like the toss of a coin to decide which movie to see.

The ability to construct such an analysis is what distinguishes the philosopher from others who assist the health-care team, such as psychiatrists, social workers, and clergy. Psychiatrists have expertise in evaluating and counseling patients, and they can also provide psychological support for staff. Social workers are skilled in communicating with patients and in eliciting information about the "psychosocial" aspects of a case, information often critical for a successful outcome in the total care of the patient. Clergy are often described as providing pastoral care, which includes ministering to a patient's spiritual needs, but may also include the sort of counseling done by psychologists or psychiatrists for patients who exhibit no psychopathology but who have emotional needs. As important as these roles played by other professionals are in the hospital setting, they should not be confused with the special expertise in ethical analysis that the bioethicist has to offer.

Few cases in the medical arena involve clear rights and wrongs. Most are more ambiguous. But however clear or ambiguous the ethical situation, one thing should be perfectly obvious: the medical expertise of physicians does not automatically confer moral expertise on their decisions and actions. Any reflective, thoughtful person is potentially as good a decision-maker as any other. There are no moral experts, in medicine or anywhere else. Philosophers have expertise *about* ethics, in the sense that they are familiar with the leading treatises in moral philosophy and can identify ethical principles, showing which ones are in conflict in a dilemma. Philosophers are also good at reasoning, and therefore are able to detect fallacies, ambiguities, and logical errors better than those who have not acquired these skills. But those abilities do not amount to expertise *in* ethics, in the sense of having moral knowledge gained by intuition, insight, or some other means. Anyone can learn to think clearly and systematically about practical moral choices and adopt a framework for addressing them rationally. This does not mean we need to ignore moral emotions. Moral sentiments do play a role in our moral life, but they cannot be counted on as a sure guide to ethical conduct.

Applying
Moral Principles

A LTHOUGH THE FIELD of bioethics has matured in the years since I first entered a hospital to discuss the dilemma of Jehovah's Witness parents who refused blood transfusions for their child, this type of problem has not disappeared. My colleagues on a hospital ethics committee and I are currently drafting a policy for Jehovah's Witness patients who enter the hospital. The policy must address the dilemma posed by the adult, competent Jehovah's Witness patient who refuses blood, as well as those of the child of Jehovah's Witness parents, the patient with uncertain mental capacity such as the one whose case led Judge J. Skelly Wright to order the lifesaving transfusion, and the patient who is unconscious or otherwise clearly incapable of participating but whose family refuses on the patient's behalf.

Another category of patients that poses an ethical problem for physicians and hospital administrators is pregnant women. According to one moral view, pregnant women should be treated just like all other competent, adult patients—their autonomy should be respected and their right to refuse treatment honored. But another view holds that the rights of a pregnant woman are tempered by the existence of the developing life within her. In this view the pregnant woman has a strong moral obligation to the fetus, one she should not be allowed to shirk. In a series of ongoing developments, the moral standing of the fetus has come under constant scrutiny, and not only because the emotionally charged topic of abortion infects other areas of medical practice. Technological and scientific advances in medicine have also contributed to the confusion and to changing perceptions.

One example is the sonogram, which uses ultrasound waves to "see" the fetus in the womb and to detect any abnormalities in it. A couple expecting a baby can now view a sonographic image as their first "baby picture," which gives the fetus a personal identity. Another example lies in increased scientific knowledge about embryonic development and the awareness that maternal behavior such as smoking or drinking alcohol poses health hazards to the fetus. These and other developments create the need to rethink the moral rights and obligations of pregnant women, especially when caregivers in the hospital perceive a conflict between the rights of a pregnant woman and the interests of her fetus.

A subject that commanded great attention in the early 1970s, when my colleagues and I began to teach bioethics and to engage in teaching "rounds" in hospitals, was how to deal with the tragedy of infants born with mental and physical handicaps. The medical specialty of neonatology had only recently been established, and the dramatic capability of pediatricians to save lives and correct birth anomalies was impressive. But concurrently, a growing but undocumented perception was emerging that neonatologists were too aggressive in their efforts to save the lives of infants born very prematurely, pursued without the full participation of the anguished parents, and perhaps without sufficient regard to the quality of life of those infants whose biological survival they were able to ensure. Infants born so prematurely that their lungs are not fully developed often suffer severe lung damage from being kept on a ventilator for a long time. A considerable number are afflicted with neurologic damage that will leave them profoundly retarded. The presumption of family autonomy and the right of parents to help determine a treatment plan for their babies (which might include selective nontreatment) appeared to be violated by neonatal specialists zealously pursuing their art.

Yet at the same time, a disturbing phenomenon of the opposite sort came to light. Some physicians were allowing some babies in special-care nurseries to die, and were failing to perform surgery on others, in response to parental refusals of treatment. In one case, the father of the baby was a busy surgeon with three teenage children. The newborn was diagnosed as having microcephalus, an abnormally small head, and a defect in the formation of the anus. The father decided against surgery, and the infant died two days later.[1] Other cases were reported in which infants with Down's syndrome had other birth defects that could be easily corrected by surgery, but were not operated on because of parental refusal.[2] Still another child had meningomyelocele, hydrocephalus, and major abnormalities of every organ in the pelvis. The parents believed no treatment should be given, and the baby died at five days of age.[3] It became evident that although some neonatologists were applying their special skills without regard to parental wishes, others were acceding to those wishes perhaps too readily.

In conducting an ethical analysis of these complex issues, it is necessary to begin by clarifying concepts and making some critical distinctions. One such distinction identifies two different sorts of value questions: substantive moral questions and procedural ones.

Substantive questions are rooted in moral principles, most of which have their basis in philosophical ethical theories or in religious precepts. Substantive moral questions ask "What is the ethically right thing to do?" Is it ethically permissible to allow some infants to die, rather than make every effort to preserve their lives? What criteria should be used for selecting those babies whose quality of life is so low that it is not morally obligatory to save them? If it is morally permissible to allow some babies to die by not intervening aggressively, is it also morally permissible to hasten their death by active means? Of course, these substantive moral questions can be asked not only about infants, but about adults as well. In an effort to resolve the moral tension between respect for human life and the need to reduce pain and suffering, physicians, patients, and their families throughout the nation are raising such questions.

Issues surrounding the imperative to prolong life and the quest for criteria to define the elusive concept of "quality of life" are the most pressing but by no means the only substantive questions addressed in bioethics. Others focus on the ethics of disclosing information to patients, preserving confidentiality in the physician-patient relationship, assessing the risks versus the benefits of therapy or research maneuvers, and allocating scarce or expensive medical resources.

Procedural questions, despite their critical importance when decisions have to be made and actions taken, rarely have a theoretical basis. Procedural questions ask "Who should decide in morally troubling cases?" These questions pertain more to process than to substance. What procedure should a hospital use to arrive at decisions to withhold or withdraw life-preserving treatment? How should treatment refusals by patients be handled? How should patients' capacity to decide for themselves be assessed when their mental status is in doubt? And if they are found to be mentally incompetent, who should make decisions on their behalf? Is it necessary to go to court to have a guardian appointed for an elderly patient no longer capable of making decisions about medical treatment or aftercare? What should be the role of the family in deciding for patients suffering from senile dementia? And what about patients with no family at all, or those whose families are estranged or far away? May those adults presume to act on behalf of their relatives? These procedural questions often raise as much doubt and cause as much controversy in the clinical setting as the substantive questions. They may seem less weighty from a moral point of view, but that does not diminish their importance, or the need to find a satisfactory resolution when conflict occurs.

It is not uncommon for substantive and procedural questions to be lumped together in discussions about cases, but it is important to keep them distinct. Often, when a clear and relatively uncontroversial answer can be given to a substantive moral question, procedural questions either disappear and become irrelevant, or should be given a lower priority. To illustrate the point:

Mr. DiS., an eighty-two-year-old man who had been in good health all his life, was admitted to the hospital with unusual symptoms. His wife and middle-aged daughter accompanied him to the hospital and visited him regularly. After a full workup and numerous tests, cancer was discovered in the bowel. When Mrs. DiS. and her daughter were informed of the diagnosis, they were adamant in maintaining that the patient not be told. The daughter was insistent to the point of becoming strident, and she threatened the physicians with a lawsuit if they revealed the diagnosis to the patient. Since surgery to remove the cancerous portion of the bowel was a possibility, the doctors told the family that the patient would have to be informed so that he could grant consent for the surgery. To which the daughter replied that it wouldn't be necessary at all. She would grant consent for the surgery if physicians recommended that course of treatment, so her father needn't be informed about his condition, nor need he be troubled with having to sign a form to authorize the surgery.

Although that plan of action was entirely unacceptable to the physicians, as they recognized the moral and legal requirement that adult, mentally competent patients must grant informed consent to their own treatment, the recommendation for surgery was not yet definite. Intimidated by the patient's daughter, the young doctor in charge of the case was uncertain how to proceed. His encounters with Mr. DiS. became increasingly uncomfortable. Although the patient had never asked directly what was wrong with him, he became less communicative with the medical staff and with his family, and soon appeared depressed. The family, meanwhile, continued to visit regularly but sat in silence for hours in the patient's room. Conversation became stilted and forced, and the daughter remained adamant that her father not be told of his diagnosis.

The doctor asked himself whether he nonetheless had an obligation to disclose the diagnosis to Mr. DiS. Or did he owe a duty to the family to honor their wishes? More generally, he wondered, do patients have a right to know their diagnosis and prognosis, even when they do not ask explicitly? The doctor was pondering substantive moral questions, questions about rights, duties, and obligations in the medical setting. If clear answers can be given to these questions, the procedural issues raised by the daughter could not even arise.

Although it might be unwise, on rare occasions, to disclose a diagnosis to an alert, competent patient, in the majority of cases patients have a right to be told that information and physicians have a duty to inform them. Those rare occasions include situations in which patients themselves have given an unequivocal message that they do not want to be told bad news about their condition. They also encompass the unlikely combination of circumstances in which disclosing the diagnosis to a patient is significantly likely to worsen his medical condition. An example might be a massive heart attack, after which the patient is not yet stabilized, and is known by his physician to be a profound worrier. It might jeopardize the patient's recovery to disclose bleak news about the extent of the damage to his heart in the immediate aftermath of his attack.

But it is rare that disclosure of information itself is likely to worsen a patient's medical condition. It is usually in response to their own discomfort, or to the demands of family members, that physicians choose not to inform patients of their diagnosis or prognosis. The justification is almost always that the patient is not being told "for his own good." This is a classic instance of *paternalism* in the medical setting.

Put simply, paternalism is the denial of autonomy. It is direct interference with an individual's exercise of self-rule, through either coercion or deception. A key element in paternalism is the reason given for the coercion or deception: it is alleged to be for the welfare or in the best interest of the person being coerced or deceived. Whether acts of paternalism can ever be morally justified, and if so, under what conditions, is a general substantive question on which reasonable people disagree. Specific cases are analyzed by examining the facts and applying an appropriate moral principle to those facts.

If any issue in bioethics is now settled, it is that only patients themselves, when they are alert and competent, may grant informed consent for medical or surgical interventions. So the answer to the procedural question—May the daughter of a patient grant consent for her father's surgery?—is "Certainly not!" Procedural questions about informed consent on behalf of marginally competent patients, or those who clearly lack the capacity to participate in their own treatment decisions, remain thorny. Even more preposterous than her offer to consent to her father's surgery was the daughter's threat to sue the physician who sought to disclose to the patient his diagnosis of cancer of the bowel. So intimidated are physicians by the ever-present threat of a lawsuit that they sometimes take such threats seriously and refrain from acting in ways they know to be morally right. To his credit, the young doctor in this case continued to explore his obligation to his patient.

One day, when communication between Mr. DiS. and his family had reached a low ebb, the patient turned to the physician and asked, "Can't you tell me what's wrong with me?" Seeing no chance to wriggle out, and feeling certain the patient should know what was wrong with him, the doctor told Mr. DiS. gently but clearly that he had cancer. The patient, much relieved, said, "Thank you. I thought so," and the discussion then turned to prognosis, treatment options, and what should be done next. The physician dreaded his encounter with the family, but knew he had to admit at once that he had disclosed the information to the patient. Communication between Mr. DiS. and his family improved immediately and dramatically. The patient's depression melted away. With no need to hide anything any longer, and having begun to discuss matters openly, everyone was in better spirits. When the daughter did confront the physician who had disclosed the information, she apologized for her earlier behavior, thanked him for his patience and dedication, and acknowledged that it had been best, after all, to tell her father the details of his condition.

HOW MUCH CAN BE LEARNED from a case like this? It would be a mistake to conclude that all or even most similar cases will be resolved in the same way. There is surely no guarantee that patients will take bad news about their medical condition as Mr. DiS. did, nor that families will react as this one did after a disclosure is made against their wishes. What this case does illustrate, however, is that worse consequences, such as Mr. DiS.'s depression, can sometimes flow from nondisclosure, or from continued withholding of information from patients, than from actually telling them bad news.

It is impossible to foresee all the consequences of alternative courses of action. Yet it would be an error to omit a careful review of the likely results of contemplated actions. One of the leading methods of moral decision-making requires an assessment of the probable consequences of each alternative facing the decision-maker. The decision is then based on the course of action likely to yield the best consequences. However difficult it is to predict those consequences accurately, it is a worse failing to ignore the task altogether. Another leading method of moral decision-making requires a determination of the rights and obligations of all relevant parties. The decision is based on respect for rights, even if the chosen action fails to bring about the best consequences. If it is difficult to predict the probable consequences of actions, it is even harder to make a clear determination of who owes what to whom in complex moral situations. Although both modes of making decisions rely on general moral principles, the application of fundamental principles to individual cases is not a straightforward exercise like following a recipe.

Ralph W. was a man in his mid-twenties who had become medically addicted to opiates while undergoing a series of operations and rehabilitative therapy following a bad accident some years earlier. As a result of the addiction, he is now in a methadone-treatment program and comes regularly to the outpatient clinic at City Hospital. The staff knows that he also gets other drugs outside the hospital, but only pills and tablets of various sorts. On a recent visit to the outpatient clinic, the patient was mistakenly given ten times his usual dose of methadone. He went into cardiac arrest, and was successfully resuscitated. Suspecting a methadone overdose, the physician in charge immediately ordered that an antagonist drug be given to counteract it. After careful monitoring and continued treatment, Ralph recovered, with no sign of adverse effect from the cardiac arrest.

This is a case of medical error. Some medical errors are a result of negligence or carelessness, and a person who commits such errors is morally culpable. Other errors arise from human fallibility and are usually not preventable. The information provided by the nursing staff in this case suggested that the error could have been prevented. But whichever type of error is committed in caring for patients, the inevitable question is posed: Should Ralph W. be told what caused his cardiac arrest? Should he be informed that he received an overdose of methadone, and that the overdose was the result of a medical error?

Consider the reasons in favor of nondisclosure: Telling the patient about the mistake will not undo the error, nor will it produce any other good consequences. Since no permanent harm resulted from the episode, and no good is likely to result from telling him, is it better to keep silent? Furthermore, some undesired results are likely to flow from disclosure.

First, he may sue the hospital, a suit he may very well win, thus costing the hospital unnecessary money and causing grief to the affected employees. Second, the patient may lose confidence in physicians and hospitals generally, and this hospital and its personnel in particular. This loss of confidence could then lead to greater problems with his addiction, since if Ralph abandons the methadone-treatment program, he becomes a candidate for street addiction, surely a worse overall situation for him. Looked at in terms of these consequences of disclosure, there seems to be nothing to recommend telling the patient the truth about the medical error, and everything to gain by remaining silent. It is hard to think of good consequences likely to result from disclosure, and easy to list the potentially undesirable results.

When we learn more of the story, however, it becomes even harder to predict the likely consequences and even more difficult to weigh the good consequences against the bad.

But even before more of the story is told, a nagging objection comes to mind. Isn't there a moral obligation to tell the truth? Doesn't that obligation hold even when a person doesn't ask directly for the truth to be told? Especially when someone has been harmed—even by mistake, and even where no permanent harm is done—doesn't the victim have a right to know the facts surrounding the harmful act? According to this objection, it's bad enough that someone has been harmed through medical error, but if the person is also intentionally kept in the dark, that person is *wronged* as well as harmed. Not just one, but two, species of unethical conduct are involved: harm and wrong.

People can be harmed physically or psychologically, and they may also be harmed financially or even socially—for example, when their good name is damaged or when they are treated unfairly. But even when people are not harmed, they still may be wronged, for example, by being lied to or deceived by the withholding of information. In Ralph's case, the fact that the harm was unintentional and only temporary does not erase it from the slate of harms. And the harm is surely not undone by keeping it secret.

Is this objection valid? Is there a moral obligation to tell Ralph W.

what happened, despite the bad consequences that may well flow from that disclosure? This is a classic moral dilemma, with applications far beyond this case. The classical statement of the dilemma is: If following what appears to be a moral obligation is likely to result in more bad consequences than shunning the moral obligation, should one act on the moral obligation or not? Does it even remain a moral obligation in that case? Or instead, is it morally right to strive to bring about the best consequences of our actions whenever possible?

A TALE IS RARELY as simple as it first appears, and this one is no exception. When a case conference was held to discuss the ethics of withholding information from Ralph about his cardiac arrest, the staff claimed that the patient's behavior toward them had changed since the episode, and that he now expressed a fear of obtaining drugs on the street. Prior to his cardiac arrest, Ralph had manipulated the staff, had demanded their time and attention, and had seemed unconcerned about the possible dangers of using drugs obtained through nonmedical channels. Since the episode, however, he had become more humble and accepting of the staff's regimen, and was now much less manipulative. Apparently, Ralph believed his own behavior was responsible for bringing on the cardiac arrest, probably from pills he had consumed outside the methadone-treatment program. His belief that he had "done it to himself" seems to have contributed to his improved behavior toward the staff, as well as instilling in him a fear of taking drugs without medical supervision.

Now, the staff reasoned, if this assessment of the patient was accurate, even more potential harm could result from disclosing that it was not he but the medical staff who had caused the overdose and subsequent heart attack. Ralph's belief that he was the culprit not only made him more compliant, the staff argued; it also was likely to keep him from self-medicating and from dangerous drug abuse. So, they concluded, an additional reason existed for nondisclosure: to keep him in the dark would most likely benefit him medically, while to reveal the staff's error would return him to his former self-destructive behavior. The balance of good to be achieved so far outweighed whatever negative consequences might flow from remaining silent that the morally right course of action seemed obvious.

But is it really so obvious? It takes little effort to imagine a quite different set of consequences that could flow from disclosing the truth to the patient. In the case conference, I suggested the following alternative picture. Suppose Ralph's false belief—that he had caused the cardiac arrest by taking an overdose—were changed to the true belief that the arrest had come about through an error on the staff's part. The patient might very well reason as follows: This almost fatal episode resulted from a mistake by the staff. Luckily, it all took place in the hospital, where doctors and nurses were available. But what if this happened at home, or in the street? There probably would be no one around to assess what was going on, and surely no one able to administer cardiopulmonary resuscitation (CPR) expertly. So, he might conclude, I'd better stick to the methadone treatments and avoid self-medication in the future. Although the hospital did make a bad mistake in giving me an overdose, they were honest in telling me about it and there are no permanent effects from the mistake. They saved my life, and I'm grateful for that.

Here, then, are two possible scenarios. The staff traces one set of possible consequences, while another picture can also be drawn, projecting different consequences of disclosure. Which picture is accurate? Which set of consequences is more likely? Alas, there is no crystal ball for an accurate prediction. And even if the staff's scenario is the more likely one, the question remains whether it is ethically justifiable to lie, or even to withhold information, in order to bring about desired consequences. This is an old ethical dilemma, one that often rears its head in the medical setting.

BOTH OF THESE CASES focus on the ethics of disclosure: Must the truth always be told? Or do the bad consequences of disclosing information to patients (or for that matter to anyone) outweigh whatever moral obligation exists to tell the truth? It is hard enough to resolve such ethical dilemmas in the abstract, but concrete cases typically pose special complications. The main one is the difficulty of making accurate predictions of the consequences. With Mr. DiS., whose family insisted he not be told, disclosure of his diagnosis proved to be the best course of action, despite his daughter's objections. In the case of Ralph W., two plausible scenarios could be imagined, with no way of predicting the actual consequences. Yet uncertainty about consequences should not lead us to conclude that this method of ethical decision-making is fundamentally flawed.

Perhaps the best way to appreciate the role of principles is to see how they operate in a variety of individual cases. The next two episodes embody a conflict of principles similar to those examined earlier, but with some new twists.

A fifty-two-year-old woman has been brought to the psychiatric ward of the hospital after causing a commotion in the office of a local bank executive. The woman, known as Bunky, is well-known to the psychiatric social worker from other hospital stays. She is a member of the city's large homeless population. Bunky lives in a subway station most of the year, and survives by the good graces of local merchants and residents, who find her no threat in the neighborhood. She has one leg—the other was amputated three years ago—and gets around on crutches. She often shows up at the office of the local bank executive, making a nuisance of herself by shouting and by brandishing her crutches like a weapon.

Bunky has often been examined at the hospital by psychiatrists, who made no firm diagnosis of mental illness. The psychiatrists also determined that she posed no danger to others, nor was she judged dangerous to herself, because she demonstrated no suicidal behavior. Yet when she was brought to the hospital this time, she was dirty and disheveled, and the social worker believes she may be suffering from malnutrition. She has been observed by more than one social worker on several occasions crawling across a busy thoroughfare. The woman is an alcoholic, and has been beaten and accosted in the subway station where she lives. She is unwilling to move to a shelter for the homeless and has refused to enter other public institutions voluntarily. She seems to enjoy her periodic, short stays in City Hospital, but is eager to leave so she can return to her drinking.

The dilemma for the social worker: Should she seek to have Bunky committed to a mental hospital, despite the woman's unwillingness to change her living conditions? Because Bunky has not been determined to be dangerous to herself or to others, no proper legal basis exists for committing her. Yet the bank executive whose office she periodically disrupts is outraged, and is trying any means within his power to rid himself of this nuisance. Does Bunky pose a threat of genuine harm to others? Or does she simply offend? Does she have a "right to be let alone"? What is in this woman's best interest? Does her best interest conflict with her civil rights?

In another case of conflicting principles, twelve-year-old Annabella is admitted to the hospital and found to be in need of surgery for a life-threatening condition stemming from a hemorrhage, or "bleed," in her head. She was born with Down's syndrome and is moderately mentally retarded, but has lived her entire life with her parents, who are enjoying a brief visit to relatives in New York when the need for surgery is diagnosed. The family is from one of the Caribbean islands, and they practice a religion that forbids surgical cutting. The physicians explore the possibility of surgery with Annabella's parents, but they remain steadfast in their refusal. The social worker finds them to be devoted parents, whose love for their daughter, despite her mental retardation, is not in question. Annabella has a healthy and warm personality and endears herself to the pediatric staff, who argue vigorously for treatment. The treatment team could seek a court order, overriding the parents' refusal of surgery. Without the surgery the girl faces a high probability of another bleed in the near future, which might cause her death. With the surgery she will most likely live for several more decades—the usual life span of a person with Down's syndrome, but shorter than normal. An additional complication is the risk of surgery itself, which is known to have a 5 to 10 percent mortality rate. However, the parents' refusal is based not on the risk of surgery but on their religious convictions.

Should the physicians seek a court order to override parental refusal to consent for treatment? Could that recommendation be based on a finding of parental neglect because of the child's need for medical treatment? Or should the parents' refusal of treatment be respected, based on their religious convictions and the fact that they are visiting foreigners who should not be subjected to local customs? Does Annabella have a right to treatment, a right that overrides her own parents' right to refuse treatment on her behalf?

In the case of Bunky, the homeless woman, the relevant moral principle is the one that recognizes each individual as having dignity or intrinsic worth and mandates that autonomy be respected. The principle is known as "respect for persons." From it a set of legal and moral rights can be derived, such as the right to freedom or liberty, the right to self-determination, and the "right to be let alone." But we must recall the corollary to this principle that was found to apply to the case of the Jehovah's Witness patient discussed earlier: Persons with diminished autonomy stand in need of protection. This precept allows for a range of justified acts of paternalism—acting for the good or benefit of persons with diminished autonomy, even in the absence of their explicit consent. Mentally ill persons, the mentally retarded, elderly persons suffering from memory loss, and, most obviously, children fit this category to a greater or lesser degree. While most people readily accept the principle that persons with diminished autonomy stand in need of protection, disagreements begin at the point where assessments must be made. How is full autonomy to be measured? How far short of full autonomy must someone be before he can be said to suffer from autonomy that is diminished enough to warrant interference with his liberty?

Competing with the respect-for-persons principle is the ethical perspective known as "consequentialism." It applies both to the case of Bunky and to the Caribbean family refusing surgery for their retarded daughter. Consequentialism has several variations, but its central meaning is captured by an imperative: "Choose the action most likely to bring about the best results." Since human actions often have mixed consequences—unwanted results as well as desired ones—the consequentialist principle is sometimes cast as the formula "Choose the action likely to result in a balance of benefits over harms."

In bioethics this ethical principle is commonly called the "principle of beneficence." It directs doctors and other health-care workers to do good. The version best known to the medical profession is the ancient injunction "Do no harm." In that form it is sometimes termed the "principle of nonmaleficence," to emphasize the prohibition against doing harm. It seems like a principle that should be hard to quarrel with.

Yet problems exist with both the consequentialist principle and "respect for persons," when considered separately and especially when taken together. The principle of beneficence directs the decision-maker to choose the action with the best probable consequences. For medical professionals, the consequences almost always refer to the patient alone. Yet more generally, the consequentialist approach to ethics mandates taking into account the interests of all who stand to be affected by a decision. This is the source of the dilemma for physicians caring for Annabella. Considering the alternative courses of action (conducting surgery or refraining from surgery) and the possible consequences of each alternative (surgery with a successful or an unsuccessful outcome; withholding surgery with death the likely result) physicians reason that the likelihood of the greatest benefit to the patient lies in performing the surgery. Since the ethos of medicine and health care directs physicians, nurses, and medical social workers to focus primarily, if not solely, on the health and well-being of the patient, the principle of beneficence is as individualistic as the respect-for-persons principle.

However, some would argue that the effects on the patient's family must also be considered in the calculation of benefits and harms. Will this family be devastated by having their authority over their own child removed? Would the violation of their religious principles cause them emotional and spiritual harm? Could a judicial proceeding, followed by a court order to perform the surgery, so traumatize this family that the harms would outweigh the potential benefits to the child?

These questions were raised at pediatric ethics rounds when the case of Annabella was presented. Some argued vehemently for the right of the child to be treated, despite her parents' objections and despite the risks of the surgery. Others saw the case differently, noting that the parents were truly concerned about their daughter, and questioning the right of doctors to impose medical treatment on visitors to this country whose beliefs and values are alien to our own. No one expressed the view that Annabella's mental retardation should be a factor that disqualified her from a recommended medical treatment.

I thought of the Jehovah's Witness parents who refuse lifesaving blood transfusions for their children, and how I have no uncertainty about the right course of action in such cases. Moral consistency seemed to demand that the dilemma in Annabella's case be resolved in the same way. But are these situations strictly analogous? No analogies are perfect, and the key lies in determining just which similarities and differences are morally relevant and which are not. If Annabella's family were from the United States, caregivers would probably be less hesitant to seek to override their refusal. In trying to escape between the horns of this dilemma, the staff sought to develop a relationship of trust with the parents, hoping that once it was established they would change their minds about the surgery. Sadly, while those efforts were being made, Annabella suffered another bleed in her head and died.

THERE IS A CONFLICT between the moral perspective that emphasizes the rights of individual persons and the one that promotes the happiness or welfare of the majority. These two frequently clash, not only in the practice of medicine but in other professions as well. The conflict takes place even more prominently at the policy level, whether the policy is formulated by a hospital, a branch of the government, or any other body.

One of the most widely debated examples of this clash of values arises in cases of involuntary commitment of persons believed dangerous to others. The criminal-justice system in the United States forbids, at least in theory, preventive detention of those who have not yet been found guilty of a crime. Although the system is imperfect and violations of this prohibition are widespread, let us assume for the moment that the prohibition against preventive detention is a sound and workable premise.

But there exists another system, side by side with the criminal-justice system: the mental-health system, which can get around that prohibition by the mechanism of involuntary commitment on grounds of danger to others. Though many psychiatrists, psychologists, and other mental-health experts maintain that dangerousness in an individual is impossible to predict accurately, the practice of committing persons deemed dangerous to others persists. Strong opposition to the practice comes from civil-liberties lawyers and from a few members of the mental-health profession, who argue that taking away a person's liberty in the absence of a criminal offense is a direct violation of that individual's civil rights. Defenders of the practice appeal to a moral principle called, for short, the "harm principle": interference with an individual's freedom is justified by the likelihood of harm to others.

The "harm principle" is a specific version of the more general principle of beneficence. One way of attempting to promote the greatest welfare of society is to remove those few individuals who pose a threat to innocent persons. But how accurate is the assessment of the likelihood of harm to others? And how high must that probability be in order to justify taking away an individual's basic right of liberty if no crime has been committed?

The "harm principle" is not paternalistic. It does not justify involuntary commitment or any other intrusion into a person's freedom for that person's own sake, but only for the good of others. A paternalistic justification for involuntary commitment would be that harm is likely to befall the individual himself, because he is judged as being either "dangerous to self," which usually means "suicidal," or "in need of care, custody, or treatment." Morally speaking, then, two quite different grounds exist as a basis for removing a person's liberty and interfering with personal autonomy: the individual may be judged likely to harm others, or likely to commit some form of harm to self. These are genuine dilemmas in most Western cultures, where the tradition of liberal individualism is strong, and where individual rights have been ensconced in law, as well as recognized as part of the moral tradition. But in countries in which the individual is subordinate to either the community or the state, or where religious values predominate and override individual interests, dilemmas that pit the individual against societal values may be minimal, if they exist at all.

In my role as teacher and ethics consultant, I typically take the position of advocating for the patient. But there is ambiguity in that stance: Does advocacy mean promoting the patient's best interests, even when patients disagree with the knowledgeable medical staff about what those interests are? Or does advocacy mean protecting the rights of patients, even when the exercise of their rights undermines their best medical interests? Sometimes, as in the case of the homeless woman who regularly makes a nuisance of herself in the bank executive's office, the patient needs to be protected from being taken advantage of by powerful persons in society, who would violate her civil rights by institutionalizing her without proper cause. It would be an exaggeration to say that Bunky posed a threat of harm to others. More accurately, she was causing offense, not genuine harm. So the "harm principle" does not apply. In this case, then, advocacy means protecting the individual's right to liberty.

Yet even this conclusion is fraught with lingering doubts when we recall that Bunky is an alcoholic and an amputee, has some mental disorder, and has been assaulted more than once in her subway-station home. She has, however, demonstrated a remarkable resistance to those dangers, and seems to have manipulated the harsh world around her in a way that has ensured her continued survival. Would she truly be "better off" in an institution, especially one of the state institutions where the environment may not be much safer, on the whole, than her niche in the subway? Our society's failure to create alternatives other than the hospital and the street makes cases such as this even harder than they would be in a society that provided better options. When a patient's "best interests" are so hard to ascertain, a clear preference lies on the side of protecting her individual rights.

At a conference convened by psychiatric social workers to discuss Bunky's case, I argued for her right to liberty. As the case had been described, her autonomy did not seem to be sufficiently diminished to pose a danger to her life or health. But that judgment turned out to be mistaken, as I was later to learn when the case unfolded.

Gaining
Informed Consent

I T IS JULY 3. On July 1, recent medical-school graduates begin their internship, the first year of postgraduate training before they become full-fledged doctors. A new intern orders a nurse to bring him a Swan-Ganz line, a catheter to be inserted into a patient's heart to monitor cardiac response to medications. The nurse—an experienced practitioner who, unlike many of her younger colleagues, is not intimidated by doctors—asks the intern if he obtained the patient's consent to insert the catheter. The young doctor, impatient to begin the procedure, replies, "No, I didn't, but never mind, just bring me the line, will you?"

The nurse: "I'm sorry, but you have to get the patient's consent for this procedure. Didn't they teach you that in medical school?"

The intern: "Dammit! When a doctor gives an order, you listen!"

The nurse grabs the red-faced young man by the lapels of his short white hospital jacket. "Look here, God!" she snaps, and proceeds to lecture him about legal and ethical requirements to get consent from a patient before inserting the catheter or doing any other medical procedure that invades the patient's body.

THE FEATURES OF INFORMED consent can be stated quite simply: before invasive or risky procedures may be performed, the physician must *disclose* to the patient pertinent details about the nature and purpose of the procedure, its potential risks and benefits, and any reasonable alternatives to the recommended treatment. But it is not enough to recite a litany of facts. The patient must *understand* the information presented orally or on a written form. Furthermore, the patient's consent must be obtained without coercion; it must be granted *voluntarily*. Finally, patients from whom consent is sought must be *competent*, that is, have the mental capacity to grant it. In law, *competency* refers to the *legal* capacity to make decisions, but the term is also used more broadly to denote the psychological or mental capacity to make decisions.

In the clinical practice of medicine, the law requires that informed consent be obtained from patients for a variety of diagnostic and therapeutic procedures that invade the body. Invasive diagnostic procedures include spinal taps and insertion of catheters into the heart to monitor cardiac activity. The most familiar example of invasive therapy is surgery.

It is not only brand-new doctors who "forget" they must obtain informed consent or who disdain the process altogether. More typically, physicians with long years of experience have difficulty adapting to the changes in medical practice that now demand full disclosure to patients, and their participation in decisions about their own care and treatment. The usual justification given for the failure to disclose information or to obtain consent for every procedure is that the doctor is acting in the patient's best interests. In cases that pose genuine dilemmas, there is some truth to that claim.

A fictitious story designed to highlight the dilemma tells of a seventy-year-old man who consented to surgery for repair of his hernia. During the workup prior to the operation, the usual tests were performed, including tests for kidney function and barium-enema X rays to detect cancer of the lower intestine. The tests revealed no abnormalities. In the course of the operation, the surgeon found cancer of the colon in a very early stage, and he chose to remove it. While performing that operation, he discovered another cancerous tumor in the kidney, and chose to remove that as well. Finally, noting that the patient's prostate gland was abnormally enlarged, the surgeon thought it good preventive medicine to take it out.

A surgical intern questioned his superior, asking how he could justify doing these procedures without having gotten the patient's consent. The surgeon replied that his obligation lay in bringing about the best outcomes for his patients. In this case, the surgeon contended, he weighed the risks and benefits, and concluded that the benefits to the patient of undergoing only one surgical procedure far outweighed the risks of several operations. Given the age of the patient and the risks of anesthesia, in addition to the risks of the surgery itself and the fact that the patient had several life-threatening conditions, it was better to do all surgical procedures at one time. Also, the surgeon reasoned, if he performed only the hernia repair and waited until after this operation to obtain consent for the next series of procedures, the cancer could only worsen in the meantime. And the patient would surely grant consent to lifesaving surgery, since he had already consented to an operation for the minor hernia repair. The patient's best interest, as the surgeon saw it, superseded the need to get informed consent for the additional operations.

Reasonable people disagree on whether the surgeon in this case did the morally right thing. One source of disagreement lies in the different priorities given to the competing ethical principles: some people place the patient's right to decide, the right of self-determination, above the results obtained from the risk-benefit calculation; others hold that the doctor's chief obligation is to act in the patient's best interest, even if that means performing surgery without the patient's explicit consent.

Another source of disagreement lies in the facts and probabilities: some would argue that the additional risks involved in performing subsequent surgical procedures on a seventy-year-old patient are not as great as the surgeon made them out to be. With only slightly increased risks, there is no justification for proceeding with the operation without first obtaining informed consent from the patient.

Still another area of disagreement is the urgency of the need for surgery. The one undisputed circumstance in which the requirements of informed consent may be bypassed is that of emergency. In this case the surgeon defended his actions by noting that the patient suffered from several life-threatening conditions, and that the cancer would worsen while the patient recovered from this operation and was prepared for the next. True; but that did not make it an emergency, one that precluded the need to obtain the patient's consent.

Physicians sometimes take refuge in the notion of "implied" consent. This strategy enables a doctor to justify treatments for which the patient did not grant explicit consent. One line of defense goes like this: "The patient contracts for care and treatment by the physician, the expert in medical matters. In consenting to a particular treatment, the patient implicitly consents to whatever else the physician believes is medically necessary." The trouble with this defense is that it is simply false. Nothing in the moral or legal doctrine of informed consent supports this interpretation. Yet standardized consent forms prepared by hospitals often embody clauses that seem to demand "implied consent."

To most patients, being presented with a consent form—which looks like an official document—can be intimidating. Not to sign might bring disfavor from the doctor, or even a loss of treatment. More than a decade ago, soon after I had begun working in the field of bioethics, I entered the hospital for minor elective surgery. Proud of my newly acquired sophistication about informed consent, I studied the written consent form carefully. At the same time, in my unaccustomed role of patient, I felt subordinated, diminished, and reluctant to make trouble for the busy hospital personnel.

Nonetheless, I was troubled by a sentence on the consent form that read: "I hereby consent to this [named surgical procedure], and any other procedure my doctor deems necessary in the course of the surgery." I refused to sign. My own physician was not in the hospital at the time, as it was the evening before the surgery was to be done. The nurse called a young doctor—presumably a resident, a surgeon in training. He entered my room in a hurry, looking annoyed.

"They tell me you won't sign the consent."

"Actually," I replied, "I simply want an explanation of something on the form before I sign."

Impatiently: "Didn't your doctor explain everything to you?"

"Yes, but what does this mean?" I asked, pointing to the offending clause.

"Oh, well, that's there just in case of something unforeseen."

Now I really got worried. "You mean, if they open me up and find something abnormal—a tumor, maybe—they'll take it out? Or my doctor might judge that I need a hysterectomy and remove my female organs?"

"Oh, no," the resident reassured me. "Nothing like that."

"What then?" I asked.

"Well, you know, sometimes things can go a little bit wrong during the surgery."

"For example?" I dreaded the reply.

"The surgeon might inadvertently nick the bowel. You'd want him to repair that, wouldn't you?"

"Of course," I answered, not knowing whether to be relieved or more worried. "Anything else you can think of that might happen?"

"No, not really."

"Okay, I'll sign now," I said, and was a "good patient" for the remainder of my short stay in the hospital.

▪ ▪ ▪

THERE IS PROBABLY no subject in bioethics that has caused as much discussion, controversy, and skepticism as the topic of informed consent. Many doctors have come to accept these new aspects of their practice, and the moral requirement of obtaining informed consent from patients is by now widely acknowledged and embodied in legislation and legal precedent, but theoretical and practical problems remain. On the one hand, few would argue that it is entirely unnecessary for doctors to obtain informed consent from their patients. On the other hand, many physicians are still skeptical about the possibility of obtaining truly informed consent from most patients. Perhaps less frequently, but nonetheless loudly, doctors have been heard to proclaim that informed consent is a pernicious doctrine, that to take it seriously is to act against the best interests of patients.

Some physicians maintain that they can persuade their patients to consent to virtually anything, and so the idea that consent is wholly free or fully voluntary is a myth. Others argue that patients are very unlikely to be properly informed: either they cannot understand what they are told, or they fail to appreciate its significance, or they are so fearful and anxious that the entire process is a charade.

Still other skeptics focus on the risks of disclosing too much information to patients about to undergo a medical procedure. The well-known placebo effect may have a dark side: some patients who are thoroughly informed about the risks of procedures may needlessly develop the very side effects the consent form or the physician described. Published data show that some subjects in a drug study, when given a placebo (an inactive substance, often called a "sugar pill") after the usual informed-consent procedure, reported physiologically unlikely symptoms such as dizziness, nausea, vomiting, and even mental depression. One subject given the placebo reported that these effects were so strong that they caused an automobile accident. These and other episodes have led some skeptics to conclude that "informed consent may be hazardous to health."[1]

This is only one example of a backlash that has developed against informed consent. Another expression of that backlash challenges the voluntariness with which consent is granted. In particular, it has been questioned whether consent obtained from the donor of a kidney to a relative can ever be truly voluntary, in the sense that careful deliberation is required before one can make the decision to donate an organ.[2] Still other doubts focus on patients with language problems, those who are uneducated or unintelligent, and those who are panicky or belligerent or simply apathetic.[3]

These concerns betray a number of misconceptions about informed consent. And there are others: worry about malpractice suits leads some physicians, despite the time and trouble it takes to obtain consent, to claim that it is nevertheless smart protection.[4] But that is to misunderstand its purpose. This same misunderstanding is exhibited by another breed of skeptics, who conclude the opposite: that "informed consent isn't worth the paper it's written on." Both remarks imply that the purpose of informed consent is to protect the physician if the patient decides to sue for malpractice. Although it is true that the current legal status of informed consent came about through a series of legal actions in recent decades, it is not true that the purpose of consent is to protect the physician. The purpose is to ensure the patient's right to self-determination in the medical setting. The consent form is not a waiver. The signed form does not waive the patient's right to sue for negligence by the physician in performing a medical or surgical procedure. It does, however, stand as evidence that the procedure was explained to the patient, who granted permission for it to be performed.

It is true, nonetheless, that patients seldom understand everything they have been told. Doctors are busy with competing responsibilities and cannot spend as much time at the bedside as other health-care personnel. Medical students, who have more contact with hospitalized patients, are more likely to notice breaches in the requirements of informed consent. But they occupy the lowest rung on the medical ladder, a hierarchy of power and authority almost military in its rigidity, and it is a rare medical student who will speak out to challenge a superior. Enlightened self-interest, if not a basic survival instinct, prevents the student from directly confronting interns, residents, or attending physicians in the hospital, or from reporting their superiors' failure to disclose information, or other even more blatant acts of wrongdoing toward patients, to the physician in charge of training or to the chief of service. Students often come to me with such reports—partly out of a desire to confirm their suspicions and to learn more about medical ethics, and partly out of a need to talk to a sympathetic listener.

A fourth-year student presented the following case in class. Mrs. T. was a thirty-two-year-old Hispanic woman, married, with three children. She was admitted to the surgical service at City Hospital for the repair of a hiatus hernia, an elective operation. The patient spoke only Spanish, and communication with her was difficult for the surgical staff. The surgeons often relied on the bilingual medical student to communicate with Mrs. T.

The patient had had surgery on the same hernia two years earlier in the Dominican Republic, after several years of discomfort and difficulty swallowing solid foods. She had also had frequent pain from a peptic ulcer, and she mistakenly believed that the earlier surgery had been meant to alleviate both complaints. Although she was free from the symptoms of her hernia for a year, the pain from the peptic ulcer persisted.

Meanwhile, the discomfort and trouble in swallowing reappeared, along with a decrease in appetite, and Mrs. T. lost seventeen pounds in eight months. When she was examined before her admission, the hernia and her ulcer were detected. The patient was treated for her ulcer and told that her hernia had reappeared and that she needed what would be essentially a repeat of the earlier surgery, which had been performed by making an incision in her abdomen. This time, however, X rays showed that her internal organs had shifted after the previous surgery, so in order to repair the hernia, there was a good chance her chest would also have to be opened.

Mrs. T. was not told that her chest might be opened during surgery. The surgeons could not know if it would be necessary until the patient was actually on the operating table and her abdomen had been explored, and they chose not to inform her of that prospect. She was only made to understand that this surgical procedure would be essentially the same as the previous one. The medical student who had translated first learned of the possibility of the more extensive procedure when Mrs. T. was already under anesthesia and the surgeons were discussing the X rays as they prepared to begin. On the operating table they found there was no need to open the patient's chest. Both the surgery and recovery were uneventful.

The medical student never learned why the surgeons did not have her tell Mrs. T. that her chest might have to be opened. Perhaps they decided to take their chances that it would not have to be done and reasoned that there was no need to cause unnecessary worry in a patient about to undergo an operation. When the student herself first heard about that prospect in the operating room, she was dismayed at the thought that the patient might awake to find a huge, unexpected incision in her chest. The student also feared that the patient might blame her for failing to reveal all of the possible outcomes. Happily for all concerned, the more extensive operation was not necessary.

But the fortunate outcome does not justify the initial failure to disclose pertinent information to the patient. The surgeons probably reasoned as follows: If we tell her that her chest may have to be opened, she may refuse the surgery, and that would be a bad outcome. Even if she consents to the surgery, informing her will cause her to worry; worry is a species of harm; and we physicians have a duty to "do no harm." It could very well turn out not to be necessary to open her chest, and we will have saved her needless worry by not informing her. But even if we do have to open the chest, the patient will be so grateful to us for relieving her pain that she will not resent our not telling her. Any way you look at it, the best consequences will result from not informing the patient of this possibility.

The trouble with this "consequentialist analysis" is that it portrays the possible outcomes in the way the surgeons would like to envision them. But another distinct possibility exists, one the surgeons did not consider. Suppose Mrs. T. is not informed that her chest may have to be opened, and it turns out to be necessary. When the patient awakens, she is horrified at the size of the incision and psychologically unprepared for the greater pain and longer recovery, since her expectations were based on her previous hernia operation. She has not made arrangements for her children's care for the additional recovery time. She has obtained only a short medical leave from work—enough for the simpler operation—but now the leave will have to be extended and her employer must be informed. Her husband is upset, and decides to sue the surgeons and the hospital. Mrs. T. becomes so disillusioned with physicians that she mistrusts them in the future and fails to seek needed medical care for herself and her children. The family may even win the lawsuit, although physicians do win most malpractice suits.

True, there is no way of foreseeing which set of consequences will come about. There is no better evidence to support the surgeons' guess than for the other. However, the requirements of informed consent may not be set aside, so an appeal to consequences cannot be used to justify the surgeons' failure to disclose in cases such as this. In other areas of medical practice involving moral decision-making, a look at the likely consequences may be an appropriate part of an ethical analysis. But it is not permissible, on either moral or legal grounds, for physicians to avoid disclosing information because they believe the results of disclosure will be worse than the results of withholding information from patients.

■　■　■

ONE RECENT DEVELOPMENT, virtually unknown before the early 1970s, is the moral and legal obligation of physicians to discuss alternative treatments with patients. Disclosure of alternative modes of therapy for breast cancer is now required by state law in Massachusetts. Heated exchanges in medical journals have debated whether such disclosure is itself ethical. Some surgeons respond that there is no "real" choice here, and that doctors are acting *immorally* if they even tell patients about alternative treatments that are less than the best medicine can offer. Despite lack of solid evidence from long-term clinical trials, many surgeons continue to maintain that radical mastectomy—complete removal of the affected breast—is the "treatment of choice."

This is another example of the assumption by some doctors that they know what is in their patients' best interest, and their insistence on acting in accordance with those beliefs. Yet it should be obvious that properly obtained informed consent for an invasive, mutilating operation such as a mastectomy requires discussing alternative treatments with the patient, such as lumpectomy—simply removing the malignant lump—usually followed by radiation treatments. A patient's right to autonomous decision-making grants her the freedom to choose a procedure that is less mutilating and destructive of her body and her self-image, even if it does not hold out prospects of as long a life.

This illustrates the clash of values that often occurs in the doctor-patient relationship. In order to act in what they believe to be their patients' best interest, and based on their own superior medical knowledge, many doctors claim that a certain amount of paternalism is necessary for the proper practice of medicine. How, after all, can doctors offer anything less than the best for their patients?

But patients, not doctors, may well be the best judges of what is in their own interest. Women who reject a treatment that holds promise of a somewhat longer life, in favor of one that is less invasive, less mutilating, or less subject to known side effects, are making a judgment for themselves based on quality of life, rather than on the value of prolonging life as much as possible. If the notion of patient autonomy in medical decision-making means anything at all, it must surely include the right to refuse recommended treatments, so long as the refusal is informed and made by an individual who is mentally competent.

However, though these aspects of informed consent are clear and undisputed, the meaning of being informed remains vague. A great variation exists in both the amount and kind of information a person can be given and, beyond that, may be able to understand and recall. One key question pertains to the standard of disclosure: How much information, and of what specific sorts, must patients have before their consent can be said to be truly informed?

Physicians who argue that laypersons can never be fully informed in the requisite sense claim that in order to meet such a requirement, patients would have to know as much as doctors do about diseases and their natural course, risks of all alternative treatments, possible complications, statistics regarding similar cases, and so forth. A compassionate and humane physician confided to me somewhat reluctantly: "I don't believe patients are capable of informed consent. After all, they haven't been to medical school, have they?" If the ability to grant informed consent required knowledge of that scope and depth, consent could rarely be given for most routine medical procedures, much less for the wide variety of experimental treatments continually emerging. Clearly, a workable standard of disclosure is needed if informed consent is to have practical significance.

Recent studies have turned up other problems with obtaining properly informed consent. Poor recall by patients only one day after signing consent forms was found to be related to three different factors: the patients' educational background, their medical status, and the care with which they thought they had read their consent forms before signing.[5] But recall is not a measure of understanding at the time consent is obtained. More relevant is the readability of the consent form itself. Typical consent forms for surgery were found to be at a reading level suitable for juniors and seniors in college, and even graduate students. Some forms were written at the level of scientific journals and specialized academic magazines.[6] These studies are useful in showing just which barriers to obtaining adequately informed consent can be overcome by more care in designing consent forms, by more time and effort devoted to the process of informing, and by ensuring that patients truly understand what they have been told.

Yet other barriers remain, barriers not as easily overcome by spending more time explaining things to patients. At times patients exhibit "denial," a psychological mechanism that makes them unable to comprehend, process, or remember information about their illness and recommended treatments. Such patients don't want to believe they have a serious illness and can't accept the diagnosis or prognosis. Others, perhaps not denying their illness, are nevertheless so beset by fear and anxiety that they listen without hearing, or hear without understanding. And some patients simply refuse to listen, abandoning their decision-making role. Such patients have no interest in participating in decisions on their own care and treatment. They are perfectly willing to leave everything to the physician.

I am sometimes asked whether informed consent means that unwanted information must be forced upon patients, or whether doctors should insist on involving the unwilling patient in decisions. A colleague puts the answer best when she advises, "You can't drag a person kicking and screaming into autonomy."

Even physicians who respect the autonomy of their patients and want to comply with the requirements of informed consent are unsure just how much information to disclose, how many details to enumerate, and whether to tell patients about remote risks or rare side effects. Although some guidance is provided by the laws of informed consent, specific judgments still need to be made by doctors in each situation. However, the law does set a standard of disclosure—a standard that has changed in a few short years from a physician-centered criterion to one that is patient-oriented.

It wasn't until 1960 that courts addressed the question of what standard should be used in disclosing information to patients before they receive medical treatment. A Kansas case, *Natanson* v. *Kline*, set the standard known as the "professional community" standard—what responsible medical practitioners in similar situations would tell their patients. In that case the patient underwent cobalt radiation treatments, which were at the time relatively new. After suffering serious side effects from the therapy, the patient sued the physician. The court's opinion stated:

> The duty of the physician to disclose . . . is limited to those disclosures which a reasonable medical practitioner would make under the same or similar circumstances. . . . So long as the disclosure is sufficient to assure an informed consent, the physician's choice of plausible courses should not be called into question if it appears, all circumstances considered, that the physician was motivated only by the patient's best therapeutic interests and he proceeded as competent medical men would have done in a similar situation.[7]

This ruling now seems old-fashioned, both in substance and in language. Not only did the judge defer to the general practice of doctors, however paternalistic they may be and no matter how little information they typically disclose to their patients. The wording also presumes that all competent physicians are medical *men*, but many, of course, are women.

A patient-centered standard of disclosure was articulated in a landmark court case in 1972, *Canterbury* v. *Spence*. In this case the physician performed a procedure known as a laminectomy without informing the patient of a risk of paralysis. On the day following the operation, the patient fell out of the hospital bed, only then discovering that the lower half of his body was paralyzed. Although his condition subsequently improved, he never completely returned to his normal condition. The patient sued the physician, and the court affirmed the right of patients to self-determination in the medical setting: "True consent to what happens to one's self is the informed exercise of a choice, and that entails an opportunity to evaluate knowledgeably the options available and the risks attendant upon each."[8]

The standard of disclosure established in this case became known as the "reasonable-patient" standard—what the reasonable patient would want to know before granting consent to a recommended therapy. The patient's ability to make an intelligent decision rests on the disclosure of all "material" information regarding "the inherent and potential hazards of the proposed treatment, the alternatives to that treatment, if any, and the results likely if the patient remains untreated," said the court.

It is important to note that the standard established in the Canterbury case does not require full disclosure of the risks of therapeutic or diagnostic procedures, but rather, all information that is "material" to a patient's ability to make an informed decision about medical treatment. The court was realistic in not requiring full disclosure, but the standard it chose to adopt is subject to varying interpretation. Physicians must exercise their judgment concerning just which facts are "material" to patients' ability to make an informed choice and which are not. It is neither a simple nor a straightforward judgment to make. But that is probably the price to be paid for having a realistic standard of disclosure, one that does not mandate full disclosure of all risks of harm, however small or remote, that could conceivably occur.

It would be optimistic to conclude that these judicial precedents changed the long-standing medical tendency toward paternalism—physicians acting in what they believe to be their patients' best interests, without those patients' knowledge or consent. Even if the practice of ignoring patients' autonomy were to change out of fear of litigation rather than out of more noble ethical motives, it would still be a change in the right direction. Yet such changes, after literally thousands of years of medical paternalism, still proceed by tiny increments, not by leaps and bounds.

Even though informed consent does not require doctors to disclose every conceivable risk, they continue to worry that patients will refuse needed treatments out of fear or anxiety about the risks they are told about. There is little basis for this worry. Indeed, quite the contrary, one study of treatment refusals revealed that *lack* of information can cause some patients to refuse. The study was conducted in a university teaching hospital and a community hospital. In both hospitals it was found that in many instances little or no information was provided to patients about proposed diagnostic and therapeutic procedures. Among patients who refused, lack of information was one factor, though often not the sole cause of their refusal. Some patients who knew or learned that procedures were very risky refused treatment at first, but later consented, once reasonable justification and assurances were provided.[9]

Empirical studies such as this are important in demonstrating the actual reasons why patients refuse to grant consent—reasons that may be quite different from what physicians imagine them to be. The studies reveal some useful data about problems in communication between doctors and patients. But this does not necessarily mean that patients who first refused, then consented, changed their minds solely on the basis of the new information. A much more likely explanation is that in the process of informing these patients, physicians developed a relationship with them that had been absent before. Talking to patients helps to form a good doctor-patient relationship, but very little in medical-school education focuses on that aspect of patient care. Medical students are taught how to do procedures, not how to disclose bad news to patients or how to obtain a properly informed consent. When physicians advise trainees, "You have to help the patient maintain hope," they interpret that to mean "Don't give bad news about diagnosis, prognosis, or risks of treatment."

But another interpretation can be given, one that focuses on the nature of the relationship between doctor and patient. The physician can help the patient maintain hope by instilling confidence and gaining the patient's trust. That trust is likely to grow as a result of talking frankly to patients about their condition. In the medical situation, as in any other, people who speak brusquely, who are always hurried in their communications, and who are evasive in their answers are less likely to be trusted or to instill confidence than those who take the time to explain things and, especially, to listen. The doctor who takes the time and makes the effort to develop a good physician-patient relationship by communicating with patients is more likely to gain their confidence and, ultimately, obtain consent to treatment.

Here, too, lies an ethical danger. The better the doctor-patient relationship, the more readily consent will be granted. Recall the physicians who say they can get their patients to consent to anything. The ethical worry now switches from concern with the information provided to the voluntariness with which consent is granted. Ironically, the better the doctor-patient relationship, the less likely patients are to deliberate a lot. This is not to say that physicians intentionally coerce their patients into consenting (although many do threaten in some manner). Even when physicians do not behave in a coercive manner, people who are sick, anxious, or debilitated tend to become dependent and may unwittingly give up their autonomy. This is one possible consequence of a patient's placing trust in the healer with whom a relationship has been formed.

I find much less to worry about in this aspect of informed consent than in inadequate disclosure of information. It is a feature of the human condition that the voluntariness of decisions and actions decreases as the relationship between people becomes closer. This was illustrated in the report that questioned whether consent obtained from a relative for a kidney donation is ever truly voluntary. Yet it would be a mistake to conclude that it is ethically wrong to seek consent from family members because the voluntariness of their consent is compromised by their eagerness to aid a loved one who might otherwise die from kidney failure. The correct conclusion is that informed consent can still be valid, even if less than wholly voluntary, so long as full information is provided and the prospective donor is counseled in a careful and sensitive manner.

The same holds true for the voluntariness of consent in a good doctor-patient relationship. If one of the inevitable consequences of developing such a relationship is that patients are less free in granting consent to recommended treatments, it is a trade-off that comes out best, on the whole. If physicians are conscientious and careful in assessing the risks and benefits of treatments and engage in full and open communication, then the autonomy of patients will be preserved.

Aggressive Treatment

MRS. F. WAS A ninety-four-year-old woman with a history of heart disease, brought to the emergency room complaining of shortness of breath. She responded well to the treatment given in the emergency room, but was still admitted as an inpatient so her condition could be monitored. After three days on a regular hospital floor, she again had trouble breathing and was found to be lethargic. Nurses called for a resuscitation, which resulted in tubes being inserted in Mrs. F., and again she responded well. After another three days in the hospital, the same series of events recurred. Although the patient again recovered heart and lung functions, this time she lapsed into a coma and was transferred to the intensive-care unit, where she remained comatose and showed no response to pain. After two days in the ICU, a fever developed and a urinary-tract infection was treated with antibiotics, given intravenously. Her condition remained unchanged for several days, and Mrs. F.'s niece was consulted in order to set a policy for future resuscitative efforts. The niece asked that her aunt not be resuscitated if the need arose again. On her twelfth day in the ICU, the patient was found to be unresponsive. In accord with the earlier decision, no resuscitative effort was made and Mrs. F. died.

CLARA M. WAS AN EIGHTY-FOUR-YEAR-OLD DIABETIC woman with a history of heart failure. She came to the emergency room one day complaining of chest pains. She was admitted to the intensive-care unit with orders to "rule out MI," which means to monitor her closely in order to rule out the probability that she had suffered a myocardial infarction, or heart attack. The next morning a bed was needed in the ICU for another patient. Clara M. was asked if she minded being moved, and when she said she did not, was moved to a regular floor. There she was put in a bed with no cardiac monitor, where she remained despite test results that indicated she had suffered a myocardial infarction. At one point she tried to get out of bed to go to the bathroom, fell, and was put back in her bed. Later that day she suffered a cardiac arrest and was resuscitated. She died in the hospital two days later.

MR. R. IS A forty-nine-year-old man who has undergone both conventional and experimental treatment for leukemia over the last nine months. On this hospital admission he has decided to refuse all further treatment, including "supportive measures"—antibiotics, blood transfusions, and other elements of routine care. When asked, Mr. R. said he did not want to be resuscitated in the event of cardiac arrest. His only request was that he be made comfortable and "sleepy." His family, on the other hand—especially his daughter—could not accept this decision. They continued to pressure both Mr. R. and the physicians and nurses caring for him. Mr. R. signed a statement in the medical record confirming the requests he had made orally. His wife and daughter told the staff they must resuscitate him if he suffered a cardiac arrest. With reluctance and misgivings because of the family's demands for continued treatment, the physician respected the patient's wish and wrote an order to administer an intravenous morphine drip until the patient becomes lethargic.

HOW AGGRESSIVE SHOULD medical treatment be? This question comes up in a hospital more often than any other. Case after case in rounds and conferences recounts situations in which physicians and other decision-makers must determine an appropriate level of care for a patient. Although it is true that no general answer can be given to this question, the reason is often misstated. It is common for doctors to assert, "Every case is unique," or, "You can't generalize about treatments." There is a core of truth in these observations, but it would be a mistake to conclude that therefore no general principles could be found to guide decision-making.

The rejection of those ethical perspectives that seek to apply general moral principles to medical cases is known as "situation ethics."[1] A reaction against dogmatic forms of morality, especially those derived from rigid religious teachings, this approach argues that each situation is different and that recognizing the uniqueness of every situation demands that decision-makers abandon doctrinaire rules and inflexible principles. What is required is to seek a "loving and humane solution" in every situation that poses an ethical dilemma. This view has its roots in the Christian ethics of love, and thus does not reject religion altogether. It does, however, seek a methodology for ethical decision-making that does not rely on moral rules or universal principles.

Although situation ethics has the virtue of being nondogmatic in its approach to ethical dilemmas, it fails to give clear guidance to the individual perplexed about the morally right thing to do. To tell the pediatrician who is in a quandary about how aggressively to treat an infant born with several birth defects to "choose the most loving and humane solution" is simply to restate the problem the physician faces. The pediatrician is agonizing over just which is the more loving and humane solution: to artificially prolong the infant's poor-quality life or to "let nature take its course."

If situation ethics requires the abandonment of all general principles, on what basis can one make a decision? Does one appeal to moral intuition? Is it by looking very hard at each case that a person comes to a flash of ethical insight? Does the "loving and humane solution" present itself when the decision-maker introspects, consulting inner moral feelings? None of these methods provides a useful guide to action. Nor does this approach lend itself to informed discussion and the ability to provide a moral justification for a preferred course of action. Situation ethics is little more than an affirmation of the subjective biases of the decision-maker: whatever feels right *is* morally right. That stance is at best unhelpful and at worst morally dangerous. The more situation ethics acknowledges the need to call on some principle or other to guide decision-making, the more it resembles perspectives derived from traditional ethical theories.

The proposition that every situation is unique is true, but its truth is almost trivial. The correct conclusion to draw is not that *no* general principles can be found, but rather that it is necessary to choose from among a variety of potentially applicable principles the one that best applies to the case at hand, given its individual features. Even so, no simple or automatic procedure exists for choosing the most applicable principle. This is partly because a number of different, perhaps conflicting, principles can be simultaneous candidates. It is also because procedural considerations enter the picture and sometimes override a substantive moral principle in the process of decision-making. A look at the similarities and differences between the three cases described earlier will illustrate these somewhat abstract points.

All three cases involve patients with life-threatening conditions. All require decisions about an appropriate level of care, and questions were raised in each situation about whether the patient should be resuscitated in the event of a cardiac arrest. Medical and nursing personnel inquired whether it was acceptable to omit some medical treatments while administering others. They also asked what counts as "aggressive" care, and what should be considered "routine."

Obvious differences exist among the three cases, despite these similarities. Mr. R. is still in the prime of life, far from having lived out a normal life span. Mrs. F. had already lived well beyond that statistical life span, while Clara M. was old but not very old. Is the age of the patient a morally relevant factor in seeking to determine the appropriate level of care? Is it morally relevant in deciding whether a patient should be placed in the ICU, where beds are always scarce?

Another difference in the cases is the role played by family. Clara M. entered the hospital with no family present, and apparently none could be found. Mrs. F. also came in without any family, but a niece was later contacted to assist in decision-making. Mr. R., in contrast, was accompanied by a devoted wife and daughter whose demands for aggressive treatment were unceasing. Should the presence or requests of family members be a factor in the level of care delivered to patients?

An ethical analysis begins by identifying the morally relevant factors. For any medical case the most important feature is the patient's prognosis. That should be determined at the outset and reassessed continually. Is the illness terminal? Are there several concurrent diseases, any one of which could worsen and threaten the patient's life? Is the patient's medical condition so poor that aggressive treatments could only prolong the dying process? The answers to these questions rest on objective facts. Although medical science contains many uncertainties, it also relies on an understanding of the natural history of diseases, the efficacy of standard treatments, and published data in the literature about similar cases.

Of the three cases, Mr. R.'s situation provides physicians with the clearest objective evidence about prognosis. The patient is suffering from the advanced stages of a terminal illness. He has undergone the complete course of conventional and experimental therapies for leukemia, and death is now imminent. Mrs. F. came into the hospital with a less certain prognosis, but during the course of her stay, the evidence mounted in support of a bleak prognosis. Having responded to initial therapy, the patient deteriorated, suffering multiple cardiac arrests and lapsing into a coma. Experience with patients such as this convinces the doctors that death from one cause or another is likely, even if efforts are made to prolong the patient's life. In the case of Clara M., however, the prognosis is neither as poor nor as certain as in the other two cases. The patient entered the hospital with a history of heart failure, complaining of chest pains. While her status was still being evaluated, she was moved out of the intensive-care unit to a place in the hospital where only less-aggressive care could be administered. It was not known whether Clara M.'s condition was terminal, so reliable information about her prognosis was yet to be confirmed.

Despite the uncertainties involved in making predictions about the future course of a patient's illness, the task is nevertheless based on objective medical information. From a moral point of view, it is more problematic to determine a patient's quality of life. Judgments about quality of life contain a subjective element, one that differs from person to person, and may even vary for a particular person from one time to another.

The distinction between subjective and objective should not be confused with the problem of uncertainty in making a diagnosis or prognosis. Objective considerations rest on observations and the known data of medical science. All scientific matters contain some uncertainty, which is why their truths are said to be probabilistic rather than absolute. But their lack of certainty does not make such matters any less objective. Subjective considerations, on the other hand, are based on the perceptions, feelings, and values of individual persons. The problem involved when one person seeks to determine another person's quality of life is entirely different from the difficulty of making judgments when uncertainty about the facts complicates a decision. A quality of life that for one person is unendurable may be acceptable for another. To base a treatment decision on the patient's quality of life is, therefore, more ethically problematic than to base it on objective facts about the patient's prognosis.

There is a world of difference between situations in which quality-of-life judgments are made by patients themselves and those in which family or medical caregivers make the assessment. In general, the one most qualified to judge quality of life is the person whose life it is.

There is little doubt that Mr. R. was the best judge of his own quality of life. Both his disease and the side effects of months of chemotherapy left him ravaged by pain and discomfort. Nearing death, he requested only that he be made as comfortable as possible. His wife and daughter, quite understandably, were not yet ready to let him go. It is not so much that they assessed his quality of life as better than Mr. R. himself judged it to be. Rather, desperate in their hope for a last-minute reprieve, a miracle of remission, they demanded that physicians continue to treat the patient as aggressively as possible. But do they have the right to make that demand? The answer is a clear no when, like Mr. R., the patient is awake, alert, and oriented. Only when a patient lacks the capacity to speak for himself may family members become the primary decision-makers about medical care.

When someone attempts to overrule the decision of a competent patient, procedural questions become entangled with substantive ethical questions about the right thing to do. The substantive question relates to the appropriate level of medical care: How aggressively should a particular patient be treated? The procedural question asks: Who should decide? One reason (but not the only one) that no universal answer can be given to the question about administering aggressive treatment is that the procedural question trumps the substantive one in cases of awake, alert adult patients. If this is part of what is meant by saying that "every case is unique," the statement is true, but all too obvious. Even if two patients have virtually identical medical conditions, if one is capable of participating in decisions while the other is not, then decisions about how aggressively to treat may differ in the two cases.

When the case of Mr. R. was presented at ethics rounds, nurses involved in the patient's care raised these questions: How does one choose between the patient's wishes and the family's? What if the patient becomes unresponsive? Are blood transfusions and antibiotics aggressive treatment? Are fluids and food aggressive treatment? Is administering a morphine drip to the point of lethargy euthanasia? Should the patient be resuscitated if his heart stops?

The answer to the first question is unequivocal: The competent patient's wishes must prevail. As hard as it is for doctors and nurses to reject the demands of family members, that is what is required by the respect-for-persons moral principle. Of course, family members should always be treated with consideration and with recognition of their own emotional turmoil when a relative is dying. But compassion for a family undergoing anticipatory grief should not lead to acceding to their wishes about treatment when those wishes conflict with what the patient himself has expressed.

When the nurses ask, "What if the patient becomes unresponsive?" they are inquiring whether it would continue to be necessary to adhere to the patient's previously stated wishes. It is one thing when an alert, adult patient requests less aggressive treatment. But what about that same patient when he lapses into unconsciousness? May caregivers then treat more aggressively, in response to the family's requests or their own medical judgment? Here, too, the answer is unequivocal. Neither caregivers nor family members may seize that opportunity to do what they think is best for a patient who has recently and clearly expressed his own wishes about the level of care. To wait until a patient becomes unresponsive and then begin aggressive treatment is to violate the respect-for-persons principle. This holds true also for "routine" treatments for unconscious patients, such as a blood transfusion that had been refused by a Jehovah's Witness while still alert. Although an unconscious person lacks autonomy, if that same person, while conscious, has recently exercised his autonomy in his stated preferences about medical treatment, those wishes must be respected.

The next pair of questions posed by the nurses—Are blood transfusions and antibiotics aggressive treatments? Are fluids and food aggressive treatments?—are requests to classify various modes of therapy. Such requests are problematic. The problem with such attempts to classify forms of treatment, whether the term used is "aggressive" or "heroic," or whether the familiar distinction between "ordinary" and "extraordinary" measures is invoked, is that there is no accepted meaning of the terms and therefore no agreement among health-care professionals about which treatments should be classified under which category. It is even less clear what patients or their families mean when they use these terms.

One well-known effort to specify a meaning for these concepts is the statement of Pope Pius XII delivered in 1957.[2] The pope noted that we are normally obliged to use only ordinary means to preserve life, and that "a more strict obligation would be too burdensome for most men and would render the attainment of the higher, more important good too difficult." While this statement makes it clear that, from the standpoint of the Roman Catholic Church, physicians need not do everything possible to preserve and prolong life, it does not help in distinguishing between what should be considered ordinary and what extraordinary.

Despite the vagueness and ambiguity of these concepts, patients and doctors alike continue to invoke them in discussions about treatment plans. In one case the question of resorting to "heroic measures" had been discussed by the patient, members of her family, and the physician who had previously been treating her at another hospital. When she was admitted to City Hospital on an emergency basis, the staff argued about what procedures could or could not be performed in complying with the patient's wishes.

A physician discussing the case made the following observations:

> We tend to define "extraordinary" by the scarcity or cost of the treatment, its technologic complexity, or its potential for discomfort and injury. I do not find this a satisfactory definition; yesterday's heroics quickly become today's routines. If you are treating a cancer patient with acute renal [kidney] failure, and your goal is to get him home for the holidays one more time, *and* if careful balancing of fluids, electrolytes, and calories still leaves him dangerously hyperkalemic [having elevated potassium], then hemodialysis [cleansing the blood in an artificial kidney machine] is not extraordinary, but is in fact medically indicated and, in 1985, perfectly ordinary. If a patient had clearly stated an unwillingness to continue to suffer from truly intractable pain and then develops hemorrhagic shock [from loss of blood], not only blood transfusion but the use of any volume expander constitutes extraordinary therapy, because it does not advance that patient's management goals. For any given patient, any treatment, however complex, can be considered ordinary, and any treatment, however simple, can be considered extraordinary. The difference lies in the purpose of the treatment, not in its cost or complexity.[3]

These observations, although perfectly sound from a theoretical standpoint, may not succeed in changing the practice of doctors who adhere to the dubious rule "Always treat what's treatable." Nor do they answer thorny legal questions about which life-prolonging treatments may be withheld or withdrawn. The legal issues surrounding decisions to forgo life-sustaining treatment have been evolving over the past decade, and while some trends can be detected, the law fails to provide absolute guidance in these matters. The rule "Always treat what's treatable" signifies much of what has been criticized when doctors practice medicine by following a technological imperative.

Some physicians believe it is part of their obligation to treat what's treatable. How should that belief be assessed? Certainly, physicians do not have an obligation to treat what's treatable in an alert patient who has completely refused treatment and has repeatedly expressed that wish. In such cases, like that of Mr. R., the physician's obligation is to honor the patient's request. In many instances, including ones in which patients lack the capacity to participate in their own treatment decisions, doctors who feel they must treat what is treatable only ensure that the patient will suffer a protracted period of dying—say, from cancer—rather than from the treatable infection that physicians so zealously eradicated. It is not a simple matter to determine just which obligations are binding on physicians. In general, the doctor's obligation is to bring about the best outcome for the patient, which means striving for a cure, when possible, or restoring the patient to his pre-illness level of functioning. But it can also mean relieving the patient's suffering. It is the patient who should be the object of concern, and not the medical condition that brought the patient to the hospital. The physician whose governing rule is "treat what is treatable" is more like a body mechanic than a doctor caring for a patient.

Despite the inability to draw a clear and workable distinction between ordinary and extraordinary treatments or between heroic and routine measures, the questions posed by the nurses in the case of Mr. R. call for reflection. To ask whether fluids and food constitute aggressive treatment may be to inquire whether they should be considered medical therapies at all. Long before the technological capabilities of modern medicine, indeed before the healing arts developed in civilized man, people sought to satisfy their basic nutritional needs. Food and liquids, and probably blood as well, occupy an important symbolic role in human life. At the heart of the nurses' request to classify forms of medical treatment is a commonsense query: How can something as instinctual, as fundamental as eating and drinking be considered "aggressive" or "heroic" in the medical setting? And doesn't the denial of these basic human needs deserve to be called "inhumane" medical practice?

Perhaps not. If the nutrients can be delivered only by means of a tube inserted into a patient's esophagus, a tube that produces continuous discomfort, the burdens of feeding may begin to outweigh the benefits to the patient of continued life. If the purpose of tube feeding is to sustain life, yet the procedure succeeds only in prolonging the process of dying, it is the provision, rather than the denial, of these basic human needs that deserves to be called "inhumane." Although most of us recoil at the thought of death by starvation or dehydration, we need to consider whether our distaste is prompted by the symbolic importance of food and fluids in human life, or whether we believe that the process of dying by this means is actually more painful, more uncomfortable, or more undignified than death from other causes. The sort of evidence that could settle the matter, evidence drawn from personal experience, is necessarily absent.

In all three cases—Mr. R., Clara M., and Mrs. F.—it was questioned whether cardiopulmonary resuscitation (CPR) should be performed if the patient had a cardiac arrest. Now if any procedure in modern medicine deserves to be called "aggressive," it is CPR. As commonly practiced, a resuscitation team rushes to the bedside, where one member of the team jumps onto the patient and pounds on his chest while others insert lines and tubes, give injections, and do whatever is necessary to get the patient's heart beating again. It is usually a messy affair, with blood and other body fluids spattering everyone within reach. Most patients are deemed to be candidates for CPR, and when they are discovered to be in cardiac arrest, either by a monitor that signals when a patient's heart has stopped, or by a nurse or other caretaker who discovers the patient in that condition, everyone rushes into action. The act that triggers the emergency response is someone's "calling a code": a preselected word or set of numbers announced over a loudspeaker paging system in the hospital. Perhaps the best-known is Code Blue, a widely used phrase to signify that a patient has suffered a cardiac arrest, which summons the resuscitation team.

The language surrounding CPR has taken on a life of its own in the hospital and may come as a surprise to the layperson unacquainted with terms used by insiders. Understandably enough, the phrase "call a code" replaces the lengthier "call for the cardiopulmonary resuscitation team" by busy hospital workers. Shortening often-used words or phrases is common practice everywhere, like the use of "peds" (pronounced "peeds") instead of pediatrics, "meds" in place of "medications," and a slew of alphabet-soup abbreviations: MI for myocardial infarction, IV for intravenous and IM for intramuscular, UTI for urinary tract infection, PID for pelvic inflammatory disease, OMS for organic mental syndrome, and the acronym ROMI (pronounced "row-me") for "rule out myocardial infarction."

These are shorthand expressions, intended only to make communications more concise, although they may serve the additional purpose of defining an in-group vocabulary, words and phrases not likely to be known to patients and families. When the primary purpose is to keep full information about the situation from patients, however, other words and phrases are available. "Cancer" has been a taboo word for a long time and has been replaced successively by "CA" (abbreviation for carcinoma), "malignancy," and now "neoplasm." As patients have learned the in-group's terminology, new, obscure terms are introduced to enable doctors to keep from revealing everything to patients. One expression continues to amuse me, despite the fact that I've heard it countless times. Instead of saying, "The patient went into cardiac arrest" or "The patient's heart stopped" or simply "The patient died," physicians, nurses, medical students, and others now typically say, "The patient coded."

Cardiopulmonary resuscitation is a good example of a therapy once considered heroic or extraordinary but now routine. To perform CPR on hospitalized patients who suffer a cardiac arrest is standard care. However, some patients are judged not to be candidates for this aggressive yet routine procedure, based on their medical condition and prognosis. Still other patients refuse CPR in advance when physicians frankly discuss treatment plans. When is it ethically permissible to withhold this aggressive treatment from patients who are unable to decide for themselves? Should the wishes of patients who decide against CPR always be honored?

Before these questions can be answered, another question must be addressed: Is a decision not to perform cardiopulmonary resuscitation a decision to use less aggressive measures within a range of acceptable therapeutic options? Or is it a decision to withhold life-sustaining treatment? Practically speaking, these amount to the same thing. But morally and legally, a lot can depend on what terms are used to describe actions that may, in fact, turn out to have the same consequences. Causing the death of another person could be a justifiable killing, as in self-defense; it could be manslaughter; or it could be first-degree homicide, as in a premeditated murder. When a patient is judged not to be a candidate for CPR, a do-not-resuscitate order (DNR) is written. This means that if the patient's heart stops, nurses will not "call a code," the resuscitation team will not leap into action, and the patient will be allowed to die. Described as a decision to adopt a nonaggressive treatment plan, a do-not-resuscitate order appears to be one of several acceptable options. But described as a decision to withhold life-sustaining treatment, a DNR order might appear to be an act of medical negligence, perhaps even an act of criminal negligence. Does the difference lie in what we choose to call it?

Both descriptions are accurate. A decision not to resuscitate a patient *is* a decision to withhold a particular, aggressive therapy. It is also a decision to withhold a therapy that could prolong a patient's life.

The rightness or wrongness of this action depends not on how we describe it, but rather on how we decide on it. If a decision not to perform CPR is arrived at in the same way other treatment decisions are reached—by involving the patient in the process when the patient is capable of participating, and if not, by consulting the family—then a DNR decision is not a morally culpable one and should be legally permitted. The problem with the law is that it lags behind existing practices in medicine, as in other areas of human life.

Although cardiopulmonary resuscitation is an aggressive, invasive procedure, it is nevertheless a routine aspect of medical care in today's modern hospital. Similarly, a decision not to engage in CPR, but instead to write a DNR order for a patient, also falls within accepted standards of care. In the past several years, state and local medical societies, hospital associations, and individual hospitals have begun writing guidelines and policies governing DNR orders. These efforts are a result, in part, of the recognition that hospitals have had no clear policies and, even worse, have permitted inconsistent practices concerning decisions not to resuscitate. In addition, attempts to develop morally sound policies have been mounted in response to unfavorable publicity and legal actions taken against several hospitals found to engage in shady practices.

An infamous incident that was reported in the media and resulted in a grand-jury indictment involved a hospital on Long Island in which patients who were not to be resuscitated had a sticker, a purple dot, placed on their charts. No written DNR orders were used, and doctors made the decision without consulting patients about whether they wished to be resuscitated if they suffered a cardiac arrest. This episode, which became known as "the purple-dot case," created a furor, and other hospitals rushed to their lawyers to try to avoid similar legal liability. Lawyers for the hospitals gave conflicting advice: some asserted that the hospital *must* begin to have DNR orders written in patients' charts, while others said just the opposite—it's legally risky to place a note in the chart.

The conflicting advice in this situation is a consequence of the uncertainty that prevails in state law (in this case the laws of New York State). Because no existing state statute addresses the issues involved in decisions not to resuscitate, and because no court cases have set a precedent for this medical procedure, chaos and uncertainty dominate the picture. The only clear guidance that was forthcoming related to the role of the patient in decision-making: if an alert adult patient is a party to the decision to write a do-not-resuscitate order, then such an order does not depart from the standard of care for medical treatment. Despite the fact that the situation regarding other patients is still in legal limbo, most hospitals in New York and other states have been actively seeking to develop clear policies for their own institutions.

It is evident from the discussions surrounding the appropriateness of administering CPR to certain patients that a decision to be less aggressive is frequently a decision to withhold a life-prolonging therapy. Cast in that form, the issue is transformed from that of physicians' clinical judgment and patients' informed consent into the more problematic question of when it is permissible to withdraw or withhold life supports from patients. This question deserves careful scrutiny, since it raises fundamental conceptual, moral, and legal questions about suicide, assisted suicide, and euthanasia.

As difficult as it is for physicians to ignore or reject requests from family members for aggressive treatments, doctors must recognize the primacy of the patient's wishes, such as those expressed by Mr. R. Yet lingering worries continue to surround the nurses' question: Is administering a morphine drip to the point of lethargy euthanasia? Patients may refuse treatments, even life-sustaining ones. But may they demand a course of action that is ethically unacceptable to their caregivers, and that could place doctors, nurses, and the hospital at legal risk?

Mrs. F., having become comatose, was in no condition to express wishes of her own. Yet as her poor prognosis became manifest, along with the futility of further resuscitations, the patient's niece was consulted about continued aggressive treatments. Although there is still considerable legal uncertainty in situations in which patients have expressed no wishes about medical care before becoming unable to participate in decisions, the practice almost everywhere is for physicians to consult family members and be guided by their wishes.

Most troubling, from an ethical standpoint, is the case of Clara M. The patient was consulted about being moved from the intensive-care unit to a regular floor. But did she understand what that move meant? Did she realize that she would not be monitored as closely on the floor, that there were fewer nurses than in the ICU, and that she was less likely to be resuscitated in case of cardiac arrest? Probably not. In the rush to make room for another patient, Clara M. was asked "if she minded being moved." With no family to ask additional questions, and with no private physician to stand firmly behind this patient's best medical interests, she was moved out of the ICU despite test results that were positive for myocardial infarction. Had she remained in the ICU, she would not have been allowed to get out of bed unattended, leading to a fall. Was the removal of this patient from the ICU ethically suspect?

When this case is considered in isolation, suspicion mounts that the patient was treated less aggressively than she should have been. Had there been someone—a family member, a private physician—to advocate strongly for her, the decision to remove Clara M. from the ICU might have been different. But these considerations, weighty as they are, are not the only morally relevant ones. Beds in the ICU are a scarce resource. More patients await entry to the ICU than there are available beds at any time. There are not enough beds in the ICU for all patients who are suspected of having had a myocardial infarction, so a selection needs to be made.

The need to make allocation decisions also arises in other areas of medical practice, such as selecting patients to be recipients of organs for transplantation. In these situations the particular patient's prognosis is only one of the factors to be taken into account. When more than one patient is involved in a situation requiring a decision, a different sort of moral problem arises: a problem of distributive justice.

Distributive justice is a matter of the comparative treatment of individuals. Not only the needs, interests, or stated wishes of an individual patient must be thrown into the decision-making hopper, but a just distribution of scarce resources requires that everyone's needs and interests be taken into account. The respect-for-persons principle is not at all applicable to such situations. And the utilitarian principle, while applicable, is only one among several that could be used to make decisions about allocating scarce resources.

So it is unresolved whether it was ethically questionable to remove Clara M. from the ICU to a room where she received less aggressive care and died shortly thereafter, or whether that move could be justified because a more acutely ill patient needed her ICU bed. Allocation decisions are among the most difficult ones physicians confront, partly because they require choosing among several patients, all of whom have some medical needs, and partly because the basis for deciding fairly remains fuzzy and controversial. The one thing that is clear about Clara M. is that she did not refuse aggressive treatments; it also seems clear that the decision to remove her from the ICU was *not* based on a judgment that it was in her best interest to withdraw life-sustaining treatment.

Patients' refusals of life-sustaining treatment continue to be unacceptable to many physicians. Yet it is becoming more common for physicians themselves to question whether insisting on such treatments is in some instances more inhumane, and therefore less ethical, than withholding or withdrawing life supports.

5

Forgoing Life-Sustaining Therapy

F EW WOULD ARGUE against the proposition that modern medicine has brought untold benefits to millions of people. Most would agree that cures for diseases, relief from pain and suffering, and the ability to prolong life are advances for which we can be grateful. But for some patients the burdens of modern medical treatment outweigh the benefits, with the result that an increasing number are now claiming the "right to die."

If the "right to die" seems like an odd sort of right, it is easy to see why. Our society not only opposes suicide, but it spends a considerable amount of money and effort on prevention. It appears to be inconsistent, then, to denounce suicide on the one hand, and yet to proclaim that there exists a "right to die." But the inconsistency is only apparent, as can be shown by first identifying clear, undisputed cases of suicidal behavior, and then comparing these cases with the circumstances in which patients and their families seek to exercise the newly recognized "right to die."

Ann B., a seventy-year-old woman, was admitted against her wishes to the psychiatric ward at City Hospital. She was found by a housekeeper in her apartment, playing with a knife at her wrists. The housekeeper called the emergency medical service, and Ann B. was whisked by ambulance to the psychiatric emergency room, where a psychiatrist evaluated her and found her to be "dangerous to self," meaning "suicidal." The psychiatrist also made a diagnosis of depression. Once she was admitted, Ann B. revealed that she had made a suicide pact with her sister, who had recently fallen ill and was a patient in another unit at City Hospital. The two sisters had had little contact with the outside world and, it appears, had led a somewhat eccentric life in isolation from anyone but each other. Ann B.'s actions with the knife, along with her disclosure of the pact with her sister, make this a clear, undisputed case of genuinely suicidal behavior.

Soon after her admission Ann B. developed a fever and was found to have pneumonia. She said she wanted to die and had to be restrained to keep her in the hospital bed. From that point on, her medical condition deteriorated: a catheter, or thin tube, had to be inserted into her bladder because she was retaining her urine; her respiratory status declined, and a breathing tube was placed; she developed skin infections over her whole body, as well as localized bedsores; and she became incontinent, unable to control her bowel functions. Although the patient had been mentally alert and oriented when she was admitted to the hospital, by this time her mental status had changed. She became lethargic and unresponsive. She lay in bed all day staring at the ceiling. Caregivers rarely found her in any other position. They wondered: Is this patient mentally capable of making decisions on her own behalf? Does her suicidal behavior suggest that she suffers from diminished autonomy, thus opening the way for justified paternalism on the part of her caregivers? Or, on the other hand, does the onset of multiple medical problems change the picture, so that now Ann B. has a rational reason to refuse life-prolonging medical treatments?

Psychiatrists consider depression to be both a life-threatening condition and a "treatable illness." The incidence of suicide attempts among depressed persons is high, and so clinicians in psychiatry and other medical specialities consider it their obligation to treat depression. They tend to dismiss refusals of treatment made by such patients. By definition, it is claimed, a diagnosis of depression means the patient has a bleak outlook on life, decision-making is impaired, and paternalistic behavior toward the patient is warranted. If the depression can be cured, the patient's outlook will improve and he will most likely cease to refuse life-prolonging medical therapies. This reasoning demonstrates the need to distinguish between refusals of medical treatment that stem from suicidal wishes and those that emanate from patients' rational judgments about their own quality of life.

Patients can be kept alive hooked up to respirators, dialysis machines, and other devices that keep their vital organs functioning; terminally ill cancer patients suffering intractable pain are given che-

motherapy, blood transfusions, radiation, and other treatments to prolong their lives by a few weeks or months; severely demented elderly
patients must often have a tube inserted through the nose and esophagus to the stomach, in order to receive medicines and food. To equate
the right to die with suicide would be to fail to recognize that such
treatments can sometimes make continued life an excessive burden.
Many patients on life supports, who are not depressed, judge the
quality of their own life to be so poor that they do not want it prolonged further by artificial means. And those patients whose depression results from learning their diagnosis of terminal illness may wish
to die sooner rather than later. Such a wish might then be entirely
rational.

Suicidologists have devised the category of "rational" or "logical"
suicide to apply to such cases. This approach recognizes a distinction,
one that has ethical implications, between suicidal wishes or actual
attempts to end one's life that are a consequence of mental illness
or emotional disorder and those that arise from a miserable quality
of life or a hopeless prognosis. To mark these distinctions, better
than the simple phrase "the right to die" are two alternative descriptions: "the right to die a natural death" and "the right to die with
dignity."

Hospitalized patients have come up against two formidable barriers in seeking to have treatments withdrawn or withheld. The first is
the unwillingness of physicians to allow their patients to forgo therapies that could preserve their lives. Doctors are dedicated to curing
disease and to prolonging life. They have traditionally seen it as their
duty to pursue these goals, even in the face of refusals by patients who
are fully competent to decide about their own treatments. The second
barrier has been the law, which until quite recently stood behind
physicians in their reluctance to allow patients to refuse treatments
when the likely result would be death.

Now, however, much has changed, because of some leading court
decisions as well as more assertive actions by patients and their families. Physicians are acknowledging, alongside their obligation to preserve and prolong life, another equally valid goal of medical practice:
to relieve suffering. As in any practice having multiple goals, these
two noble aims of medicine may sometimes conflict. Even when a life
could be prolonged, a physician might question the wisdom of continuing treatment, as in the case of Martha T.

The patient was a sixty-one-year-old woman with a history of
heart failure, who several years ago suffered a stroke. Three months

before this hospital admission, she became increasingly weak; she showed evidence of aphasia (loss of the ability to transmit ideas through speech), and her overall mental status declined. Following another neurologic episode, Martha T. was brought to the hospital with hydrocephalus, an accumulation of fluid that exerts pressure on the brain, and a shunt was performed to drain the excess fluid from her skull. She was placed on a respirator and given medication to control seizures. For a while she was unable to speak, and her mental status reached zero; then she improved. At the time her physician believed a decision was called for, the patient's mental status was fluctuating from one day to the next. Her husband, who came to visit occasionally, reported that his wife did not recognize him.

As a patient in the intensive-care unit for two months, Martha T. underwent repeated procedures: tube feedings, delivery of medications through an intravenous line, insertion of a Swan-Ganz catheter into the heart in order to monitor cardiac response to medications, and regular blood drawings for laboratory tests. Her attending physician, judging her to have a very poor prognosis, suggested that the heart medications be withdrawn and that she be mercifully allowed to die. The resident in the ICU disagreed. She said a new experimental drug had been used on some patients, whose condition then improved. Martha T.'s husband, who had granted consent for all procedures recommended so far, now seemed willing to accept the cardiologist's judgment that nothing more could benefit his wife. Was it beneficial to this patient for physicians to administer an experimental drug and continue invasive procedures and life supports in the ICU? Her cardiologist did not think so, and ordered the heart medications stopped. Martha T. died the next day.

Matters of life and death involve law as well as ethics. This is because of the legal notion of "the state's interest in life," a notion that goes back many years. Two separate legal developments—one judicial and one legislative—have granted patients and their families the right to forgo life-sustaining treatments. Beginning in New Jersey in 1976 with the landmark case of Karen Ann Quinlan, courts in many jurisdictions have permitted the removal of respirators from comatose patients. At the time of that decision, twenty-one-year-old Karen had fallen into a coma, apparently caused by a combination of alcohol and tranquilizers. She remained alive on a respirator but was judged by physicians to be irreversibly comatose. Specifically, expert medical opinion held that there was no reasonable possibility of her ever emerging from her comatose condition to a "cognitive, sapient state." Based on this prognosis, her parents sought to have the respirator that artificially sustained her breathing withdrawn. At first denied by a lower court in New Jersey, the Quinlans' request was eventually granted by the New Jersey Supreme Court in a unanimous decision. Although the judicial case set an important precedent, an irony of nature ensued: despite medical predictions to the contrary, Karen Ann Quinlan survived removal of the respirator. She remained alive in a coma for ten years, and died in June 1985.

Although Karen Quinlan was not the one who requested that the respirator sustaining her life be withdrawn, the court in her case nevertheless distinguished between cessation of life supports and suicide. The court stated; "We would see . . . a real distinction between the self-infliction of deadly harm and a self-determination against artificial life-support or radical surgery, for instance, in the face of irreversible, painful and certain imminent death."[1]

That view was echoed in a Massachusetts case decided the following year. This case also involved a patient unable to make decisions on his own behalf. The patient, Joseph Saikewicz, was a profoundly retarded man, age sixty-seven, who had a form of leukemia that is invariably fatal. Unlike Karen Quinlan, who was in a coma, Mr. Saikewicz was conscious. Yet it was evident that he would be unable to understand the reason for the pain and suffering he would experience as side effects of chemotherapy, and that he would have to be physically restrained in order for doctors to administer drugs and perform blood transfusions. The court was petitioned to appoint a guardian to make the necessary medical decisions, and it eventually ruled that life-prolonging treatment could be withheld from the patient.

The Massachusetts court wrote:

The interest in protecting against suicide seems to require little if any discussion. In the case of the competent adult's refusing medical treatment such an act does not necessarily constitute suicide since (1) in refusing treatment the patient may not have the specific intent to die, and (2) even if he did, to the extent that the cause of death was from natural causes the patient did not set the death-producing agent in motion with the intent of causing his own death. . . . Furthermore, the underlying State interest in this area lies in the prevention of irrational self-destruction. What we consider here is a competent, rational decision to refuse treatment when death is inevitable and the treatment offers no hope of cure or preservation of life. There is no connection between the conduct here . . . and any State concern to prevent suicide.[2]

The Quinlan and Saikewicz cases are two of the earliest in an increasing number of cases brought to courts for a decision about whether life-sustaining therapies may legally be withheld or withdrawn. Although most of these judicial opinions contain moral as well as legal reasoning in support of their conclusions, it is the nature of judicial findings that they must rely on precedents set in earlier cases. This fact, along with differences among judges in the experience and values they bring to the bench, has resulted in variations from one state to the next in both the substantive and procedural aspects of the courts' rulings.

In a related series of developments, precipitated in part by these court cases, state legislatures have enacted so-called "right-to-die" laws. The first of these was the California Natural Death Act, a living-will law passed in 1976. By the end of 1985 thirty-six states had passed legislation giving legal validity to the living will, a statement made by competent persons concerning what they want done in the event they become incompetent to make decisions about their own medical treatment. An advocacy organization, the Society for the Right to Die, uses the phrase "living will" as a generic term applied to legislation identified by a variety of descriptive phrases—"natural death," "death with dignity," "right to die."[3] But in more general terms, the phrase is used to refer to documents drawn up by individuals even in states that have not passed living-will or natural-death legislation.

Here is such a document, devised by a physician, a colleague of mine. It is based on a standardized form but expanded to include elements he wanted made explicit.

MY LIVING WILL

To My Family, My Physician, My Lawyer, and All Others Whom It May Concern:

If the time comes when I can no longer take part in decisions for my own future, let this statement stand as an expression of my wishes and directions while I am still of sound mind.

If at such a time the situation should arise in which there is no reasonable expectation of my recovery from extreme physical or mental disability, I direct that I be allowed to die and not be kept alive by medications, artificial means, or "heroic measures." I do, however, ask that medications be mercifully administered to me to alleviate suffering even though this may shorten my remaining life.

This statement is made after careful consideration and is in accordance with my strong convictions and beliefs. I want the wishes and directions here expressed carried out to the extent permitted by law. Insofar as they are not legally enforceable, I hope that those to whom this will is addressed will regard themselves as morally bound by these provisions.

In the face of impending death, which I define as the reasonable likelihood of death occurring within three months, I specifically refuse:

- Electrical or mechanical cardiac resuscitation.
- Nasogastric-tube feeding or feeding gastrostomy.
- Mechanical respiration involving tracheal intubation.
- Any surgical procedure except that directed specifically to the relief of actual pain or other physical distress.

In the event that I should become comatose, or should enter a permanent vegetative state, or should become so impaired mentally or physically that I am incapable of meaningful communication with other persons, and if two consulting neurologists believe that recovery from this state is not likely to take place, I direct that my physicians treat me as if I were actually dying, with all the requests and restrictions listed above. It is my strong belief that such states are, for me, the equivalent of death itself. I do not wish my body sustained by artificial feeding, antibiotics, blood transfusions, or cardiopulmonary resuscitation, nor do I wish to undergo any diagnostic studies likely to cause physical distress.

Further, if I should be so impaired, all reasonable efforts should be made after two weeks in that state to transfer me to a chronic-disease facility or nursing home, and all efforts on my behalf thereafter limited to maintenance of cleanliness and relief from pain and other physical distress.

If any of my tissues or organs are thought to be of value to others as transplants or for tissue-banking, I freely give my permission for such donation.

Should I become incompetent temporarily or permanently, I designate my wife Carol to serve as my attorney-in-fact for the purpose of making all medical treatment decisions. If she is not able to do so, then I designate my daughter Elizabeth, and if she cannot perform this function, my daughter Laura. I ask them to do so in the spirit of my requests and directions stated above. This power of attorney shall remain effective indefinitely unless I recover competence to make treatment decisions.

Signed: Martin L——, M.D.
Dated:

Witness:
Address:

Witness:
Address:

Copies to be given or sent to: Carol L.
Elizabeth L.
Laura L.
My lawyer
My physician

The legal developments surrounding patients' rights to refuse life-sustaining treatments are not without their moral problems. Although the trend in living-will statutes suggests that formerly competent patients can now have their wishes honored once they are no longer able to decide for themselves, what about individuals who have never stated what they would want done medically when they are no longer capable of making decisions? Is it morally acceptable for others to make decisions for them? And if so, who should those others be: Doctors? Family members? Judges? Hospital ethics committees? Is there an objective basis for making such decisions? And is there a danger in allowing any person to decide for another based on "quality-of-life" considerations?

These now-familiar questions have no simple answers. But they can be approached in order of decreasing certainty about what is the morally right thing to do. The greatest certainty lies in cases involving mentally competent adult patients. There is little or no difference between the general situation regarding decisions about how aggressive treatments should be and specific decisions to forgo life-sustaining treatments. Neither a moral nor a legal justification exists for ignoring patients' clearly stated wishes to withdraw or withhold those treatments, even if the family begs the doctor to "do everything possible." As in the case of Ann B., exceptions to this rule arise when patients are depressed and therefore lack proper judgment to decide about forgoing life-prolonging treatment. But in nondepressed patients, and especially when the patient suffers from a fatal illness, even the tradi-

tional reluctance of the courts to go against physicians' recommendations has all but disappeared.

A case decided recently in California upheld the right of a competent patient, William Bartling, to have life-support equipment disconnected, despite the fact that withdrawal of such devices would surely
hasten his death. Mr. Bartling was seventy years old and suffered from
emphysema, a condition that causes severe difficulty in breathing;
chronic respiratory failure; arteriosclerosis; an aneurysm (ballooning
of an artery) in his abdomen; and a malignant tumor of the lung. He
also had a history of "chronic acute anxiety/depression" and alcoholism. The patient entered Glendale Adventist Medical Center in April
1984 for treatment of his depression. A physical examination revealed
a tumor on his lung. A lung biopsy caused the lung to collapse, and a
breathing tube was inserted. Because of his emphysema, the hole
made by the biopsy needle did not heal properly and the lung did not
reinflate. A tracheotomy was performed, and Mr. Bartling was placed
on a ventilator, where he remained until his death, despite efforts to
"wean" him from the machine.

On several occasions the patient tried to remove the ventilator
tubes, and his wrists were placed in "soft restraints." Despite requests
from Mr. Bartling and his wife, the hospital and treating physicians
refused to remove the ventilator or the restraints. The patient himself
signed a living will, which stated in part:

> If at such time the situation should arise in which there is no
> reasonable expectation of my recovery from extreme physical or
> mental disability, I direct that I be allowed to die and not be kept
> alive by medications, artificial means or heroic measures.

He also signed a declaration stating in part:

> While I have no wish to die, I find intolerable the living conditions
> forced upon me by my deteriorating lungs, heart and blood vessel
> systems, and find intolerable my being continuously connected to
> this ventilator. . . . Therefore, I wish this Court to order that the
> sustaining of my respiration by this mechanical device violates my
> constitutional right, is contrary to my every wish, and constitutes
> a battery upon my person.

In that declaration Mr. Bartling said he understood that removing the
ventilator would likely cause respiratory failure and ultimately lead to

death. He stated his willingness to accept that risk rather than continue the burden of "this artificial existence which I find unbearable, degrading and dehumanizing."[4]

Despite these strong and unequivocal statements from Mr. Bartling and his family, his treating physicians refused to remove the ventilator and the restraints. In a deposition the patient said that he wanted to live but not on the ventilator. Attorneys for the hospital and the physicians questioned the patient's ability to make a meaningful decision because of his vacillation.

Another feature of the case was the nature of the hospital itself: Glendale Adventist is a Christian hospital devoted to the preservation of life. Spokesmen claimed that it would be unethical for that hospital's physicians to disconnect life-support systems from patients whom they viewed as having the potential for cognitive, sapient life. The California Court of Appeal reversed the decision of a lower court, a decision that, in the words of George Annas, a lawyer who worked on the case and assisted in preparing the appeals brief, "sentenced William Bartling to spend the rest of his life in an intensive care unit. His crime seems to have been that he suffered from fatal diseases instead of 'terminal' ones, and that his desire to live seemed at odds with his desire to have the mechanical ventilator that sustained his life removed."[5] The California Court of Appeal ruled that the earlier trial court was incorrect when it held that the right to have life-support equipment disconnected was limited to comatose, terminally ill patients, or representatives acting on their behalf. The court held that Mr. Bartling was competent in the legal sense to decide whether he wanted to have the ventilator disconnected. He wanted to live but preferred death to his intolerable life on the ventilator. The fact that the patient periodically wavered from this posture because of severe depression or any other reason does not justify the conclusion that his capacity to make such a decision was impaired to the point of legal incompetency, the court ruled.

The major issue, according to the court, was the right of the patient, as a competent adult, to refuse unwanted medical treatment. The court stated that in California, "a person of adult years and sound mind has the right, in the exercise of control over his own body, to determine whether or not to submit to lawful medical treatment." Moreover, that legal right predates the state's Natural Death Act. It derives from a long line of court cases dealing with informed consent, one of which, *Cobbs* v. *Grant*, was decided in California in 1972. The court in the Bartling case concluded that

if the right of the patient to self-determination as to his own medical treatment is to have any meaning at all, it must be paramount
to the interests of the patient's hospital and doctors. The right of a
competent adult patient to refuse medical treatment is a constitu-
tionally guaranteed right which must not be abridged.[6]

Somewhat less certainty surrounds the situation of patients who
are no longer mentally competent at the time a decision must be made
but who had given indications about desired medical treatment while
still competent. Although evidence of patients' wishes need not be in
the form of a written living will, such a document probably offers the
most solid evidence. However, a statement made orally to family
members might be equally valid.

In an important precedent in New York State, the court accepted
as evidence of the wishes of a comatose patient, a clergyman known as
Brother Fox, an oral statement he had previously made to his religious
brethren that if he were ever to fall into a situation similar to Karen
Ann Quinlan, he would not want to be kept alive by "extraordinary
means," in accordance with the dictate of Pope Pius XII. Some time
after making that statement, Brother Fox, an eighty-three-year-old
member of the Society of Mary, suffered a cardiac arrest and was
placed on a respirator. The New York Court of Appeals considered
Brother Fox's earlier statement to be "clear and convincing evidence"
of his refusal of treatment. Basing its conclusion on the right of a
competent adult to refuse treatment, the court authorized the removal
of the respirator.

In contrast, however, a never-competent patient, one who had
been mentally retarded all his life, was denied that right at the same
time and by the same court that decided the Brother Fox case. The
patient, John Storar, was a fifty-two-year-old man who was profoundly retarded, having a mental age of about eighteen months. He
had cancer of the bladder, which had progressed to a terminal stage.
He initially received radiation treatments and, after internal bleeding
had begun, was being given regular blood transfusions. Consent for
treatment was granted by Mr. Storar's mother, who had been appointed his legal guardian.

Eventually, she requested that her son's blood transfusions be discontinued. He could not understand what was happening to him or
the need for the transfusions and at times had to be put under sedation
and physically restrained in order for the procedure to be done. It was
estimated that even with the transfusions John Storar would live only

about three to six months. In denying his mother's request to discontinue the blood transfusions, the court argued that there was no way to determine what the patient himself would want done. To ask that question, the court said, was like asking, "If it snowed all summer, would it then be winter?"[7] Since the patient was mentally an infant, he should have the same rights as minors: protection from decisions by others—even their legal guardians—who seek to refuse life-saving blood transfusions.

The court's motivation in this ruling is commendable. It seeks to protect people like John Storar, a mentally retarded person who cannot speak for himself, from relatives' or guardians' decisions that run contrary to the patient's best interest. Those unable to express their own views stand in need of such protection. But not all decisions to terminate life-sustaining treatment go against the patient's best interest. John Storar was suffering from both the pain of his cancer and the discomfort of being tied down for the blood transfusions. To require the life of a terminally ill patient to be prolonged in this way seems cruel. It suggests the need for a proper mechanism that would allow life supports to be withdrawn and at the same time erect safeguards against abuse.

The court that decided the cases of Brother Fox and John Storar found the crucial difference between the two cases of withdrawing life-sustaining treatment to lie in a characteristic of the patient: one had been mentally competent to state what he would want done if he became incompetent to decide, while the other had never been competent. Another dissimilarity between Brother Fox and John Storar lay in the nature of the treatment each was receiving. Brother Fox was on a respirator, a form of medical treatment that he as well as others deemed "extraordinary." John Storar was receiving blood transfusions, a therapy usually considered "routine" and one that the court said was analogous to feeding. But if there is good reason to question the moral relevance of the distinction between ordinary and extraordinary treatments, then there must be some way of determining what is in a patient's best interest, regardless of the specific therapy being administered.

In the Massachusetts case decided two years earlier, Joseph Saikewicz, another mentally retarded patient who had never been competent, was granted the right to have life-sustaining treatment withheld. The Supreme Judicial Court in Massachusetts determined that "the substantive rights of the competent and the incompetent person are the same in regard to the right to decline potentially life-prolonging treatment."[8] Cases that are apparently similar may be decided differently by courts in different jurisdictions.

The Saikewicz case was decided in 1977, and the Fox and Storar cases in 1981. In the few years since then, the discussion in bioethics has moved from considering the ethics of withdrawing respirators to the permissibility of withholding food and fluids from patients. Like blood—perhaps even more so—the symbolic role of nutrients in sustaining human life prompts further reflection on what may ethically be withheld from patients unable to decide for themselves. Some would draw a line at blood, others at food and fluids. This is to make the mode of treatment the basis for drawing a line between when it is acceptable to forgo therapy and when it is unacceptable. It is to base the decision on the rather dubious distinction between ordinary and extraordinary treatments. But other factors have much greater moral significance.

A factor of considerable moral importance is the mode of dying. The process of dying can be peaceful and easy for the patient, or it can be painful and frightening. For many patients, prolonging their lives amounts to prolonging an agonizing dying process, one fraught with discomfort, nausea, shortness of breath, or mental confusion. In deciding which treatments may be withheld or withdrawn, physicians should consider the manner of death and, if possible, choose a plan of selective therapy that will result in the "least worst death."[9]

In the years since courts were first brought into cases involving termination of life supports, there has been a gradual progression from greater to lesser moral certainty. Early cases dealt with removal of respirators from patients in permanent coma, or withdrawing treatment from patients who had clearly stated their wishes about life prolongation. The final court case to consider here is one in which these features were absent, and in which several important precedents were set. In January 1985, nine years after the Quinlan case was decided, the New Jersey Supreme Court permitted the withdrawal of life supports from a nursing-home patient who was not comatose. The patient had no written living will, the "treatment" in question was food and fluids rather than a respirator or other high-technology device, and the life-sustaining measures had to be withdrawn rather than simply withheld.

Claire Conroy was an eighty-four-year-old nursing-home resident who suffered from serious and irreversible physical and mental impairments, including arteriosclerotic heart disease, hypertension, and diabetes. Her condition eventually reached a point where she could not speak and could not swallow enough food and water to sustain herself. She was fed and medicated through a nasogastric tube inserted through her nose and extending down into her stomach. She was incontinent. She could, though, move to a minor extent, and occasionally smiled and moaned in response to stimuli. The patient's nephew, her guardian, sought court permission to remove his incompetent aunt's feeding tube. This request was opposed by the patient's court-appointed guardian, known as guardian *ad litem* (a guardian appointed solely for the purpose of making specific decisions during a limited time period). The patient's own physician stated that he did not think it would be acceptable medical practice to remove the tube and that he was in favor of keeping it in place. Ms. Conroy's nephew, based on his knowledge of his aunt's attitudes, said that if she had been competent, she would never have permitted the nasogastric tube to be inserted in the first place.

Ms. Conroy was a Roman Catholic. A Catholic priest testified in the case that acceptable church teaching could be found in a document entitled "Declaration of Euthanasia" published by the Vatican Congregation for the Doctrine of the Faith, dated June 26, 1980. The test that this document used required a weighing of the burdens and benefits to the patient of remaining alive with the aid of extraordinary life-sustaining medical treatment. The priest said that life-sustaining procedures could be withdrawn if they were extraordinary, which he defined to embrace "all procedures, operations or other interventions which are excessively expensive, burdensome or inconvenient or which offer no hope of benefit to a patient." The priest concluded that the use of the nasogastric tube was extraordinary, and that removal of the tube would be ethical and moral, even though the ensuing period until Ms. Conroy's death would be painful.

A long-standing debate in bioethics revolves around the question of whether a valid moral distinction can be made between withholding life-sustaining treatments from a patient and withdrawing them once they are in place. Although many physicians act as though there is a moral difference, their reaction probably reflects their own emotional discomfort at withdrawing a treatment already begun rather than an ethical position that can be convincingly defended. The court in the Conroy case explicitly rejected the validity of "the distinction some have made between actively hastening death by terminating treatment and passively allowing a person to die of a disease. . . . Characterizing conduct as active or passive is often an elusive notion, even outside the context of medical decision-making." The court went on to state, "The ambiguity inherent in this distinction is further heightened when one performs an act within an overall plan of non-intervention, such as when a doctor writes an order not to resuscitate a patient." Thus, the court concluded, "whether necessary treatment is withheld at the outset or withdrawn later on, the consequence—the patient's death—is the same."

The court also found unpersuasive "the distinction relied on by some courts, commentators and theologians between 'ordinary' treatment, which they would always require, and 'extraordinary' treatment, which they deem optional. The terms 'ordinary' and 'extraordinary' have assumed too many conflicting meanings to remain useful," the court said.[10]

Among the observations made by the Conroy court was the fact that people who refuse life-sustaining medical treatment may not harbor a specific intent to die. This view concurred with that of judges in earlier cases, who held that refusals of life supports should not be equated with suicide. Yet the court noted the difficulty involved in making such determinations regarding incompetent patients. It recognized a number of different types of evidence and information that might bear on an incompetent person's intent or prior wishes; nevertheless, the court said, in the absence of adequate proof of the patient's wishes, "it is naive to pretend that the right to self-determination serves as the basis for substituted decision making."

Situations involving great ethical and legal uncertainty are those in which a patient is no longer competent, had never clearly stated any preferences while still competent about what sorts of medical treatment should be administered or withheld, but had provided some bit of evidence through attitudes or behavior during prior illnesses. Even more troubling are situations in which no evidence whatsoever is available about what the patient would have wanted. The standard in such cases should be the "best interest" of the patient. But that is precisely the problem: Is there any objective way of determining what is in the best interest of someone lacking the mental capacity to decide about continued life?

The court in the Conroy case tackled this problem head-on. It did not want to rule out the possibility of terminating life-sustaining treatment for persons who had never clearly expressed any desires but who are now suffering a prolonged and painful death. Judge Schreiber, who wrote the opinion in the Conroy case, articulated two best-interest tests for determining when life-sustaining treatment may be withheld, tests that supplement the "subjective test" (what the patient would have wanted).

The two standards are a "limited-objective" test and a "pure-objective" test.

Under the "limited-objective" test, life-sustaining treatment may be withheld or withdrawn from a patient in Claire Conroy's situation when there is some trustworthy evidence that the patient would have refused treatment, and the decision maker is satisfied that it is clear that the burdens of the patient's continued life with the treatment outweigh the benefits of that life for him. By this we mean that the patient is suffering, and will continue to suffer throughout the expected duration of his life, unavoidable pain, and that the net burdens of his prolonged life (the pain and suffering of his life with the treatment less the amount and duration of pain that the patient would likely experience if the treatment were withdrawn) markedly outweigh any physical pleasure, emotional enjoyment, or intellectual satisfaction that the patient may still be able to derive from life.

The pure-objective test is similar to the limited-objective test but omits the element requiring evidence of the patient's prior wishes. Thus,

the net burdens of the patient's life with the treatment should clearly and markedly outweigh the benefits that the patient derives from life. Further, the recurring, unavoidable and severe pain of the patient's life with the treatment should be such that the effect of administering life-sustaining treatment would be inhumane.

These two tests—limited-objective and pure-objective—constitute a bold step in interpreting the vague notion of "best interest," and the Conroy decision sets an important legal precedent. This is not to say that it will always be an easy matter to apply the tests. The court's wording makes it appear that determining a patient's objective best interest is a matter of arithmetic calculation: the net burdens of his prolonged life (the pain and suffering of his life with the treatment less the amount and duration of pain that the patient would likely experience if the treatment were withdrawn) markedly outweigh any physical pleasure, emotional enjoyment, or intellectual satisfaction that the patient may still be able to derive from life. Yet even if this cannot be accomplished by means of simple calculations, it is a step forward in trying to explicate the notion of "best interest" as it applies to incompetent patients.

As important as the court's positive attempt to give meaning to the best-interest doctrine is what it explicitly ruled out when such determinations must be made. The opinion stated quite clearly that it would not be appropriate for a decision-maker to determine that someone else's life is not worth living simply because, to the decision-maker, the patient's "quality of life" or value to society seems negligible.

It is widely agreed—but with objections voiced by some—that decisions to forgo life-sustaining treatment should not be based on assessments of the personal worth or social utility of another's life, or the value of that life to others. A morally acceptable reason to withdraw or withhold life supports exists when continued life would not be a benefit to the patient. This description clearly fits patients who are irreversibly comatose. With perhaps less certainty it also applies to patients on life supports who have deteriorated mentally to the point where they can no longer recognize their loved ones, cannot experience any pleasure, and can engage in no human relationships. Although safeguards should always be in place for the protection of patients, sound moral principles support the view that it is sometimes permissible to forgo life-sustaining treatments.

Determining
Incompetency

DOCTORS ARE TRAINED to act in the patient's best interest. The long-standing medical practice of deciding what is best for their patients leads many physicians to become impatient, frustrated, and even angry at patients who seem not to respect their medical expertise. But doctors need not face an either-or choice between two moral evils: permitting patients to sicken or die as a result of respecting their autonomy, or violating their autonomy by forcing them to accept a recommended treatment. One way out of the quandary is to find the patient a victim of diminished autonomy, which could then ethically justify overriding the refusal. This third choice allows the physician to escape between the horns of the dilemma. But it does not get the doctor entirely off the moral hook.

When I was called to a case conference to deliberate about what should be done with Bunky, the homeless woman with one leg who made a nuisance of herself in the bank executive's office, I found that much of the discussion revolved around determining the patient's competence. Although the case did not initially involve a refusal of treatment by a patient with diminished autonomy, it posed the equivalent problem of placing her in a mental hospital against her will.

Many state laws now permit involuntary hospitalization of mental patients only if they are judged dangerous to themselves or others. Bunky's case was complicated by the fact that she had been legally declared incompetent to manage her own affairs some years earlier. According to this ruling, her court-appointed guardian, an attorney, could make all decisions on her behalf. But the lawyer, to his credit, insisted on considering Bunky's own wishes in the matter. He was reluctant to assume automatically that she lacked the capacity to make decisions for herself or to continue to manage her marginal existence on the streets. He explored the options in consultation with mental-health workers at City Hospital, where Bunky awaited a decision about her fate.

My own view was that patients should be treated as competent unless they are clearly shown to be incapable of deciding and acting for themselves. In Bunky's case psychiatrists had not come up with a clear diagnosis of a psychiatric disorder. And even if they had, that diagnosis would not be sufficient in itself for a determination of her incompetence.

On the one hand, there was evidence of her ability to survive from the fact of her subsisting in the subway for the past few years. On the other hand, there was evidence to the contrary: she had been beaten and abused, and had suffered the accident that led to the loss of her leg. I argued for Bunky's right to liberty, her "right to be let alone." But my judgment about how capable she was of managing her existence proved wrong.

Bunky's legal guardian, the court-appointed attorney, decided to allow her to be taken to another municipal hospital, which contained a long-term-care facility, until a final decision could be made. While at that hospital, the patient refused psychiatric medications, and the guardian supported her in that refusal. However, Bunky drove her wheelchair down the steps in the hospital and broke her collarbone. She was transported back to City Hospital (an acute-care facility) for medical care, and although she had not previously been diagnosed as psychotic, she now developed unmistakable psychotic symptoms.

After being treated for her broken collarbone, Bunky was placed once again in the psychiatric ward, where she rapidly deteriorated. The staff saw no alternative but to make arrangements for her admission to a state psychiatric hospital. That facility would accept the patient only if she was receiving psychiatric medications, which she continued to refuse. Because of the pressure exerted by the bank executive, a powerful person in the community, and also because it was thought to be in her own best interest, Bunky was given antipsychotic medications—against her will but with the approval of her legal guardian—while arrangements were being made to transfer her to the state hospital.

■ ■ ■

THE IMPORTANCE OF making accurate assessments of competency
—the capacity of a person to grant or refuse permission for therapy—
is crucial for obtaining properly informed consent. The entire procedure would be a sham if patients who consent to treatment lacked the
capacity to understand the information presented before signing a
consent form.

The notion of competency used in the context of informed consent
is a legal as well as a psychological concept. An official determination
of incompetency can be made only by a judge, and usually rests on a
recommendation by a psychiatrist following an evaluation of the patient; as one expression puts it, "The psychiatrist proposes, the judge
disposes." Despite the fact that competency is strictly a legal concept,
in that it requires a judicial declaration, it is used loosely and infor-
mally in the hospital to refer to the mental capacity of patients to grant
properly informed consent.

Because an assessment of competency is typically made when a
question arises about a patient's ability to grant properly informed
consent, efforts to determine competency should focus on the patient's
understanding of the nature and purpose of the treatment, its risks
and benefits, and the alternatives—including no treatment. Yet what
actually happens when patients are thought to have impaired judgment often has little connection with these basic elements that must
be comprehended by the patient.

When a psychiatric consultation is called for the purpose of evaluating a patient's competency, one or more standard tests of "mental
status" are commonly used. Devised originally for other purposes,
these mental-status tests bring an air of mystique to the process. In
one test, known as "serial sevens," the patient is asked to count backwards from one hundred, subtracting by seven. On another test the
patient is told to copy simple geometric figures. A third test requires
the patient to offer an interpretation of standard proverbs, the point
being to determine the person's ability to think abstractly or to generalize. The most basic "test" is referred to as the patient's "orientation
to time, place, and person." The patient should know the date (at least
the year), where he is (in the hospital, not at the Hilton), and who he
is. Patients who pass this test are described in the shorthand lingo of
the hospital as "oriented times three." Although being "oriented times
three" is usually necessary for a patient to be evaluated as competent,
it is often not judged to be sufficient.

Since I am convinced that a person's ability to grant informed
consent to treatment is a commonsense notion that does not require

special psychiatric expertise to evaluate, I have remained puzzled about the use of these mental-status tests. The ability to copy a single geometric figure seems relevant neither to understanding information nor to reasoning about that information. (The original purpose of this test was to reveal and locate possible organic brain lesions, such as tumors or injuries.)

Interpreting proverbs is a highly culture-bound task, and it requires certain factual knowledge as well. In order to supply a general meaning for the expression "A rolling stone gathers no moss," a person has to know whether having moss is considered a good thing or a bad thing. Even in cases where the meaning of a proverb is nearly universal, it is still unclear how the ability to interpret it bears on a patient's competency to grant or refuse consent for treatment.

As for the serial-sevens subtraction test, someone who spent a lifetime as a retail clerk may perform superbly when asked to count backwards from one hundred by units of seven, but the task might be accomplished by rote. Conversely, a young adult raised on electronic calculators could be very slow at simple arithmetic. I've tried this test on a number of highly educated friends, and some, to their embarrassment, fumbled, were slow, or made errors in subtraction.

Orientation to time, place, and person does seem to be a necessary condition for a minimal level of understanding. Occasionally, some physicians who are giving the test cannot pass the time portion if they are not wearing a digital watch with date and day-of-the-week display. If a patient thinks that he's Napoleon, that the year is 1812, and that he's in France, it takes no psychiatric expertise to judge that he is out of touch with reality. But what does this person's "orientation times zero" have to do with his ability to grant informed consent for a leg amputation? The answer depends on the relation between the delusional beliefs and the decision regarding treatment. If the patient refuses surgical amputation on the grounds that he could not lead his troops in battle without both legs, or because it is 1812 and anesthesia has not yet been invented, then his false beliefs are causally related to the refusal to grant consent. In that case there is good reason to presume incompetency even before any further psychiatric tests are administered. Curiously, however, despite this patient's delusional belief system, he is nevertheless able to offer relevant reasons, within the context of that delusional system, for refusing treatment.

But suppose he refuses consent for the amputation and, when asked why, replies with cogent reasons that would or should be respected if offered by a nondelusional patient. In that case his delusional state and its accompanying irrationality could be separated from his competency to grant or refuse consent for treatment.

This suggests that psychiatrists called upon to make competency evaluations should keep the patient's capacity to grant informed consent distinct from a diagnosis of mental illness. Determining the competency of psychiatric patients such as Bunky is often problematic. Despite a diagnosis of mental illness, many individuals may nonetheless be found competent when given a mental-status examination. It is certainly true that some patients who are schizophrenic or have other psychiatric illnesses lack the capacity to understand the information necessary to grant properly informed consent. Psychiatrists are expert at diagnosing and treating mental disorders. Their education and experience enable them to diagnose schizophrenia, depression, and a host of other disorders for which there are biological or behavioral criteria. But "incompetency" is not a mental illness, so psychiatrists who are called upon to assess competency must draw on something other than their expertise in diagnosing psychiatric disorders.

More problematic is the apparent fact that even well-trained psychiatrists lack a firm, consistent basis for evaluating competency. Some psychiatrists take mental illness to be an automatic guarantee of a patient's incompetence, while other psychiatrists make no such assumption. Some patients are lucid at some times and confused at others. There are people who appear competent when judged by some criteria and incompetent according to other criteria. And then there are patients who are marginally competent, making it impossible even for trained psychiatrists to make a definitive evaluation. Elderly patients are often treated as incompetent because they react and speak slower than younger patients, or because the house staff—resident physicians typically in their late twenties—tend to assume that people in their eighties, debilitated from illness, must be somewhat demented and therefore lacking full mental capacity.

There is, in actual practice, no single standard of competency. The seriousness of a patient's condition is often a factor that tips the balance one way or the other in cases of uncertain competency. Yet objections can be raised against having multiple standards of competency. The main objection is the inconsistency that would result from a shifting standard of competency, an inconsistency that could result in unfairness—failure to treat like cases alike.

Still, for other reasons, it may be ethically desirable to have multiple standards of competency, or even a "sliding scale." A higher standard of competency is more appropriate when the likely consequences of a treatment refusal are the patient's death or rapid deterioration. And a lower standard is appropriate when the behavior of a marginally competent patient is consistent with that person's attitudes and values prior to the mental decline, a common situation with elderly patients.

Just as in the criminal-justice system, where an accused person is presumed innocent until proven guilty, so too in the hospital, a patient must be presumed competent until proven incompetent. Because of the inconvenience of seeking a judge's ruling, and the delays in treatment that would occur, that practice is rarely followed. Instead, psychiatrists from the liaison psychiatry service are summoned to make informal competency evaluations, frequently because a patient has refused a recommended treatment. Surgeons, who tend to be paternalistic anyway, are frustrated by patients' refusals. "The patient is refusing surgery, he'll die without the operation, so he must be crazy. Call liaison psych." This is a prevailing rationale, but there is no good reason to infer from a patient's refusal of treatment that he must be incompetent, as the following case demonstrates.

Mr. McL., fifty-eight, was blind and had undergone amputations of his legs, both because of complications of diabetes. He had also suffered a heart attack, and was admitted to City Hospital on this occasion because of nausea. He was found to have an infected sore on one of the stumps, and gangrene was diagnosed. The doctors recommended another operation to amputate more of his leg, but Mr. McL. refused. He remained in the hospital and was treated with antibiotics for several days, and then was asked again to grant consent for surgery. Again he refused. This time a psychiatrist from the liaison psychiatry service was called to evaluate the patient's mental capacity to consent to treatment. The psychiatrist judged Mr. McL. capable of granting or refusing consent.

Mr. McL. gave a reason for refusing the surgery. He felt he had suffered enough over the past fourteen years. Meanwhile, his condition continued to worsen, and he wanted to sign out of the hospital and go home to die. The physicians caring for him felt uncomfortable about allowing Mr. McL. to go home, not only because they knew they could treat him successfully with surgery, but also because he couldn't walk and caring for himself until death would be difficult, if not impossible.

Repeated attempts were made to convince the patient to submit to surgery. Finally one physician took the time to hold a long discussion with Mr. McL. Following that conversation, he consented. As it turned out, he had thought he would need a prosthesis, an artificial leg, following the surgery, and was opposed to that. It emerged that his reason for refusing the surgery was his belief that the prosthesis would be necessary. Once convinced that he could get by without the artificial leg, he willingly signed consent for the surgery. The amputation was performed, and Mr. McL. was discharged from the hospital.

Mr. McL.'s case posed a problem for his doctors, but it was not a genuine moral dilemma. The patient's refusal of surgery triggered the call for a psychiatrist to evaluate his mental status. Yet even his initial reason for refusal could be seen as rational, not only from his own perception of his quality of life, but also according to the objective factors of his blindness, his double amputation, and his heart condition. The ability to make a choice based on "rational" reasons is widely recognized as an appropriate measure of a patient's competency. It emerged, however, that what led Mr. McL. to refuse at first was his lack of understanding of the consequences of the surgery rather than his present quality of life. Better communication with his caregivers revealed the real reason for his refusal of surgery and led the patient to accept the recommended therapy. Problems like this might be avoided if doctors would allow more time for talking with their patients, yet the hospital setting still presents barriers to real communication.

NOT EVERY CASE of questionable competency can be resolved as clearly as Mr. McL.'s, however. Mary F., a seventy-seven-year-old woman, was admitted to City Hospital with shortness of breath. She was living alone and was entirely independent. She was given a complete workup, and a lump was found in her left breast. When informed of this, and the need for a biopsy to determine if the lump was malignant, Mary F. said she knew her breast lump wasn't cancer. She knew about lumps, she said, and would go to a faith healer for her condition. She thought a combination of the faith healer's efforts and her own will would make the lump go away.

A psychiatric consultant was called. The psychiatrist found Mary F. to be alert, animated, talkative, with an intact memory. However, the patient did admit to having occasional auditory hallucinations, hearing voices from time to time. She said someone was "putting thoughts into my mind" and believed she had special powers given by God. The psychiatrist, with some hesitancy, judged Mary F. to be competent. Because the patient's medical condition was not an emergency, and immediate intervention was not necessary, it was easier to allow this patient to refuse further treatment and to seek help from a faith healer than it would be if a lifesaving procedure had been recommended.

Yet the psychiatrist was uneasy about her decision. She might just as easily have judged Mary F. to lack the mental capacity to decide for herself, based on the fact that she was hallucinating from time to time, and the voices she heard in those hallucinations were what led her to refuse the standard medical treatment for the lump in her breast. But because no urgent treatment was indicated to preserve the patient's life or health, the psychiatrist chose to respect her autonomy, even though it was somewhat diminished. The psychiatrist had implicitly adopted a "sliding scale" in making this competency evaluation.

The psychiatrist's assessment of Mary F. was an exception to the general rule that competency depends, at least in part, on the sorts of reasons a patient gives in refusing a recommended treatment. But even that may be too high a standard of competency, since it requires an assessment of the patient's reasons as "rational" reasons, and a physician's assessment of what counts as a rational reason may differ from a patient's. Under certain circumstances, there may be more than one interpretation of what is rational.

Mr. W., an elderly man who had been in good health and had no previous history of cardiac disease, was brought to the hospital emergency room in acute distress. He was diagnosed as having suffered a myocardial infarction, a heart attack. Immediate treatment was administered, and in preparation for giving Mr. W. medications, the resident planned to insert a Swan-Ganz catheter to monitor the patient's response to the drugs.

Insertion of a Swan-Ganz line is invasive but relatively simple. When the details of the procedure were explained to the patient, he refused and rejected any other invasive treatment. He was willing to take the drugs but rejected the monitoring device that physicians deem necessary when cardiac medications are given. When queried about his reasons for refusing the Swan-Ganz line, Mr. W. replied that his son had died not long before as a result of medical mismanagement, and his daughter-in-law, the wife of the deceased son, had also suffered bad consequences as a result of misdiagnosis of a brain tumor. The elderly patient expressed his fear of invasive medical procedures, a fear that stemmed from these tragic episodes in which close relatives were harmed, one of them mortally.

The physicians in charge claimed that Mr. W. was being irrational in refusing the procedure, since all available evidence indicates that insertion of a Swan-Ganz line carries a low risk when performed by skilled personnel. But was the refusal clearly irrational? It depends on how the notion of "available evidence" is construed. According to the evidence available to the physicians—published data in the medical literature—it is irrational for a patient to refuse a low-risk procedure that is clearly beneficial. According to the evidence from Mr. W.'s own experience, however, the risks accompanying invasive medical treatments far outweighed the benefits.

This patient's decision could be considered rational if based on the evidence he himself used in refusing the Swan-Ganz catheter. But the question remains: Ought he have accepted the evidence the physicians were basing their recommendation on, once they informed him of the statistics about risks and benefits of the procedure? When a consultation was called from the liaison psychiatry service, Mr. W. was found competent to participate in medical decisions regarding his own care, despite the uncertainty about whether his reason for refusing was "rational." This illustrates why an attempt to base competency evaluations on the rationality of a patient's reasons is not likely to resolve many difficulties. After a couple of days of pleading, cajoling, and urging by his wife, Mr. W. eventually consented to the insertion of the Swan-Ganz line. His condition improved, and he was soon able to go home.

A MODEL HAS BEEN proposed for making clinical assessments based on a "sliding scale" rather than a single standard of competency.[1] The rationale for the sliding scale is to avoid two types of error: disqualifying a competent person from participating in treatment decisions, and failing to protect an incompetent person from the harmful effects of a bad decision.

According to this model, standard 1, the least stringent standard of competency, applies to medical decisions that are low-risk and are objectively in the patient's best interest. The cognitive requirement of informed consent is satisfied when the patient is *aware* of the general situation, and the decisional component is satisfied by the patient's *assent* to the recommended intervention. Those who would obviously fail to meet this standard of competency are infants, unconscious persons, the severely retarded, and psychotic patients who are so out of touch with reality that they cannot meet the cognitive requirement of being aware of the general situation. Most patients who appear "marginally competent" would probably succeed in meeting this standard.

For standard 2, the patient must be able to *understand* the risks and outcomes of alternative treatment options, and then be able to make a choice based on this understanding. The patient need not be able to articulate conceptual or verbal understanding, but should be able to grasp the physician's explanation with strong feelings and convictions. Patients who would be incompetent according to this standard are those suffering from severe mood disorder or severe shock, short-term memory loss, delusion, dementia, and delirium. But those who would be competent include mature adolescents, the mildly mentally retarded, and some individuals with personality disorders. This standard should be applied when the illness is chronic rather than acute, or if the treatment is more dangerous or offers less certain benefit to the patient. The chief difference, then, between the applicability of standard 1 and standard 2 lies in the the level of risk and the amount of uncertainty regarding the risks and benefits of the recommended treatment.

Standard 3, the most stringent, applies to treatment situations in which there is very little uncertainty about a correct diagnosis, the available treatment is effective, and death is likely to result from treatment refusal. This standard of competency requires that the patient have the capacity to *appreciate* the nature and consequences of the decision being made. The elements of understanding are both cognitive and affective, or emotional. Although the patient need not conform to what most rational or "reasonable" people do or would do under the circumstances, the patient must nevertheless be able to give reasons for the decision. Persons suffering from mental or emotional disorders that compromise their ability to appreciate their situation or to make rational decisions would fail to meet this standard.

The adoption of multiple standards of competency and the use of a "sliding scale" can succeed in avoiding some problems created by a single, rigid test of competency to consent to treatment. But it does not eliminate the need to make value judgments in the process of assessing competency. When a single standard of competency is employed, the person assigned to make the assessment is confronted with an either-or choice that results in violating the autonomy of some patients whose autonomy should be respected, or the reverse error of treating as competent some patients whose autonomy is so diminished as to require protection. The use of multiple standards of competency builds the values directly into the tests of competency and requires the physician to select the appropriate standard for the particular patient. Yet there is the danger that the more the doctor disagrees with the patient's decision, the more stringent will be the standard of competency selected. Even this complex approach does not resolve all the value dilemmas of determining incompetency.

JENNIFER WAS A twenty-year-old woman admitted to the hospital with a diagnosis of anorexia nervosa, the eating disorder common in young women with a poor body image who succeed in remaining very thin by a combination of undereating and self-induced vomiting. When she entered the hospital, she weighed fifty-five pounds and had no menstrual periods. She had been treated as a psychiatric patient from the age of nine, but has received no psychiatric treatment in the last two years. She has been attending a local university and had a work-study position in a faculty office.

Before being admitted to the hospital, Jennifer had been taking potassium without medical advice. She came to the screening clinic at City Hospital and was found to be apathetic and lethargic. Two psychiatrists examined her and learned that she has few friends, spends her spare time at home, and does not drink alcohol or use drugs. The psychiatrists evaluated Jennifer's mental status as "oriented times three," but noted that she exhibits bizarre appearance and behavior, including an agitated emotional state, infantile whining, and no eye contact. They decided to admit her involuntarily for medical treatment. Before that treatment was completed, Jennifer tried to leave the hospital in the middle of the night. Physicians responded by committing her to the psychiatric ward.

Was it right to commit Jennifer involuntarily to the hospital? Should she be considered incompetent? Although still in late adolescence, Jennifer was not a minor. She was in good standing in college and was holding down a job, so there was evidence of her ability to function independently. According to the standard mental status exam, she could be considered competent. And her psychiatric diagnosis was not one that presumes her to be out of touch with reality. Nevertheless, anorexia nervosa is generally thought of as a "self-destructive" disorder, despite the fact that Jennifer had made no attempt at suicide and did not exhibit suicidal intent or ideation.

Just which tests of competency could Jennifer pass? She certainly could meet the least stringent test embodied in standard 1: awareness of the general situation and the ability to assent to the proposed treatment. She could also meet the requirements of the next higher standard: the cognitive aspect, understanding the risks and benefits of treatment, and the alternatives; and the ability to grasp the explanation with strong feelings and convictions. She does not, however, appear to fully pass the highest test, standard 3: the capacity to appreciate the nature and consequences of her decision and action. Although she possesses a cognitive understanding, the missing dimension is the affective, or emotional, one. A rational person in similar circumstances would most likely not reject medical treatment. But even this highest test does not require that a patient conform to what most rational people would do under the circumstances. Jennifer's failure to demonstrate "reasonableness" is not at all surprising, given the nature of her disorder, anorexia nervosa. Her eating behavior is not "reasonable." Why should anyone expect a "reasonable" response to forced hospitalization and treatment designed to correct that behavior?

One difficulty with the most stringent standard of competency is that it contains several different criteria, some of which may be present and others absent in a particular case. That is precisely the situation in Jennifer's case. Standard 3 is used when certain background conditions are present: diagnostic uncertainty is minimal, the available treatment is effective, and death is likely to result from treatment refusal. In Jennifer's situation two out of three of these background conditions are present. The diagnosis of anorexia nervosa is undisputed, and the likelihood of her death from continuing this eating pattern is quite high. But is there an effective treatment for anorexia? Decidedly not. The prospect, then, is for indefinite hospitalization during which the patient is force-fed. Given the moral unacceptability of that coercive approach, the conclusion emerges that since there is no effective treatment for Jennifer's disorder, not all the conditions for applying the highest standard of competency on the "sliding scale" model are present. The result is uncertainty in how to apply the standard and uncertainty about whether Jennifer should be considered incompetent to make decisions regarding her own medical care and treatment.

What looked like a way of avoiding this moral dilemma now appears blocked. The unacceptable choices are, on the one hand, to permit a patient to sicken or die as a result of respecting her autonomy or, on the other hand, to violate her autonomy by forcing her to accept the recommended course of action. The hoped-for escape is to find the patient incompetent, which would then ethically justify overriding her refusal to accept hospitalization and treatment. But despite the fact that Jennifer does not clearly meet the criteria for incompetency, she appears nevertheless to suffer from somewhat diminished autonomy. If that lessened autonomy is still not sufficiently low to justify finding her incompetent, an unhappy but possible moral choice remains: acknowledge her competency and decide to override her autonomy anyway. Her life would be preserved, and with psychiatric treatment she may come to view herself differently and eventually cease her anorexic behavior.

Although indefinite hospitalization and force-feeding is morally unacceptable, as a temporary measure it falls into the same category as detaining a suicidal person. Temporary intrusions into autonomy can be countenanced in the interest of promoting long-term autonomy. The fact that Jennifer is only twenty years old is an undeniable factor in a moral argument that concludes with a justification for overriding patient autonomy. Why age should matter is a complex issue, but one that does have a place in decision-making. To detain Jennifer in the hospital temporarily, against her will, is a clear violation of her autonomy. Yet it remains the least bad solution to a troubling moral dilemma.

A case that appears similar in a number of respects can have a different moral resolution. Mrs. Y. was an eighty-three-year-old woman brought to the emergency room by ambulance after a neighbor found her on the floor of her apartment, where she lives by herself. On a recent visit to the emergency room, Mrs. Y. had signed herself out of the hospital against medical advice. She was widowed, she had no children, and her only relative was a sister living in Florida. Although Mrs. Y. managed reasonably well on her own, the neighbor reported that she buys food and does other errands for her. Mrs. Y. was able to tell the physicians that she had lost between twenty and thirty pounds over the past several months, that she often suffers from weakness, and that the bruises found all over her body were caused by frequent falls. She emphatically did not want to be admitted to the hospital, saying she "hates doctors and hospitals."

Despite the fact that a mental-status examination was given and Mrs. Y. was found to be "oriented times three," the psychiatric report stated that her mental status and judgment were grossly impaired. Based on that report, a decision was made to admit her to the hospital. The intern said he felt as if he were kidnapping her. But the resident in charge insisted on admitting her "for her own good," because she lacked insight into her problems. Her diagnosis after examination was malnutrition and dehydration. The ethical questions are identical to the ones in Jennifer's case: What are this patient's rights? Is it permissible to admit her to the hospital involuntarily and force medical treatment on her?

My own moral inclination is to set a high standard of competency in Jennifer's case and a somewhat lower standard for Mrs. Y. Both patients suffer diminished autonomy, Jennifer in connection with her anorexia nervosa, and Mrs. Y., with the causes unknown, has "grossly impaired judgment." Both patients have had serious weight losses resulting in malnutrition, and both have life-threatening conditions. Jennifer's cognitive abilities are much superior to Mrs. Y.'s, yet despite the psychiatric assessment of "grossly impaired judgment," the elderly woman was able to articulate her hatred of doctors and hospitals—reasons that are directly related to her refusal of hospitalization and treatment. The ability to give reasons for a decision meets one of the requirements of standard 3, the highest test of competency.

The fact that Jennifer is twenty years old and Mrs. Y. is eighty-three does make a difference, but not because young people deserve more of society's resources than do the elderly. If Mrs. Y. had been willing to accept hospitalization and the food and fluids necessary to restore her to her former state of health, she would be as deserving of medical resources as any other patient. Although feeding and hydrating her would succeed in restoring her strength temporarily, the likelihood is great that once discharged, she would return to her former patterns of behavior. To force her to remain in the hospital, overriding her autonomy and failing to respect her clearly stated distaste for the institution and its personnel, is to imprison her with little hope of any permanent improvement in her already deteriorating health. Abundant evidence has shown that even mentally alert elderly patients tend to become disoriented in the hospital, and those who enter with some mental impairment typically become worse. Add to that the risk of acquiring infections in the hospital and the probability of her developing bedsores. It then becomes apparent that Mrs. Y.'s best interests would not be served by hospitalization. As morally questionable as it is to override the autonomy of a marginally competent patient, it is even less acceptable to do so when it is not clearly in her best medical interest.

PATIENTS WHOSE CAPACITY for decision-making is impaired pose special problems for medical caregivers. Even those physicians who respect their patients' autonomy, and are therefore prepared to accept treatment refusals by competent patients, are reluctant to allow marginally competent patients to make decisions that go against their best medical interest. A recognition that different levels of competency exist, and that a "sliding scale" model can serve patients' best interests and at the same time respect their autonomy, can lead to a more enlightened approach to patients of uncertain competence.

Even the marginally competent patient may be able to express values that medical caregivers should respect in the treatment setting. This possibility becomes even more critical when decisions have to be made once those patients are no longer able to participate at all. With elderly patients, such as Mrs. Y., such values might include a lifetime of dislike of doctors and hospitals. Ascertaining the values and wishes regarding medical treatment of patients who still retain some mental capacity can be a great help for the next phase: deciding for those who are clearly unable to decide for themselves.

Deciding
for Others

P ARENTS POSSESS AWESOME decision-making power on behalf of their minor children. For the most part, our society supports that power, recognizing that affection and concern for their children usually lead parents to make decisions in their children's best interests. But there are limits to how parents may decide to act. Those limits are stated in the court's ruling in a 1962 case in Ohio, in which Jehovah's Witness parents sought to refuse lifesaving blood transfusions for their child:

> It is true that parents exercise a dominion over their child so mighty and yet so minute as to be sometimes frightening. For example, they determine whether and whom the child may marry . . . ; whether and where he goes to school or college; which, if any, religious faith he may espouse; where he shall live; whether and where he may work, find his recreation, and so on; even whether he wears his rubbers, his pink tie, or she has her hair bobbed. Parents may, within bounds, deprive their child of his liberty and his property.
>
> But there are well-defined limitations upon this appalling power of parent over child. . . . No longer can parents exercise the power of life or death over their children. . . . Nor may they abandon him, deny him proper parental care, neglect or refuse to provide him with proper or necessary subsistence, education, medical or surgical care, or other care necessary for his health, morals, or well-being. . . . And while they may, under certain circum-

stances, deprive him of his liberty or his property, under no circumstances, with or without religious sanction, may they deprive him of his life![1]

When parents make a decision regarding medical care that clearly goes against their child's best interest, the state does not usually take custody of the child or seek foster care. This differs from cases of child abuse and neglect, in which parents forfeit their right to keep their own children and the state assumes custody until a suitable home can be found for those unfortunate children. Typically, in medical situations, a guardian *ad litem* is appointed for the specific and limited purpose of making treatment decisions on behalf of the child. The authority of the guardian ceases once the recommended therapy is completed.

The chief examples of deciding for others occur when infants and children become patients. But they are not the only examples. The need often arises to decide for adults who cannot decide for themselves: comatose or unconscious patients, profoundly mentally retarded persons and those whose mental disturbance is so great as to sever their contact with reality, and severely demented elderly patients all fit this description to some degree. As hard as it is to arrive at a clear, agreed-upon standard for assessing a person's mental capacity to decide for himself, once that difficulty is resolved by a determination that the patient is incompetent, a new set of moral problems arises. Someone must be empowered to decide on the patient's behalf.

Who-should-decide questions are largely procedural, in contrast to the substantive nature of questions about the moral rightness or wrongness of decisions. But the fact that a question is procedural rather than substantive does not mean that people do not hold strong opinions about it. The controversy over Annabella, the mentally retarded girl whose family was visiting this country from the Caribbean, is a case in point. The "merely procedural" issue sharply divided the pediatric staff: whether to seek a court order to override the parents' refusal of surgery for Annabella. The general question of whether parents ought to have the final say in matters concerning medical treatment of their own children, whatever the actual substance of those decisions may be, is surely a value question. But it is an entirely different question from that of the rightness or wrongness of the decision itself.

The familiar procedural question "Who should decide?" has several possible answers. One traditional answer lies in the *parens patriae* doctrine, the legal principle that grants the state broad authority to act in the incompetent person's "best interest." That doctrine—literally, "the state as parent"—supports involuntary-commitment statutes that permit persons in need of care, custody, or treatment to be forcibly placed in institutions. That is the basis for hospitalizing Bunky, the woman who lived in the subway station, and for eventually medicating her against her will and placing her in a state mental institution.

The *parens patriae* doctrine also underlies the authority of the state to override parental decisions alleged to go against the best interests of their children, as well as the right of the state to remove abused or neglected children from the custody of their abusing parents. Yet critics of this doctrine as it pertains to children argue that the state is too crude an instrument to become an adequate substitute for parents.[2]

The traditional, informal answer to the who-should-decide question is "the family." In most cases involving infants and minor children, the child's parents or guardians should be the decision-makers. And typically in the case of married people, it is the spouse who is presumed to be the natural one appointed in the role of decider. For an elderly person whose spouse is no longer alive, or who is mentally impaired, adult children are usually the ones who serve as surrogates for the patient. But just as the decisions of parents are sometimes thought to go against their childrens' best interests, so, too, can decisions made by other family members on behalf of their relatives be called into question.

When the content of an ethical decision is questioned, it is the substantive moral position that is under attack. True, cultural values of some sort give rise to the procedural mechanisms a society adopts for handling such problems. In our society, family values occupy a high place, so surrogate decision-makers are usually relatives of the incompetent person, unless they disqualify themselves. But it is not hard to imagine a society (anthropologists have described some) in which authority resides in some unrelated individual—a prophet, healer, or panel of elders. History provides a good example of the extreme of parental power in the father of the family in ancient Rome.

The head of the family, the *paterfamilias*, was the only full person recognized by the law. The extent of his power was remarkable. His children of whatever age, though citizens and therefore the bearers of rights in public law, were subject to the unfettered power of life and death wielded by the *paterfamilias*. Sons were regarded as the property of their father, to be disposed of in any manner he wished. In early Roman law the *paterfamilias* could as freely sell his sons as his slaves.

By the end of the classical period in Rome, the power of life and death had probably become obsolete except for one practice, interesting because of the contemporary debate that rages over the proper treatment of handicapped newborns. This is the practice, common in the ancient world and still found in some cultures today, of exposing newborn babies to the elements. This practice was made criminal in A.D. 374 but apparently still survived beyond that time. In Roman law, if a father could kill his child, he could also sell him. Tales dating from the later Empire recount the sale of newborn children, but the father always retained the right to redeem any child he had sold.[3] The absolute power of the *paterfamilias* exceeded by far the authority granted to parents in contemporary society, and even those who would like to see less intrusion by government do not urge a return to that extreme.

Parents are generally presumed to be the ones who are "best equipped" to make decisions about medical treatment for their children. Yet doubts can often arise. Simply the fact of their being the little boy's parents did not render the Greens "well equipped" to refuse the standard medical treatment for their son Chad.

Chad Green suffered from leukemia, a disease that is often fatal. His parents, believing in the efficacy of nutritional therapy and laetrile, abandoned chemotherapy, which is known to have an 80 percent rate of cure for children in Chad's age range with his type of leukemia. According to reliable medical data, Chad's "chances" were around eight out of ten for complete recovery if chemotherapy had continued and if the leukemia had remained in remission for eighteen months. Although a court ordered the Greens to resume conventional chemotherapy for Chad, they fled to Mexico to seek the treatments they believed would help. The child died some time later, and it will never be known whether he would have profited from the standard treatment.

Whatever the Greens' "equipment" may have been for making that decision, and whether or not there is a right decision in such cases, many people would argue that Chad's parents had the right and the responsibility to decide for their son. A charitable interpretation would view the Greens not as fanatics seeking a quack therapy but instead as loving parents who wanted to abandon conventional therapy, with its unpleasant side effects, in a desperate search for unproven remedies.

In another highly publicized case the parents of Phillip Becker were far from well equipped to decide to refuse lifesaving heart surgery for him at age thirteen, surgery that could easily correct his heart defect but would not, of course, improve his mental retardation—the ground on which his parents chose to refuse the proposed surgery. Among other things, Phillip Becker had been in a home for handicapped children since birth and was visited by his parents only infrequently. The notion that no one can be presumed to be in a better position than parents to make treatment decisions for their children, and therefore that no one is better equipped to make those decisions, is surely flawed. Yet it remains an open question whether the right to decide nevertheless resides with parents, so long as they are not incompetent as judged by criteria independent of the decision they make on behalf of their child.

THE SOLUTIONS TO PROCEDURAL, who-should-decide questions depend more on law and custom than they do on ethical theory. No moral principle drawn from philosophical ethics dictates an answer to the who-should-decide question. The legal doctrine of *parens patriae* is a curious blend of procedure and substance. It states both who should decide and what principle should guide the decision, requiring that the decision itself be based on the incompetent person's "best interest" —a substantive standard.

Granting decision-making authority for a patient to a family member feels comfortable. Who but a close relative should presume to make decisions for those no longer able to decide for themselves? As comfortable as this "feels," though, the comfort begins to lessen when probing questions are asked. Should whatever a family member chooses on behalf of an incompetent relative be allowed to stand as final? If not, on what grounds may a relative's decision be questioned? Should the same standard be used in deciding for children as for other incompetent relatives? If not, what basis is there for treating such cases differently?

Just as parents are presumed to be decision-makers for their children, but can nonetheless make decisions that are substantively incorrect, so can other family members make "wrong" decisions for a patient. In the case of adults, two different criteria exist—one substantive, the other procedural—for judging the rightness or wrongness of a third-party decision. The substantive standard is the "best interest" of the patient; the procedural criterion rests on the "substituted-judgment" principle—what the patient would decide, or would have wanted, if he or she were capable of participating in the decision.

The substituted-judgment standard has been the most widely accepted by courts in cases over the past ten to fifteen years. It rests on a solid moral foundation, the adult person's right to self-determination, the right to exercise one's autonomy. If competent persons have that right, then when they are no longer competent their right should still be exercised. The moral and legal theory that supports the substituted-judgment procedure is the right of self-determination.

If the patient has made a living will or otherwise given specific instructions about what he or she would want done when incompetent in the future, that written document or statement is probably the best evidence of the patient's wishes. In the absence of any prior statements by the patient, family members are normally the best source of evidence about what the patient would have wanted, since they are likely to have known the person longest and most intimately.

But many people never discuss these topics with their family or anyone else. Also, families may be mistaken about what their relative would have wanted, substituting their own judgment for that of the patient. Their emotions often play a role, and when asked to consent to an aggressive treatment for the incompetent patient, some family members act out of guilt or fear, ignoring or failing to ascertain what the patient would have wanted. The substituted-judgment doctrine is often hard to apply because of these practical difficulties stemming from uncertainty or ignorance about the patient's actual wishes.

There is another problem of a different sort: the existence of groups of patients to whom the substituted-judgment standard cannot apply. Besides infants and children, who have not yet attained autonomy, others, such as mentally retarded persons or those who have been emotionally disturbed from a young age, have never been competent. These individuals will never develop autonomy in any meaningful sense. When autonomy is so severely diminished, there can be no competently stated wishes by the patient, and therefore no substituted judgment by another. In these situations the leading moral and legal principle is the old standby, the "best interest of the patient."

Some disturbed, demented, or retarded people have preferences they are able to voice. Care should be taken to respect such preferences, when they are expressed, even if the patient hovers at the border of competency. Doctors and family members should try to strike a balance between respecting the wishes of marginally competent persons and making decisions in their best interest.

As if these two principles were not complicated enough to sort out and apply in practice, the law recognizes still another problematic concept, the "reasonable-person" standard. This legal concept is used in other situations, for example, as a standard of disclosure in the process of gaining informed consent. Its value for determining what doctors should disclose to patients lies in the fact that it is a patient-oriented criterion, replacing the earlier, physician-based "reasonable-practitioner" standard. But just as it is hard to determine what a hypothetical "reasonable patient" would want to know before giving informed consent to treatment, so must it be difficult to ascertain what the "reasonable person" would actually decide.

One thing is clear, however. In situations involving incompetent patients, "reasonable" cannot be interpreted to mean "what this patient would want if he or she were competent to decide." That describes the substituted-judgment standard for incompetent patients. An actual patient may be "unreasonable," yet if competent, his wishes should be respected. The "reasonable person" is, by definition, "reasonable." So a potential for conflict exists in the use of the substituted-judgment principle and the reasonable-person standard. And either principle could yield a different decision from the best-interest standard.

Since 1976, when the New Jersey Supreme Court issued its ruling in the case of Karen Ann Quinlan, courts have sought a basis for determining what are the rights of incompetent adult patients. The trend that emerged was to base the rights of incompetent patients on the well-established right of self-determination of competent patients. Embodied in the common-law doctrine of informed consent, the right to self-determination in decisions regarding one's own medical care has been respected for the most part, but not without impediments such as those faced by William Bartling when he tried to have himself removed from a respirator. To base the right of incompetent adult patients on the same rights possessed by competent adults seems natural and consistent. Yet a look at several of those judicial decisions reveals some curious features.

There was no question about whether Karen Ann Quinlan was incompetent to participate in medical decisions. She was irreversibly comatose, in a "persistent vegetative state," with no reasonable possibility of ever returning to a "cognitive sapient state." The court tried to use the substituted-judgment standard in the Quinlan case but had difficulty doing so. "The only practical way to prevent destruction of [Karen's] . . . right is to permit the guardian and family of Karen to render their best judgment . . . as to whether she would exercise it in these circumstances."[4] But it was not known what Karen would say in these circumstances. Her family did apparently offer some evidence, referring to her attitude toward "extraordinary treatment." But the court did not find this evidence sufficient for a clear and uncontroversial application of the substituted-judgment standard.

Instead, the court resorted to some variation of the reasonable-person standard in holding that if Karen were competent, she would not wish to be kept alive on a respirator in an irreversible vegetative state. The court observed that "this decision should be accepted by a society the overwhelming majority of whose members would, we think, in similar circumstances, exercise such a choice in the same way for themselves or for those closest to them." Not only was there no clear evidence of what Karen Quinlan herself would have wanted, there was also no evidence brought forward to support the claim that "most (reasonable) people" would not want to be maintained in her condition. In the end, the Quinlan decision invoked the substituted-judgment standard but lacked the relevant evidence that would make its application clear and uncontroversial. And it employed the central concept of the reasonable-person standard without explicitly stating that principle or citing factual evidence to buttress it.

More curious was the attempt of the Massachusetts court to use the substituted-judgment principle in the Saikewicz case. Joseph Saikewicz was a sixty-seven-year-old man who was severely retarded and suffering from an incurable form of leukemia. His mental age was estimated to be about two years and eight months, and he could not communicate verbally. The proposed treatment was chemotherapy, which has many painful and unpleasant side effects. The Supreme Judicial Court in Massachusetts issued its full opinion after Mr. Saikewicz had already died. In affirming the lower court's decision against beginning the chemotherapy, the Supreme Judicial Court explicitly rejected the "reasonable person" standard. The court said:

> Individual choice is determined not by the vote of the majority but by the complexities of the singular situation viewed from the unique perspective of the person called on to make the decision. To presume that the incompetent person must always be subjected to what many rational and intelligent persons may decline is to downgrade the status of the incompetent person by placing a lesser value on his intrinsic human worth and vitality.[5]

If the reasonable-person standard is inappropriate to use in a situation involving a person like Joseph Saikewicz, who had never been competent, how can it be more appropriate to use the substituted-judgment standard? Use of that standard requires, at the very least, that the person on whose behalf the judgment is "substituted" must once have been capable of forming an opinion about his own care and treatment. But a never-competent person like Joseph Saikewicz, with a mental age of less than three years, never had that capacity. Wanting desperately to preserve the patient's right to self-determination, the court used the substituted-judgment principle "because of its straightforward respect for the integrity and autonomy of the individual."

In rejecting the use of the reasonable-person standard on moral grounds in the Saikewicz case, the Massachusetts court made an odd decision. It imputed to a never-competent, profoundly retarded person the very traits he lacked—almost by definition—that would allow the substituted-judgment standard to operate. It remains a puzzle why the court avoided using the best-interest principle. Although vague and admittedly difficult to apply, it is nevertheless a standard that makes as good sense for never-competent patients as it does for children, where it still prevails. A legal colleague of mine surmises that courts just hate to admit that they have to decide for such patients.

The trend among courts toward using the substituted-judgment standard as a basis for decision-making on behalf of adult patients is further reinforced by the leading judicial opinion in New York State. When the Court of Appeals decided the cases of Brother Fox and John Storar, its decision reaffirmed the correctness of using substituted judgment for patients who had once been competent. Brother Fox had made oral, not written, declarations about his wishes regarding treatment if he ever became incompetent. In a discussion about the Quinlan case itself, and in remarks made in classroom teaching, Brother Fox had said that "he would not want any of this 'extraordinary business' done for him under those circumstances."[6] This is precisely the sort of situation for which the substituted-judgment doctrine was devised.

Unlike the implausible attempt by the Massachusetts court to apply this doctrine to patients like Joseph Saikewicz, who had never been competent, the New York court refused to invoke substituted judgment for John Storar, another profoundly retarded patient. The Court of Appeals reversed a lower court's decision that had allowed the patient's blood transfusions to be discontinued, arguing that there was no realistic way to determine what Mr. Storar himself would have wanted. He should be granted the same rights as an infant, according to the court, since he was mentally equivalent to an infant. Parents are not permitted by law to refuse lifesaving blood transfusions for their children, so by analogy neither should John Storar's seventy-seven-year-old mother be allowed to refuse transfusions for him.

A nagging ethical question about the court's analogy remains, however: Should an infant with a terminal illness be required to undergo a blood transfusion? If a diagnosis of incurable cancer were made in an eighteen-month-old baby, whose chronological age is the same as John Storar's mental age, by what moral principle must the infant be given a blood transfusion that would do nothing to prevent its death from cancer after several months of painful treatment? The type of treatment is not morally relevant. Rather, it is the prognosis, along with the pain and suffering caused by the treatment, that should be the determinants of what is in an incompetent patient's best interest.

The New York court should be congratulated for its unwillingness to engage in the fiction the Massachusetts court created by applying the substituted-judgment principle to a profoundly mentally retarded, never-competent person. But the court's substantive decision in the case of Mr. Storar was morally questionable. It might have been different if the best-interest principle had been applied to the case. John Storar was terminally ill from bladder cancer and didn't have long to live. It may well be in a patient's best interest to undergo painful and prolonged treatment when the therapy stands a good chance of extending life for a reasonable period of time, or of restoring the patient to a former level of functioning. But it was surely inhumane to prolong Mr. Storar's dying by administering painful blood transfusions, which required tying down the uncomprehending patient.

The most thoughtful of the several recent court opinions that involved deciding for others in medical situations is the New Jersey decision in the case of Claire Conroy, the severely demented nursing-home patient whose nephew sought to have her feeding tube removed. Noting the absence of proof of what the patient herself wanted, the court honestly acknowledged that "it is naive to pretend that the right to self-determination serves as the basis for substituted decision making."

When the judge articulated the two best-interest tests, which he termed "limited-objective" and "pure-objective," he made a significant contribution to the body of legal writings that deal with decision-making for incompetent patients. Since Claire Conroy's nephew presented some evidence that she would have refused treatment, the limited-objective standard applied to her case. In cases like those of Joseph Saikewicz and John Storar, where no evidence of what the patient would have wanted could exist, in principle, the pure-objective best-interest test would presumably apply. For those patients the reasoning used in the Conroy decision should lead to the conclusion, as the court put it, that "the net burdens of the patient's life with the treatment [would] clearly and markedly outweigh the benefits that the patient derives from life. Further, the recurring, unavoidable, and severe pain of the patient's life with the treatment [would make] the effect of administering life-sustaining treatment . . . inhumane."

DESPITE THE RECENT DECLINE in the use of the best-interest standard for incompetent adult patients, that standard has prevailed in medical situations where the patients are children. But both the concept of "best interest" and its application to those cases have been attacked. It has been argued that not only is the principle vague and hard to apply, but it is also inappropriate to disqualify parents from their traditional role. The once-simple picture of parents as the sole and proper decision-makers for their children has been altered by a number of different developments. One is the rise of the children's-rights and children's-liberation movements, leading to a call for increased decision-making autonomy for adolescents and even younger children. A related development is the idea that children need advocates who will speak on their behalf when parents decide or act wrongly.

Judicial decisions and statutes enacted by state legislatures have lowered the age of consent for a number of medical procedures, particularly those that involve sexuality: obtaining contraceptive information and devices, receiving treatments for venereal disease, and procuring abortions. Despite these exceptions, the general rule holds true that minors (defined as under eighteen in some states, under sixteen in others) cannot grant consent for themselves for medical treatment or to participate in research. Unlike adults, who are presumed competent until determined otherwise, children are held to be incompetent by virtue of their age alone. In addition to matters related to sexuality, other exceptions to the age of consent include treatment for drug abuse, and all forms of therapy for minors who are emancipated, or financially independent, and for "mature minors," ones who are married or who have borne a child.

It is obvious why the substituted-judgment standard does not apply to decision-making on behalf of young children, despite the fact that it is ethically appropriate and has been adopted by courts for adult patients whose wishes before becoming incompetent can be known.

However, older children and adolescents should be consulted and their wishes taken into account by parents and physicians. Just as absolute incompetence is rare in adults, the clearest cases being patients who are comatose or profoundly retarded, so, too, with children competency is rarely an all-or-nothing affair. A need exists to draw a line somewhere for legal purposes, so the age of majority is chosen as the time at which an individual is permitted to make his or her own medical decisions. That point is not completely arbitrary, yet it fails to reflect the wide differences in maturity, understanding, and experience among persons growing to adulthood. Any attempt to individualize the notion of competency for children as self-deciders would be so difficult and controversial from a practical standpoint that, as inadequate as chronological age is for marking the distinction between the legally competent and incompetent, it is probably the best that can be devised.

Wherever the legal age of competence is set, cases are bound to arise in which parents make decisions for their children that others deem wrong, misguided, or against the best interest of those children. Inevitably, the question arises whether parents have the unqualified right to make those decisions, or whether mechanisms should be in place to allow unwise parental decisions to be overridden.

A cluster of conflicting values lies at the heart of the controversy about whether parental decisions may be justifiably overridden by the state. One source of conflict is the disagreement about whether there exists a single right answer that can be objectively determined. A second major source of conflict stems from the value of preserving family autonomy and privacy against state intrusion, versus the value of protecting children, when they cannot speak for themselves, against potentially harmful decisions made by their own parents. This second source of conflict can easily become the type of rock-bottom clash of values for which no rational resolution is possible. In that case it falls into a realm of disputed values, where reasonable people disagree in their most deeply held moral commitments. As this controversy illustrates, procedural issues concerning the appropriate decision-maker can give rise to as much disagreement and conflict as substantive disputes about whether a decision itself is morally sound.

A FINAL STANDARD for deciding for others is known as "identity of interests." This principle holds that the interests of the third party and those of the incompetent person are so close that in choosing his or her own interests, the decision-maker will protect the interests of the incompetent individual. Many people would take this to be the proper standard when decisions must be made for children. Yet it could support a wholesale endorsement of parental authority to decide for their own children.

According to this view, an independent determination of a child's interest need not occur or even be possible. In its extreme form this position holds that the interests of parents and their minor children are identical; whatever parents decide is in their children's interest is in their interest. This extreme is untenable, yet there is a sensible core to the identity-of-interests position.

The sensible aspect rests on several assumptions, the chief one being that because children gain a great many of their values from their parents, beginning early in life, it is reasonable to expect them to have internalized those values, and therefore for their interests to coincide with those of their parents. But this very assumption presupposes that it is meaningful to grant that children have interests of their own—interests that may or may not be identical with those of their parents or of the family unit as a whole. Whether the interests of parents and children do coincide is a matter to be factually determined in each specific case. If the idea that children have interests independent of those of their parents is meaningful, then it is possible for those interests to diverge.

A second sound assumption underlying the identity-of-interests view is that children's interests are better served when the family remains a harmonious, autonomous unit, free from the strife and turmoil that can ensue when the state intervenes. Parents can probably perform their nurturing and child-rearing tasks better when the family is intact and when its values remain strong. But this assumption, too, presupposes that children have interests that can be identified independently from those of their parents.

The problem with the identity-of-interests view is that it can too easily degenerate into an extreme position, such as that of Jehovah's Witness parents who refuse lifesaving blood transfusions for their child. If those parents, in accordance with their religious beliefs, judge that their child is better off dead as a result of not having a blood transfusion than alive with a soul condemned to eternal damnation, then the identity-of-interests doctrine would have to consider the interests of parent and child identical. If that doctrine were to prevail, it would be hard to rebut the claim that the interest of a child of Jehovah's Witnesses is precisely what the parents say it is. Fortunately for the children whose lives have been saved by court orders, their interests have been viewed as separate and distinct from those of their parents.

All things considered, I think the best-interest standard—in spite of its shortcomings—should prevail. Underlying this choice is my belief that decisions parents make on behalf of their minor children can have content that is substantively right or wrong. Furthermore, it is unlikely that the state's overriding a family's decision will destroy the family unit or make permanent inroads into its autonomy. A single invasion of family privacy must be weighed against a lifetime of health, well-being, or bodily integrity for the child on whose behalf the state has intervened. It remains important to weigh any potential damage to the child. Family autonomy can be respected, and a deep commitment to family integrity maintained, in the recognition that close and loving family units are in no great danger of being destroyed by an occasional outside intervention aimed at serving the best interests of a child.

But how can physicians, parents, judges, or ethicists know what is in the best interest of an infant or child? The quest for substantive moral answers is at least as difficult as the search for clear and uncontroversial answers to the procedural questions involved in deciding for others. That difficulty must be confronted, especially in light of the increased involvement by all levels of government in matters relating to neglect and abuse of children.

The "Best Interest" of the Child

HECTOR, a three-year-old boy with burns covering his body, was brought to the pediatric emergency room by his father. Hector's father said the burns were a day old, but the doctors who examined the boy said the burns had occurred some days earlier. Examination revealed many other things wrong with Hector: multiple fractures, scars, and older, healed burns. Most of one ear was missing, and when the hospital records were searched, it was discovered that surgery had been performed a year earlier, after the father brought Hector in and admitted having bitten off his son's ear.

The father, in his early thirties, was unemployed and lived alone with Hector. The child's mother, an alcoholic and intravenous-drug abuser, had abandoned her husband and child immediately after Hector's birth. Hector's father had been reported to the local agency responsible for handling cases of child abuse. He was indicted by a grand jury and released on bail, awaiting trial. He visited Hector in the hospital, usually late at night, when there was less supervision to monitor visits than in the daytime. Hector was being treated by a child psychologist, who judged him to be emotionally as well as physically scarred. Since his father was the only person with whom Hector had an ongoing relationship, despite the episodes of abuse, the boy was still dependent on his father and very attached to him.

Pediatric social workers called a conference to determine whether Hector's father should be prohibited from visiting him while he was in the hospital. They feared that the father would harm the child during an unsupervised visit. Efforts to have all visits monitored had not been successful. Nurses were called away to care for other sick children, pediatric residents on call had other duties, and there were no social workers on the night shift. The primary ethical issue was to determine what was in Hector's best interest.

The staff was sharply divided. Some saw a moral obligation to prevent any possibility of further abuse to this already physically and emotionally maimed child. Others claimed that if Hector were prevented from seeing his father during his hospital stay, he would be harmed by isolation and separation from the only adult with whom he had any continuity of relationship. According to this view, it can often be more harmful to an abused child to remove him from the abusing parents than to allow the relationship to continue.

An experienced physician at the conference pointed out that there was a distinct possibility that Hector would be returned to his father if the man was not convicted of child abuse. The doctor noted that judges are reluctant to remove children from their natural parents, even in the face of evidence that those children had been physically and psychologically abused in their home environment. A social worker argued that if Hector was to be returned to his father's custody after his stay in the hospital, it was not in his best interest to disturb the continuity of their relationship by preventing the father from visiting him.

On the opposing side, the child psychologist worried that the gains she was making with Hector were being undercut by the father's visits. Although the boy was progressing slowly in the hospital, all would be lost if he was returned to his father's home. The father himself was judged to be a "hopeless" candidate for counseling and therapy. He was hostile to the staff, continued to deny that he was harming his son, and demanded that his rights as a parent be respected.

During the conference I found it hard to think of this case as an ethical dilemma. Hector's father had behaved in a way that produced direct physical harm to a helpless child: maiming, burning, beating, mutilating. How could it be in a child's "best interest" to be subjected to that sort of treatment? Could that harm, and the resulting emotional trauma, be outweighed by the psychological loss of his only parent, even an abusing one? Perhaps it was my lack of psychiatric training that prevented me from seeing a dilemma here. The child's "best interest" seemed quite clear. But the staff, recognizing that Hector would probably return home, decided to permit his father to continue to visit him in the hospital.

When Hector's medical treatments were completed, the staff, concerned as they were, could do nothing more for him. In the face of imperfect legal mechanisms and the lack of better alternatives, even the staunchest child advocates had lingering doubts about whether Hector would be better off if taken away from his father.

MORE AMBIGUOUS TO ME was the case of Marita, a seven-month-old infant brought to the hospital by her mother, who said the baby refused to eat at home. Marita had gained very little weight since birth and was admitted to the hospital with a diagnosis of "failure to thrive." During her stay in the hospital, the baby ate well and gained weight. One pediatrician suspected that this was a case of neglect and suggested that child-protective services be contacted. Another doctor resisted, claiming there was too little evidence and that it was unfair to make such accusations in the absence of hard evidence. Marita was discharged, only to be brought back in three months with her mother complaining of the same feeding problems. Again the pediatric staff found little weight gain and slow physical and mental development, and once again they made a diagnosis of failure to thrive. Yet to take the next step, a step involving notification of child-protective services leading to investigation and possible removal of Marita from her home and family, would require more certainty about what caused the baby to fail to develop normally.

SOMETIMES EVIDENCE OF neglect or abuse is altogether absent, but doctors and nurses specializing in pediatrics draw on their experience in making judgments—perhaps prematurely—about a mother's ability to care for her child. A case of this type caused much debate in the neonatal unit of City Hospital when an infant with a very low weight was born to Tiffany, a fourteen-year-old unwed girl. Tiffany had diabetes, required insulin, and managed her own health care poorly. She lived with her grandmother (no one knew the whereabouts of her own mother), attended her eighth-grade school class occasionally, and received no prenatal care during pregnancy.

The baby boy weighed under four pounds and required a number of treatments in the neonatal intensive-care unit (NICU). He had to remain in the hospital for two months before he was ready for discharge. His young mother visited infrequently, sometimes alone, at other times with her grandmother. As the time neared for discharging the infant, a pediatric resident and a social worker questioned whether the baby should be sent home with Tiffany. They inferred from Tiffany's home environment and her apparent unwillingness to manage her own disease that the infant boy would most likely be neglected. Based on their experience with cases they thought were similar to Tiffany's, these staff members felt that it was in the baby's best interest to be placed in foster care. Other staff members argued that many young mothers who are immature in caring for their own health nevertheless rise to the occasion and are conscientious in seeing to the needs of their infants.

This case illustrates the zealous efforts made by pediatric staff members to protect the best interests of young patients. An ironic feature of this case, and many others like it, is that the parent of the patient was an adolescent, herself a pediatric patient. This child who bore a child now faced the responsibility of being a parent. When the case was discussed at neonatal ethics rounds, a debate ensued about Tiffany's moral and legal right to take her baby home. Some argued that her right to her own infant was unquestioned, since she had done nothing to disqualify herself from the role of parent. Others claimed that along with rights go responsibilities, and the evidence pointed to Tiffany's inability to assume the responsibilities of parenthood.

For good measure another argument was thrown in: Since Tiffany herself was a patient, the staff had a responsibility to promote her best interest in addition to that of her baby. A social worker noted that a teenager coming from a disadvantaged background would be better off finishing her education and gaining the chance to escape from the cycle of poverty and single parenthood that awaited her.

A pediatric resident replied that while all this was true, these are vast societal problems, well beyond the abilities of this group to resolve. The responsibility of pediatricians to protect the best interests of their patients should not encompass global attempts at social reform. The doctor added that those who sought to rescue the infant from a disadvantaged home environment were making a value judgment rooted in middle-class bias against the poor. The family's right to privacy, to lead their lives in accordance with their own values, should remain free from well-meaning intrusions of others.

Against this array of rights and responsibilities loomed the question of the best interest of the infant. Although uncertainty prevailed concerning the future behavior of Tiffany toward her baby, the absence of any evidence of neglect or abuse compelled the conclusion that she should take the infant home when he was ready for discharge.

Legally, there would be no grounds at all for removing this infant. Ample opportunity existed for follow-up, since Tiffany would bring the baby to the hospital's clinic for regular outpatient visits. Those frequent medical checkups would afford the opportunity to detect whatever problems might be traced to Tiffany's inability to care for her child. Although this prospect was comforting, I was left uneasy about what would happen if the baby did not gain much weight, was slow in reaching developmental milestones, or seemed understimulated. As in the preceding case, this infant might then be given a diagnosis of "failure to thrive." The uncertainty that initially surrounded the case would then recur, this time with a bit of evidence, yet still fraught with ambiguity.

No AMBIGUITY SURROUNDS the question of what is in the best interest of a neglected or abused child who can be adopted into a caring, loving family. But that is not the situation confronting most such children. More likely, they will be placed in temporary foster homes, perhaps one after another, with little or no continuity of parenting. Furthermore, infrequent as it may be, the prospect of neglect or abuse exists in the foster home itself. Many foster homes do offer family surroundings, headed by capable and concerned adults. But more often than not, such placement is merely temporary and creates disruption in the emotional life of a child. Unless these unfortunate children are permanently adopted, their best interest remains uncertain.

The difficulty of determining which of these unhappy alternatives best serves the child's interests has led to a call for abandoning the concept of the "best interest" of the child. An alternative standard is "the least detrimental available alternative for safeguarding the child's growth and development."[1] Designed to serve as an overall guideline for child placement, "the least detrimental alternative" is intended to maximize the child's "opportunity for being wanted and for maintaining on a continuous basis a relationship with at least one adult who is or will become his psychological parent."[2] This standard is easier to apply than the best-interest standard in child-custody decisions and for situations calling for placement in a foster home or an institution, an even worse alternative. As useful as it is for purposes of child placement, "the least detrimental alternative" fails to give clear guidance where the degree of aggressive medical treatment for a child becomes the ethical dilemma.

■ ■ ■

PHYSICIANS AND OTHER health-care workers have been traditionally viewed as strong advocates of their patients. Despite critics
who maintain that it is rarely in the interest even of abused and neglected children to be "rescued" from their own parents, pediatricians
have always sought to protect their young patients' physical and
emotional well-being. To discover, then, that they themselves
could be charged with child neglect for failing to administer aggressive medical treatment to severely impaired newborns comes as a
shock to the pediatric profession. Yet this is one effect of the
"Baby Doe rules" proposed by the Reagan administration in 1982
and revised several times until the final regulations were issued in
April 1985.[3]

The final Baby Doe regulations stipulate that medical neglect includes "the withholding of medically indicated treatment from a disabled infant with a life-threatening condition." Instead of viewing
physicians as the advocates for their youngest patients, this federal law
accuses doctors of neglect if they withhold treatments they judge to
impose burdens without compensating benefits to the infants. This
tale of the federal government's unprecedented intrusion into decisions
about whether to withhold aggressive treatment from infants with
severe birth defects began with an April 1982 case in Bloomington,
Indiana.

The infant who became known as "Baby Doe" was born with
tracheoesophageal fistula, a birth defect that leaves the esophagus un-
connected to the stomach, preventing the infant from eating normally.
Although this condition can be surgically corrected, the baby's parents
refused the operation, apparently because the infant had another birth
defect, Down's syndrome, which rendered the child mentally retarded. Doctors sought a court order to perform the surgical repair
despite parental refusal, but courts in Indiana upheld the parents'
decision. The court used the family's right to privacy as a basis for its
ruling, asserting that parents are best suited to make decisions for their
children, and that a long tradition in law has upheld family privacy
and autonomy in matters such as this. Baby Doe died after six days,
having been denied food, water, and surgical aid.

As a result of widespread media reports, the Baby Doe case was
thrust upon the public's attention. Many people were outraged about
what they saw as the unnecessary death of a baby who could have
been saved by a relatively simple surgical procedure. Others argued
for the family's "right to decide," probably thinking that they, too,

might choose to reject a lifesaving operation for their own mentally retarded newborn.

The case reminded me of moral problems I had been introduced to a decade earlier when I first began teaching medical ethics. At that time it was more common than it is today for doctors to defer to parental refusal of treatment for babies with Down's syndrome. The practice was reflected in medical terminology then in vogue. Such infants were called "Mongols"—a variant of the term "mongolism," which was used because the facial features of persons with Down's syndrome are similar to those of Asians. This negative label was eventually dropped, probably because it was recognized as a racial slur. Use of the term persists even today among some older doctors, and it is easy for me to criticize those health-care workers who have failed to adopt a more enlightened language when discussing patients who are not entirely normal. Yet along with many colleagues I typically referred to such babies as "defective newborns" until a medical student pointed out the callous implications of the terminology. It sounded, he said, as if I were talking about a washing machine or some other piece of equipment. I never used that phrase again.

Despite the importance of remaining sensitive to the connotation of labels, language reforms do not eliminate ethical dilemmas. On the one hand, it seemed correct that parents should play a role in treatment decisions, including selective nontreatment, for their infants. On the other hand, reports published as long ago as 1973 reveal that pediatricians in prestigious medical centers such as Yale–New Haven Hospital had regularly allowed some babies with minor birth defects to die, for reasons that had little to do with the infants' best interests but much to do with the desires of the parents.[4] Although the issues were by now familiar, what was new in the Bloomington case was the intrusion of the federal government with its Baby Doe regulations issued through the Department of Health and Human Services (HHS).

In May 1982 HHS sent out a "Notice to Health Care Providers," warning hospitals that if they withheld food or lifesaving medical or surgical treatment from handicapped infants, the hospitals could lose their federal funds. The directive required hospitals to post a notice with these requirements in each delivery ward, maternity ward, pediatric ward, nursery, and neonatal intensive-care unit (NICU). The notice was to include a toll-free, twenty-four-hour hot-line number to call in the event of suspicion that treatment was being withheld from such infants. Tips could be phoned in anonymously and would be followed by investigative teams from the federal government, which came to be called "Baby Doe squads." The rule was issued under the authority of Section 504 of the Rehabilitation Act of 1973, a statute that prohibited discrimination on the basis of handicap by any organization or program receiving federal financial assistance.

This version of the Baby Doe regulations was to be short-lived. It was ruled invalid on procedural grounds on April 14, 1983, by U.S. District Court Judge Gerhard Gesell. The narrow procedural grounds on which Judge Gesell based his ruling was the failure of the Department of Health and Human Services to follow the required procedure of allowing thirty days for public comment before a proposed federal regulation can go into effect. However, in his written opinion, the judge broadened his discussion, calling the hot-line portion of the rule "hasty" and "ill-considered," and criticizing "the invasive and disruptive police tactics used by federal 'Baby Doe squads' " and the use of an "anonymous tipster." He also faulted the rule on substantive grounds, saying there was no consideration of the rightful role of families or of the devastating nature of certain defects.[5]

Many thoughtful legal scholars and medical practitioners questioned whether a law initially intended to forbid discrimination against handicapped persons should be applied to medical-treatment decisions for infants. The law was meant to provide for ramps and wheelchair access and for nondiscriminatory hiring practices for disabled persons. Congress did not intend it as a means for intruding into the doctor-patient relationship or invading family privacy. The United States Supreme Court eventually ruled that it is a matter for the states, and not the federal govenment, to review decisions in which parents refuse treatment for their handicapped newborns.[6]

Despite the numerous procedural grounds on which the original Baby Doe rules were criticized and found to be invalid, a nagging doubt remains: Should the lives of infants like Baby Doe be legally protected, and if so, what should the mechanism be? Traditionally, the mechanism has been that of local and state courts. But that system failed in the Baby Doe case, when the Indiana courts upheld the parents' right to refuse lifesaving surgery for their mentally retarded baby. As inappropriate as it was for "flying Baby Doe squads" from Washington to come swooping into hospital nurseries, some acceptable procedure was needed to ensure that babies are not permitted to die because their survival would be inconvenient for their parents.

The federal government tried again. The Department of Health and Human Services issued a second set of Baby Doe regulations, this time under authority of a 1984 amendment to the Child Abuse Protection and Treatment Act of 1974. In its previous effort the government had defined failure to provide treatment to disabled infants as discrimination against the handicapped. In its second attempt to regulate medical treatment decisions, HHS called such practices child abuse and neglect. This placed the authority to investigate alleged cases in the hands of state-based child-protective services. It also made doctors potential adversaries of those agencies rather than the allies they had formerly been, working together to report and remedy instances of parental abuse or neglect of children. Despite these changes, the mechanisms for federal oversight remained in place.

In the midst of all these legal developments, a second infant with life-threatening birth defects was thrust into the glare of public attention. Baby Jane Doe was born in October 1983 in a community hospital in Port Jefferson, New York, and transferred to University Hospital at Stony Brook, where doctors and nurses skilled in neonatology could deliver care. The baby had a number of serious disorders associated with spina bifida. Not only did she have a meningomyelocele, a protruding sac filled with cerebrospinal fluid and containing a defective spinal cord; she also had hydrocephalus, an accumulation of excess fluid on the brain, and microcephaly, an abnormally small head. Doctors estimated that without surgery, Baby Jane Doe might live for several weeks to two years; with surgery, they said, she could survive twenty years, but with paralysis, epilepsy, and a likelihood of infections of her bladder and urinary tract, along with severe mental retardation.

Baby Jane Doe's parents were given the option of surgical treatments or a "conservative" treatment plan for their baby. Under the first option, surgery would be performed to correct the lesion on the spinal column and shunts would be inserted to drain the excess fluid from her head. Under the conservative treatment plan, antibiotics could be given to protect against infection of the spinal column, or no medical treatment could be administered but the infant would be fed and kept warm and comfortable.

The parents consulted with neurologists, nurses, a social worker, and religious counselors, and eventually chose the conservative course with antibiotic therapy. Soon thereafter, a confidential "tip" was given to a "right-to-life" lawyer named Lawrence Washburn, Jr. Mr. Washburn worked in Albany but lived in Vermont, had nothing to do with Baby Jane Doe's family or with the hospital, and had no direct knowledge of the infant's condition or the circumstances surrounding the parents' decision. Washburn sought to bring a lawsuit to have surgery performed, but his efforts were eventually blocked by the Appellate Division of the New York State court system and upheld by the New York Court of Appeals. The Appellate Division held that the decision of Baby Jane Doe's parents was in the best interests of the infant, and that therefore there was no basis for the courts to intervene. The higher court, the Court of Appeals, made its ruling on procedural grounds: Lawrence Washburn was a totally unrelated person invading the privacy of the parents and had no legal standing to intrude. Because proper legal procedures were not followed, this right-to-life lawyer was unable to carry out his efforts to have surgery performed on Baby Jane Doe.

But suppose that attempt had been procedurally correct. The substantive questions remain: How can the best interest of severely disabled newborns be determined? Was Baby Jane Doe's best interest served or violated by her parents' decision to withhold surgical treatment? Should this case, and others like it, be construed as instances of child abuse and neglect? These questions demand renewed scrutiny of the concept of the "best interest" of the child.

It is odd to think of death as being in anyone's "best interest." Yet competent adult patients have chosen to forgo life-sustaining treatment because they viewed their own quality of life to be so poor that death was preferable to continued existence. Courts have upheld those autonomous decisions, recognizing that patients have a right to act in what they see to be their own best interest. If that concept makes sense for adults who are capable of deciding for themselves, it should be meaningful, as well, for infants and children. But the Baby Doe regulations left no room for quality-of-life considerations. Nor did they grant the possibility that it may be in the best interest of some infants not to survive. The rules did, however, define a narrow range of cases in which nontreatment of newborns was allowed.

In their final form the Baby Doe rules under the Child Abuse Protection and Treatment Act prohibit "the withholding of medically indicated treatment from a disabled infant with a life-threatening condition," and term such withholding "medical neglect." The regulations explicate the phrase "withholding medically indicated treatment" as "the failure to respond to the infant's life-threatening conditions by providing treatment (including appropriate nutrition, hydration, and medication) which, in the treating physician's (or physicians') reasonable medical judgment, will be most likely to be effective in ameliorating or correcting all such conditions. . . ."

Only three circumstances are described in which withholding treatment "other than appropriate nutrition, hydration, or medication" is not "medical neglect":

(i) The infant is chronically and irreversibly comatose;
(ii) The provision of such treatment would merely prolong dying, not be effective in ameliorating or correcting all of the infant's life-threatening conditions, or otherwise be futile in terms of the survival of the infant; or
(iii) The provision of such treatment would be virtually futile in terms of the survival of the infant and the treatment itself under such circumstances would be inhumane.[7]

In other words, only when an infant is already dying and treatment will be to no avail, or when the baby is in a coma from which it will never recover, can treatment be withheld. These regulations leave little or no room for quality-of-life considerations, and no possibility of judging that an infant's best interest can lie in withholding or withdrawing medical therapy.

The federal government's Baby Doe regulations are sometimes equated with a right-to-life position. But that interpretation is misleading. It draws a picture of conflicting rights: the right to continued existence of severely disabled infants pitted against the rights of others, usually their parents, who wish for the death of such infants. But only a minority of cases of seriously ill newborns fit this picture of conflicting rights. Calling a position right-to-life does make sense in some debates in bioethics, like the abortion controversy, where foes of abortion ascribe that right to the fetus. And it also makes sense in cases where parents selfishly refuse treatment for their infant because they don't want to rear a retarded or otherwise "imperfect" child. But in dilemmas in which the ethical problem lies in the very determination of what is in an infant's best interest, the phrase "right to life" is ill chosen. A better way of describing the position held by the lawyer Lawrence Washburn and others is "sanctity of life." Washburn asserted that "he believes that every life is sacred, and that 'profoundly retarded children . . . are here [for us] to protect, . . . the children of the good God, they are given to us because it is our call to heroism, to greatness, to have a child like this."[8]

A moral stance that rests on the sanctity of life in contrast with the more moderate quality-of-life position is often associated with orthodox religions such as Roman Catholicism. Yet just as in 1957 Pope

Pius XII rejected the idea that all possible means must be employed to preserve and prolong life, asserting that we are normally obliged to use only "ordinary" means, so too have some Catholic theologians more recently adopted a quality-of-life position. One such spokesman is Richard A. McCormick, a Jesuit priest on the faculty at Georgetown University known for his insightful contributions to bioethics. In an article published in 1974, entitled "To Save or Let Die: The Dilemma of Modern Medicine," Father McCormick explains and defends a quality-of-life viewpoint.[9] Noting that modern medicine can keep almost anyone alive, he poses the question: "Granted that we can easily save the life, what kind of life are we saving?" Father McCormick admits this is a quality-of-life judgment and holds that we must face the responsibility of answering these questions when they arise.

Examining cases of grossly malformed infants, Father McCormick states that "it is neither inhuman nor unchristian to say that there comes a point where an individual's condition itself represents the negation of any truly human—i.e., relational—potential. When that point is reached, is not the best treatment no treatment?"[10] Physicians are the ones who must provide the concrete categories and biological criteria for this judgment, according to McCormick. He is careful to point out that a large gray area is bound to exist between the easily identifiable extremes. Yet he succeeds in offering a useful guideline for making quality-of-life judgments for infants with severe birth defects:

> . . . life is a value to be preserved only insofar as it contains some potentiality for human relationships. When in human judgment this potentiality is totally absent or would be, because of the condition of the individual, totally subordinated to the mere effort for survival, that life can be said to have achieved its potential.[11]

McCormick's guideline is "the potential for human relationships associated with the infant's condition." It is a guideline that can be applied as well to the incompetent adult patient who had expressed no prior wishes while still competent. Translated into the language of "best interests," an individual who lacks any present capacity or future potential for human relationships can be said to have no interests at all, except, perhaps, to be free from pain and discomfort.

Using rather different terminology, the President's Commission for the Study of Ethical Problems in Medicine and Biomedical Behavioral Research came to a similar conclusion. In its discussion of seriously ill newborns, the commission adopted what it called a "very restrictive standard." In cases where seriously ill newborns will be left with permanent handicaps, either from the underlying birth defect itself or from medical therapy, "such permanent handicaps justify a decision not to provide life-sustaining treatment only when they are so severe that continued existence would not be a net benefit to the infant."[12] The commission states explicitly that this strict standard "excludes consideration of the negative effects of an impaired child's life on other persons, including parents, siblings, and society." As an example, the handicaps of Down's syndrome "do not justify failing to provide medically proven treatment, such as surgical correction of a blocked intestinal tract."[13]

This is an infant-centered criterion, one that requires the surrogate decision-maker to try to evaluate benefits and burdens from the infant's own perspective. That requirement has provoked criticism for a reason similar to the one that rejects the courts' use of the substituted-judgment standard in deciding for never-competent patients: it is impossible for the surrogate decision-maker to adopt the required perspective.

According to both Father McCormick's guideline and the standard set forth by the President's Commission, Bloomington Baby Doe, born with Down's syndrome and a tracheoesophageal fistula that could have been surgically repaired, should have had the operation. Despite their mental retardation, which is rarely severe, persons with Down's syndrome are capable of distinctively human relationships, and usually form a close and loving bond with family members. When they live in a caring and supportive environment, their quality of life is unmistakably good. It is altogether implausible to judge the handicaps imposed by Down's syndrome to be so severe that continued existence would not be a net benefit to the individual.

Unlike the first Baby Doe, for whom the benefits and burdens of continued life could be meaningfully assessed, the case of Baby Jane Doe, who was born with spina bifida, hydrocephalus, and microcephaly, is far from clear. This unfortunate infant falls within McCormick's large gray area, an area in which the future potential for human relationships is unknown or open to dispute. No greater certainty can be gained in this case from using the President's Commission's standard, since it is virtually impossible to judge whether from Baby Jane Doe's perspective her multiple handicaps are so severe that continued existence would not be a net benefit to her.

■ ■ ■

WHEN A SUBSTANTIVE CRITERION FAILS to give clear guidance, as in cases that fall in the gray zone, then a procedural mechanism should be in place to ensure a timely and effective resolution. The President's Commission recommended that hospitals caring for seriously ill newborns should have explicit policies on decision-making procedures for such cases. The commission also urged the establishment of ethics committees that could serve an advisory role and could review the decision-making process. The use of hospital ethics committees to deal with the agonizing dilemmas surrounding the care and treatment of seriously handicapped newborns involves a mixture of substance and procedure. The procedure involves selecting a body of thoughtful individuals drawn from several disciplines to review hard cases in a careful and dispassionate manner. But such committees themselves must arrive at a substantive standard to guide their recommendations, a standard that is infant-centered and embodies moral principles to guide decision-making.

Although the best-interest standard should remain a central feature of decision-making on behalf of infants and children, it has limits. In addition to the widely noted problems of vagueness and uncertainty, there is the further question of the applicability of this standard to some of the most troubling dilemmas in the neonatal nursery. As explicated by the President's Commission, the best-interest standard would mandate treatment so long as the infant was not suffering extreme pain or the severe burdens of the treatment itself. The standard would require treatment even of those infants who would never develop the ability to interact with other people and who might live a very short life.[14]

This shows that Father McCormick's guideline, the potential of the individual for human relationships, is a notion quite different from "best interest." It is questionable whether severely neurologically impaired children can be said to have any interests to which a best-interest standard might apply. The parents of such infants may have an interest in their continued existence, and those wishes should be honored. Although prolonging their lives would not be a benefit to such infants, neither would it be a burden. In cases where an infant's best interest is nonexistent or impossible to determine, parental wishes should govern.

The hospitals in which I work have an infant bioethical review committee (IBRC), a name used by the American Academy of Pediatrics early in its efforts to work out a compromise with the federal government on the Baby Doe regulations. Our committee worked long

and hard to develop a set of policies and principles to guide our deliberations. We are almost always unanimous in our recommendations to
physicians who come to the IBRC with cases for committee review.

In one case, however, the committee was sharply divided. Parents
of a newborn with multiple birth defects refused corrective life-
preserving surgery, and the doctors thought it was proper to operate.
After all the facts had been presented to the committee by the health-
care personnel involved in the case—pediatricians, a pediatric surgeon, a nurse specializing in neonatology, and the neonatal social
worker—the committee took a straw vote on its recommendation. The
vote was split. Next, a subcommittee met with the baby's parents.
They were shocked, grieving, and disconsolate at the birth of a handicapped infant. But there was no doubt in anyone's mind that these
parents cared very much about their infant and that their refusal of
surgery did not stem from selfish motives. They simply judged the
prospects for their baby's quality of life to be miserable.

Following a lengthy, heartrending session with the parents, another vote was taken. Two committee members changed their vote,
this time supporting the parents' refusal of surgery. I was tempted to
do the same. Sympathy ran high for the plight of this unlucky couple,
who, like all prospective parents, had been looking forward to the
birth of a normal, healthy child. Some doubt existed about whether
this case fell into the gray zone, with no one able to make a reasonable
prognosis concerning the child's future quality of life.

In the end, however, I had to return to the principles our infant
bioethical review committee had adopted after months of discussion
and debate. One principle states that parents are presumed to be the
decision-makers unless they choose a course of action that is "clearly
against the best interests of the infant." The more I thought about the
facts presented to the committee by medical experts, the more convinced I was that this child clearly possessed a potential for human
relationships, despite the likelihood of some mental retardation. Based
on that prognosis, I couldn't cast my vote against the life-sustaining
surgery. Yet the meeting with the parents, and the realization of how
the committee's recommendation affected this family, haunted me for
weeks. Eventually, a follow-up revealed that the baby had done well
after surgery, and the parents were providing a warm and loving
environment at home.

Some months later I was giving a lecture to a community group on
the subject of the increasing public nature of once-private medical
matters. I had described the increasing use of hospital ethics commit-

tees, including the infant bioethical review committee on which I serve. A woman in the front row, visibly pregnant and obviously distressed, asked a question.

"Are you telling me that parents don't have control over their babies anymore? Are you saying that a bunch of strangers can force treatment decisions for an infant on its parents and even the doctors?"

Gently, I pointed out that the IBRC does not make decisions, but rather recommendations. Small consolation that would be, I realized, when the committee recommends to physicians who are colleagues within the same institution. The doctors will in almost all cases accept the committee's recommendations and if necessary seek a court order to provide treatment over the parents' refusal.

I was able to dispel the woman's worst fears by pointing out the very small range of cases in which an IBRC will get involved in the first place, and the even smaller number in which they are likely to advise a course of treatment that goes against the parents' wishes. That small number comprises the cases in which parents make a decision that is clearly against the infant's best interests. Given the existence of a large gray area, as noted by McCormick and other thinkers, and based on the fact that in the overwhelming number of instances parents decide in favor of life for their infants, I could assure the woman that fears about intrusive hospital ethics committees are largely unwarranted. But I could not deny that if an infant with Down's syndrome and blocked intestines were born at our institution, and if the parents refused consent for repair of the intestinal defect, the IBRC would recommend treatment and the doctors would almost certainly seek and obtain a court order to operate. The reason for the committee's action would not be fear of federal Baby Doe rules or any other law. The reason would be that in accordance with its own policies and principles, the IBRC tries to do the morally right thing.

Yet as valiantly as doctors and ethicists strive to elect the morally right course of action, cases arise in which it remains unclear. Sometimes the lack of clarity is a result of the diagnostic and prognostic uncertainty of medicine itself. In other cases it can be traced to moral uncertainty or ethical ambiguity. It is only in the rarest instances that physicians recommend withholding or withdrawing aggressive therapy when family members insist that "everything be done" for their infant. The parents' insistence is sometimes a result of their denial of the baby's hopeless condition or bleak prognosis. At other times parents recognize the reality of the situation but their guilt prevents them from requesting termination of life supports even for a baby whose survival is unprecedented.

In all cases of ethical ambiguity, the physician's primary obligation is to keep the interests of the patient in focus. Despite the problems inherent in determining the best interest of the child, that standard should remain the ideal toward which to strive. Doctors are often caught between their own judgment of what is in their patient's best interest and the demands of the patient's family. This is true not only for pediatricians, whose patients are infants and children, but also for geriatricians, whose patients are aged and frequently infirm. One of the hardest tasks physicians face is how to deal with the family, a task for which their medical-school education leaves them ill-prepared.

Treating the Family

M RS. M., a thirty-seven-year-old woman with diabetes, was in labor when admitted to City Hospital. This was her third pregnancy, and the patient and her husband were anxious about the successful delivery of a healthy baby. Her two previous attempts had resulted in stillbirths. This time a baby girl weighing just under four pounds was delivered by cesarean section. The infant emerged limp and lifeless, with two knots in the umbilical cord. The delivery-room team began vigorous efforts to resuscitate the baby, who was having seizures, needed to be placed on a ventilator, required the drug dopamine to sustain her blood pressure, and remained in critical condition. The doctors explained to Mrs. M. that her baby was very sick and would probably not survive. Even if she did live, there would be severe neurologic damage because her brain had been deprived of oxygen for too long. Having been fully informed, Mrs. M. told the doctors to "do everything" for her baby.

Soon after beginning aggressive measures, the neonatologist discovered that the infant had necrotic bowel syndrome, death of a portion of the intestine. Only major surgery could correct this life-threatening condition, but because the baby was critically ill, her chances of surviving the surgery were poor. Still, Mrs. M. insisted that everything be done.

After holding an emergency case conference that included an ethics consultation, doctors, nurses, and social workers agreed that surgery was not in the infant's best interest. It could only prolong the dying process, inflicting pain and suffering on an infant whose chances for survival were almost zero. The ethical dilemma revolved around the mother's insistence on surgical treatment despite the bleak prognosis and the harm that would come to the baby from the aggressive procedures.

Unlike cases in which parental refusal of treatment is clearly against the infant's best interests, the opposite problem arose in this tragic case. Although parents do not have a right to decide against lifesaving treatment for a baby who could experience a good quality of life, it remains uncertain whether they could demand treatment for an infant who had virtually no chance of survival.

One nurse argued that time was too valuable for skilled nurses to engage in extra postoperative care for an infant who would die anyway, with or without the surgery. She added that caring for very sick and dying children takes a terrible emotional toll on the nurses, and it was unfair to inflict more grief on nurses by forcing them to endure a baby's unnecessary suffering.

A hospital administrator present at the conference expressed concern about the use of expensive, high-technology resources in cases like this. Under pressure to hold down costs in the hospital, he argued that for economic reasons, futile treatments should not be undertaken. A social worker insisted that in the neonatal field it is not just the baby but the whole family who should be considered "patients." She argued that the staff had an obligation to "treat the family" as well as the infant, which in this case meant performing the surgery as requested by the mother.

I listened to all these arguments, finding some more persuasive than others. Many interests appeared to be at stake. The prevailing theme at the conference revolved around balancing those interests, a typical utilitarian approach to such problems. But I was troubled about the fact that the patient's interests were being considered on a par with all the other interests identified in the course of the discussion.

There is something vaguely disturbing about the idea of "treating the family." The notion of "treatment" is ambiguous. It can mean "the performance of therapy," but it also has a nonmedical sense, meaning "dealing with" or "behaving toward." This ambiguity was at least partially responsible for the health professionals' confusion of their therapeutic obligation to the patient with their responsibilities to the patient's family. "Treating the family" had assumed as much importance as treating the patient.

It was easy for me to dismiss the interests of the hospital as "merely economic," and to sympathize with the nurses yet give their concerns a lower order of priority than those of the patient and family. It was much harder to argue against the position that the staff should comply with Mrs. M.'s wishes that everything be done for her infant. Humane concern for the family of patients is a morally relevant consideration. But I rejected the idea that Mrs. M. should be allowed to dictate to doctors a course of treatment that would provide no ultimate benefit and might even cause the baby additional pain and suffering. An infant-centered criterion required that the patient's interest come first.

THE CASE OF WILLIE P., a fourteen-month-old baby with a degenerative disease of the spinal cord and skeletal muscles, also raised the question of "treating the family." Although the diagnosis was certain, the prognosis was unclear because each patient has an individual course. In all cases of this disease, life expectancy is shortened. But there is a wide variation in the severity of the condition and the relative shortness of the patient's life, though if the disease is manifested early, the prognosis is worse, with survival rarely extending into the teens. In Willie's case the illness had been diagnosed at three months of age, and his parents were told at that time about the disease and its prognosis.

This case was presented at pediatric ethics rounds when Willie was hospitalized with pneumonia, and the question was raised whether to put him on a ventilator. In previous hospitalizations it had taken longer for Willie to be removed from the ventilator than other patients, and the staff worried that he might have to remain on a ventilator all the time, for the rest of his life. The pediatric social worker doubted that Willie's parents fully understood their child's prognosis, because of the complicated nature of the disease and the fact that Willie's condition had not sharply deteriorated. Discussion focused on what was best for the parents, as well as what was the right thing to do for the patient. In this case, like many others, the parents were emotionally involved, yet deferred to the pediatricians when it came to decisions about their child's medical treatment. They were, quite simply, paralyzed with indecision.

Life on a ventilator is not pleasant, to say the least. But no one was willing to argue that it was a fate worse than death. In fact, everyone at the conference agreed that Willie should be intubated and placed on the ventilator if that was the only way of prolonging his life. I was surprised, then, to see the discussion turn to the issue of treating the family. One nurse asked, Why not withhold treatment now rather than ten months from now? It would be prolonging the inevitable to use aggressive means to treat this child, who suffered from a fatal, degenerative disease. As his condition worsened, the need for a decision would arise again soon and it would be harder to withdraw him from the ventilator later than it would be to withhold it in the first place.

Once again, the distinction between withholding and withdrawing a medical treatment was introduced. And once again, I argued that despite the emotional difference that distinction makes for caregivers who must do the withholding or withdrawing, it has no moral significance. If anything, the justification for withdrawing a treatment already begun is stronger, since more solid evidence exists for the patient's prognosis and ability to tolerate the treatment.

Seeing that the staff was unanimous in their belief that for now, placing Willie on a ventilator was in his best interest, and agreeing with that judgment myself, I began my customary role of summing up as the ethics conference neared its conclusion. I was interrupted by one pediatric resident, considerably older than the typical member of the house staff, who accused me of bringing a philosopher's abstract ethical principles to an emotionally wrenching situation. Nice words, he said, for an outsider to bring to a real-life problem, one in which even the health-care personnel themselves were only involved for a limited time. The poor parents have to bear the brunt of the agony of seeing their baby suffer and get worse and worse, all the while hooked up to some machine. We must be humane in treating the parents, the resident argued. We cannot let abstract philosophical theory interfere with what we feel is best for the family. It will spare the parents untold anguish if we let the child die now rather than in a year or two.

Trying not to take the attack too personally, I had to respond. It is one thing for doctors to behave paternalistically toward their sick patients, seeking to bring about the best possible medical outcomes. Medical paternalism may not be morally justifiable, yet it is surely understandable when viewed from the physician's perspective. But if doctors, when doing what they consider best for the family, treat patients as a means to that end, they are violating Kant's famous categorical imperative: Persons should be treated as ends in themselves, never as a mere means to the ends of others. The imperative warns against using people merely as a means, no matter how noble the ends may be. As important as the family is, the physician's primary obligation is to the patient, whether that be prolonging life, relieving suffering, or even withholding treatment.

Kant's principle, like other tenets of ethical theory, may appear abstract when uttered out of any context. But such principles are meant to be applied to concrete cases. To prolong the life of a suffering, dying child only for the sake of its parents, as in the case of Mrs. M. and her baby, or to withhold a treatment from a child because of the perceived benefit to its parents, as in Willie's case, is wrong. The indignant resident thought that ethical problems should be resolved by feelings rather than by principles. If he judged this use of "abstract philosophical principles" to result in cruel treatment of the parents of pediatric patients, I had to conclude that he had gotten his ethical priorities backward by paying too much attention to the family's well-being at the expense of the child's.

NOT ALL DILEMMAS involving the family take the form of conflicts between the interests of the patient and the interests of the family. One example of a different case is that of Kevin, a five-year-old boy in an irreversible coma. Kevin was the victim of a tragic accident caused by his mother's carelessness. She had thrown a lighted match into a wastebasket, which smoldered for a while and then suddenly engulfed the room in flames. Kevin was rescued from the burning room and rushed to the hospital. He had a cardiac arrest in the emergency room, and efforts to resuscitate him began immediately. Kevin lived, but medical treatment came too late to prevent severe brain damage due to a lack of oxygen. With only his brain stem functioning, he remained in an "awake coma," his eyes open in the daytime but closed at night. He required medications to prevent seizures, had a tube in his abdomen for feeding, and was having problems keeping food down, with a danger of breathing in the food and choking to death. Doctors estimated that he could probably live for a full lifetime but would never awaken and never improve.

Kevin's mother, obviously feeling massive guilt, wanted her son to be a "full code," receiving all resuscitative measures if at any time he had another cardiac arrest. Although she seemed to acknowledge that he would forever remain in his vegetative state, she nevertheless demanded that any and all treatments continue to be administered. The situation was complicated by the fact that Kevin's eyes were open and he appeared to look around, and occasionally cried. Yet experts in neurology assured everyone that this was only the appearance, not the reality, of conscious awareness.

Kevin required continuous, watchful nursing care. Because he had had recurrent vomiting, the danger persisted that he would aspirate—

breathe in the vomit—choke, develop pneumonia, and go into respiratory failure. Over and over again, the staff raised the question of whether he should be resuscitated. When the case was discussed at pediatric ethics rounds, it was first presented as a conflict between the need to "treat the mother" by making Kevin a "full code" and the dubious benefit of resuscitating a permanently unconscious patient.

The residents couched their questions in the language of the "best interest" of the child. However, I view this as a clear case of a patient having no interests at all. Kevin was in irreversible coma. A minimally necessary condition for being able to have any interests is sentience: the capacity to experience pleasure or pain. Kevin did not meet this minimal condition. His was the classic situation of a persistent vegetative state, so to ask what is in this patient's interests is to pose an essentially meaningless question.

Why not, then, consider the mother's interests and grant her expressed wish to have Kevin remain a "full code" and continue to receive all necessary medications? Unlike the cases of Willie and his parents, and Mrs. M. and her baby, this was not a case of conflict of interests between a pediatric patient and the parents. So it could not be resolved by adhering to a patient-centered criterion for treatment. The simplest solution would be to honor Kevin's mother's request. But the simplest solution may ignore other legitimate competing interests, and that is exactly what happened in this case.

The nurses stated that the careful monitoring required for Kevin took them away from other children in the unit who were acutely ill and had a much better prognosis than Kevin's. It would be unethical, they argued, to administer less than the best possible care to those sick children. In this instance the fact of limited resources in the form of skilled nursing personnel was a legitimate moral consideration, one that had to be taken into account for other patients to be treated as they deserved. Even the use of an acute-care hospital bed for this child, when others in need of that bed might be kept waiting, loomed as an ethical problem of scarce medical resources.

The inevitable mention of the costs of hospital care turned the discussion at the conference in a new direction. Is it part of the doctor's role to be a fiscal gatekeeper? Should saving money for the hospital be taken into account when making treatment decisions for patients? Someone pointed out that the financial costs of resuscitation are considerable, amounting to about $2550 for each attempt. Although it is poor policy to waste money, convincing arguments must be given before drawing the conclusion that the care and treatment of patients like Kevin should come under the heading of "wasting money."

NB: Kant — do not use a person
else's ends

The need for a decision in Kevin's case was removed by nature taking its course. One night he went into cardiac arrest and a code was called. Despite a valiant attempt to resuscitate him, Kevin died. The staff was relieved at this outcome, since it took the decision out of everyone's hands, and they turned their attention to helping the mother cope with her grief.

WHEN THE PATIENT is an infant or child, it is common for caregivers to think it proper to "treat the family" as well as the patient, partly because the interests of children are closely identified with those of their parents, and partly because parents are normally presumed to be the decision-makers for their children, unless their decisions are clearly against the child's best interests. But when the patient is an adult, especially one who has the capacity to participate in decision-making, it is remarkable that physicians may not only avoid communicating with the patient; they sometimes even go so far as to place the family's wishes above those of the patient.

I was addressing a local society of physicians when one doctor asked, "What do you do when the patient's son comes to you and insists that his father should have every known form of chemotherapy, including experimental drugs, to treat his cancer, and the patient is refusing?"

"Is the patient competent?" I asked.

"Well, yes, I guess so," the doctor replied.

"Has he had any anticancer treatments so far?"

"Yes, for a while, but it may be too soon to tell if they are effective."

"How did he tolerate those treatments?" I inquired.

"To be honest, not so well. But what am I going to do about the son? I can't just ignore his demands. He's bugging me. He stops me in the hospital every time he sees me. He calls me at home. Why, he might even sue me if I don't treat his father like he wants me to."

A familiar worry. "Is that the reason you think you ought to administer chemotherapy to your patient?" I asked.

"Well, it's part of the reason. But mainly it's the son himself. Don't patients' families have any rights in these matters?"

I was tempted to reply, "No, families don't have any rights in these matters when the patient is a competent adult," but that reply would have provoked a lengthy discussion of the distinction between moral and legal rights, and problems of grounding rights claims in an ethical theory. Also, it is difficult to discuss moral claims in terms of rights unless the rights in question are clearly established and can be substantiated. The competent, adult patient's right to informed consent, to self-determination regarding medical treatment, is one such right, but the rights of families of patients are neither clearly established nor easily substantiated.

The question the physician posed at my lecture reminded me of the wife and daughter of Mr. R., the forty-nine-year-old cancer patient who requested that he be made comfortable and sleepy when all treatments had been exhausted. Mr. R.'s wife and daughter could not accept that decision and begged the doctors to continue treatment, insisting that the patient be resuscitated if his heart stopped. It reminded me also of Mr. DiS., the eighty-two-year-old man whose wife and daughter were informed that he had cancer and adamantly maintained that the patient should not be told, threatening the doctor with a lawsuit if he revealed the diagnosis. What families do have are anxiety, fear, guilt, anger, hope, and sadness. It is these feelings that doctors have to contend with, and that some mistakenly label "rights."

AS ADVOCATES FOR their patients, physicians sometimes confront an altogether different type of situation regarding the patient's family. In these cases it is less a question of "treating" the family than of dealing with them. Not infrequently, ethical problems that arise with hospitalized patients are beyond the capacity of physicians and other health professionals to settle. Often, they revolve around the patient's discharge or placement. They are known as "disposition problems," or, in hospital lingo, "dispo" cases—a term that conjures up the unsavory image of a disposal service.

Mr. F., an eighty-four-year-old man hospitalized for six months because of severe weight loss and resulting weakness, had been home for one week during that period and was then readmitted to the hospital. Mr. F. lives with his thirty-five-year-old single son. They share the house and each has his own apartment. Tony, the son, provides meals for his father and cares for him at home. In the past year Tony has been arrested several times on drug charges and for fighting but has managed to beat the charges.

The senior physician in charge of the case identified the following issues that culminate in an ethical dilemma:

> Mr. F. wants to live and die at home and does not want to be placed in a long-term-care facility, nor does he care what the conditions are at home.

Tony is willing to let Mr. F. live and die at home.

Tony works all day, and so he's not at home to care for his father and says he can't afford caretakers.

Tony needs his father's income to cover household expenses and probably other expenses as well.

Mr. F. had Meals on Wheels and another home health-care program. But he refuses to eat food brought by Meals on Wheels. He likes only spaghetti, hamburger meat, and potato chips.

Mr. F. has given Tony control of his finances. If his son "doesn't go along" with Mr. F's wishes, Mr. F. threatens to take over his own money. Tony then threatens that he will not take care of his father, and their home will be lost to both, so Mr. F. never follows through on his threat.

When Mr. F. is home alone, he does not eat and gets ill. On his last admission to the hospital, he weighed sixty-four pounds. Now he weighs ninety-three pounds. He eats very well in the hospital.

The physician summed up the dilemma: So we have an eighty-four-year-old patient who easily becomes malnourished living with a thirty-five-year-old son who only partially cares for him. Their relationship is very manipulative and the patient refuses to go anywhere else but home. At home he doesn't eat and they won't pay for a full-time caretaker. Do we send the patient home, knowing from past experience that he will quickly worsen, or do we keep him here against his will?

The dilemma arises out of the familiar clash of moral principles: respect for persons, which dictates that competent adults should be free to decide for themselves, even if their decision is contrary to their best interests; and the principle of beneficence, which instructs moral agents to bring about the best consequences. The consequence that quite properly concerned the physician who framed this dilemma was the malnourishment and deterioration of his elderly patient. But a brief reflection on all the other possible consequences in this case leads to a moral quagmire. The social situation and the manipulative behavior of this father and son toward each other lie beyond the reach of the medical profession's capacity for help. These "psychosocial problems," as the term implies, are a function of both the interpersonal relationship of father and son, and an inadequate social-support system.

Although I have some ambivalence about this case, my moral judgment lies on the side of Mr. F.'s autonomy. Not only is he mentally alert and fully competent; he quite explicitly stated that he wishes to live and die at home. There is no guarantee that if kept in the hospital indefinitely he will not deteriorate from causes other than malnutrition. From a narrowly medical point of view, it appears to be in Mr. F.'s best interest to remain in the hospital in order to be well fed. But a broader conception of "best interest," conjoined with Mr. F.'s undisputed right to self-determination, yields the conclusion that he should be sent home.

ANOTHER CASE INVOLVING similar issues was brought by a social worker to a conference to which I was invited, along with a lawyer, several hospital administrators, and other health-care workers. The patient, Mrs. C.L., has been widowed for many years and has three unmarried sons. Two of them, Sam and Ike, live with their mother in a two-bedroom apartment. The third son, Jack, lives in another part of the city. Mrs. C.L. was admitted to City Hospital because of constipation and "dispositional status"—the need for placement in a proper environment. She had been admitted to the hospital numerous times following visits to the emergency room, but no aggressive treatment was rendered. She needs and wants nursing care, since she is unable to walk and is so debilitated she cannot transfer herself from her wheelchair to her bed or to the toilet. However, Mrs. C.L. feeds herself and is alert, mentally oriented, and verbal.

Sam and Ike visit daily. Sam is loud, hot-tempered, threatening, and often speaks nonsensically. He has admitted to having been placed in a "nursing home" in another state sometime in the past. The social worker reported that Ike has not communicated with her and appears to be actively hallucinating and delusional. Both brothers are chain-smokers and unkempt. A city caseworker claims that both sons have long psychiatric histories at a nearby state psychiatric facility. The third son, Jack, communicates with the social worker through Sam, often promising to come to visit, but never showing up. Other social workers who have visited the apartment have judged it to be unsafe and unfit for Mrs. C.L. after discharge. A psychiatrist made a home visit and questioned the competency of the sons, Mrs. C.L.'s only caregivers at home.

Mrs. C.L. does not have Medicaid, and her sons have been uncooperative about applying. They have insisted that their mother be discharged to her home. A hypothesis presented at the conference was that the sons are fearful they will not be able to share the patient's

Social Security income if she is transferred to an after-care facility. The staff is uncertain whether they can place the patient in a facility without Medicaid and whether the courts will have to become involved.

The social worker identified the following ethical issues raised by the case:

Who is competent to make the decisions for this family regarding discharge plans, Medicaid application, and court involvement?

Can Mrs. C.L. be held in the hospital without legal authorization?

Can the hospital social-service department apply for Medicaid despite the sons' resistance?

Is Jack the one who should be considered responsible, despite his failure to take responsibility after his mother's last discharge? Why should the staff look to him for help, since he is irresponsible and may be incompetent as well?

Only some of these questions pose ethical issues. Others are legal, administrative, and psychiatric. Who is competent to make decisions for this family? The several meanings of the term "competent" are shown by this question. Mrs. C.L. underwent a psychiatric evaluation and was judged competent by the usual method: she was oriented to time, place, and person. A hospital administrator at the conference questioned whether Mrs. C.L. was competent in a broader sense, a sense that requires her to stand up to her aggressive, controlling sons. Does she have the fortitude and stamina to go forward with a Medicaid application and seek nursing-home placement, even with the assistance of social workers? The social workers think not. Nevertheless, this is no reason to consider her incompetent. Being unassertive or susceptible to being bullied should not be confused with being incompetent.

Can the patient be held in the hospital without legal authorization? This does happen, but it is ethically wrong. There are ways to "beat the system," but they involve deception and dishonesty. But should Mrs. C.L. be kept in the hospital, even if it requires dishonest means? In an ideal world, no; perhaps yes, for a poor, elderly, debilitated patient with mentally ill sons, caught in a legal and administrative tangle.

To apply for Medicaid for the patient despite the sons' resistance would take some courage on the part of hospital social workers. While this action could be ethically justified as being in the patient's best interest, it might also be an invasion of family privacy. For such an intrusion to be morally permissible, the patient's interest must be placed above all other considerations.

The final question, relating to Jack's competency and responsibility, looks like a psychiatric question but is primarily a value question. In one obvious sense Jack is competent: he lives alone, manages his affairs, and has apparently not been hospitalized for psychiatric reasons. But he has demonstrated no sense of responsibility for his mother, and in all likelihood never will. Irresponsibility is not the same as incompetence. The first is a moral failing, the second a psychological inability. Yet a person who is irresponsible can be considered socially incompetent, even if not psychologically so.

To discharge a patient who is debilitated and unable to walk to an unfit home, to be cared for by selfish, emotionally disturbed, or unconcerned sons, is hardly in her best interest. Mrs. C.L. never expressed any clear preferences of her own, or indicated whether she would rather be with even abusive family members than with strangers. The social workers, mired in administrative regulations, continued to search for an alternative for her. In the meantime, she remained in the hospital, where she was well cared for. An acute-care hospital is not the proper place for a woman like Mrs. C.L., yet it was the only ethically acceptable alternative available.

THE CASES OF MR. F. AND MRS. C.L., as well as those of Mr. R. and Mr. DiS., raise ethical problems for physicians who must deal in some way with the family of a competent adult patient. But only when the patient is marginally competent, or wholly lacking the capacity to participate in decision-making, may the family assume a legitimate role in decisions about treatment or placement. These situations give rise to dilemmas of a different kind, as illustrated in the case of Mrs. C.

Mrs. C. was seventy-four years old when she was admitted to a nursing home from the hospital. A year earlier she had fallen and injured her head, resulting in a brain concussion. She is doubly incontinent, is being tube-fed, requires total care, and is developing bedsores. She has a tracheostomy, a surgical opening through the neck into the windpipe, and is severely demented. The medical record lists her prognosis as poor.

Mrs. C., who obviously cannot make any decisions on her own behalf, is currently caught in the middle of a legal battle between her two daughters, both of whom are seeking legal guardianship. The legal struggle resulted from family disagreement over where the mother should be placed. One daughter wants the mother to remain in the nursing home, while the other wants her to return to the hospital. The second daughter refused to consent to treatment for her mother in the nursing home.

A geriatric nurse presented this case at a seminar for health-care professionals. The nurse posed the following two questions: Who is to give consent for the patient while the legal battle ensues? If one party gives consent and the other eventually becomes guardian, does the consent become invalid, raising legal concerns for the nursing home? I was unable to answer either question. Although both questions were important for the caregivers and the institution involved, they are primarily legal matters to be resolved by an appropriate legal mechanism. Underlying the legal questions, though, is a pervasive ethical problem: When family members disagree about the management or placement of an incompetent patient, which family member—if any—should the doctors listen to?

The nurse reported that at the suggestion of Mrs. C.'s physician, her daughters agreed to submit their dispute to legal arbitration rather than seek an outcome through protracted litigation. Their mother was eventually kept in the nursing home, with one daughter assuming legal guardianship and the other daughter concurring with her sister's decisions.

The factors typically considered in such cases are the kinship relation of the family member to the patient and the geographical closeness of the relative to the patient. These factors often do not coincide, leaving doctors uncertain about whom to listen to. In one case two sons disagreed about their mother's treatment plan. The one who had been visiting most frequently urged aggressive intervention, while the other son, who rarely visited, suggested that his mother's suffering not be prolonged. This combination may seem most obvious, but the opposite situation is just as common: the adult children who visit their parents in the hospital most frequently are the ones prepared to let go, while those who occasionally visit demand that "everything be done."

A different kind of consideration is the substantive content of what the family member requests: withholding or withdrawing a therapy versus instituting aggressive treatment. The law gives little guidance about these matters, and so conflicts unfortunately are often resolved in favor of the party who speaks the loudest, threatens the doctors with a lawsuit, or makes the biggest fuss in the hospital. But there is another important factor, often overlooked by health-care workers: The soundest ethical choice is to seek advice from the relative most familiar with the patient's values and prior expressed wishes, if any. This choice recognizes the extension of the patient's autonomy to the family member best able to render a "substituted judgment": what the patient would want in this situation.

GERIATRIC PATIENTS, especially those in nursing homes, pose the most intractable problems for both caregivers and family members. In earlier times, when elderly persons lived with relatives until they became terminally ill and were hospitalized, or died at home, it was typically the grown children with whom they lived who took responsibility for their care and were considered the appropriate decision-makers. Changes in family living patterns have left a gap in society's ability to handle these decisions in a relatively simple manner. The geriatric nurse who presented the case of Mrs. C. and her daughters at my seminar offered some examples she and her colleagues had encountered in the nursing home, examples that are not limited to elderly patients.

A young adult is admitted from the hospital following severe trauma from an automobile accident. The patient is comatose and married but is admitted to the nursing home by his parents, who state that the patient (age twenty-seven) is "separated" from the spouse. They agree to give consent for treatment.

A middle-aged patient is admitted to the nursing home by his parents, who report that their child is married but against their wishes and they do not want the spouse involved. They state that they are paying for the treatment, so therefore they will give the consent. The parents say they will take the son home with them after treatment in the nursing home.

A middle-aged man is admitted by the spouse, who resides at a different address. The spouse reports that they are separated and have lived apart for twelve years, but never got around to getting a divorce. The staff finds it difficult to assess whether the spouse's involvement is motivated by potential financial advantage or by a sense of guilt.

A patient is admitted by his "wife." Actually, they have never been legally married but have lived together for thirty-five years. She considers herself his wife and the appropriate party to give consent. Is she?

These cases pose dilemmas for health-care workers, who some-times wonder whether to believe the family. Can their true motives be known? Which relative should speak for the patient? The last case is easy. Most states have laws recognizing common-law marriages when couples have lived together for a number of years, as defined in the statute. Even in the absence of explicit laws, changes in living arrange-ments in the past few decades have led physicians to recognize one who is the patient's "significant other" as the person to grant consent, even if related family members are present. That, of course, can create problems when the relatives and the "significant other" disagree.

One procedure for which a clear legal ordering does exist is consent for autopsy. First comes the deceased patient's spouse, if the patient was married; adult children of a deceased patient come before the parents, who are next in the ordering; in the absence of a spouse, adult children, or living parents, the siblings of the patient are the ones to grant consent for autopsy, and after that, other relatives. Although this ordering strictly applies only to consent for autopsy, informal practice has adopted a similar hierarchy for consent to treatment.

One of the most bizarre situations I've encountered was a case in which a middle-aged man was hospitalized and had not regained con-sciousness. His wife and children showed up, and the doctors con-sulted them in the first few hours of his hospitalization. The next day another wife and children showed up from a neighboring state. Each family claimed to be the "real" family, and both "wives" asserted that they had been married to the patient for over fifteen years. The doc-tors didn't know what to do about that one. Nothing in my study of ethical theory or in my experience as a bioethicist equipped me to address this problem.

While the staff was pondering which spouse to treat as the "real" wife, the families met in the ICU. One wife asked the other, "Who are you?" The second replied, "I've been married to this man for thirty years." The first woman retorted, "He's been my husband for the past fifteen years." The doctors learned that the patient had, in fact, been living with one of these wives for fifteen years but had never divorced the first wife. Every Thursday night he left home, saying he had to have dinner and spend the night with "relatives." The two families continued to visit the unconscious patient in the ICU and got along very well with each other. When it came time to make a decision, the wives discussed the possibilities and agreed amiably on nursing-home placement for their husband.

▪ ▪ ▪

WHEN FAMILY MEMBERS become active participants in treatment decisions, they sometimes demand more aggressive therapy than doctors think is appropriate for the patient, and they sometimes request less. Physicians are generally more ready to give in to a family's request for more aggressive therapy than the reverse, in part because of their abiding fear of lawsuits, but also because they recognize how hard it is for a concerned family to accept their relative's illness or impending death. Even when there is no perceived need to "treat the family," doctors who show compassion for the family as well as for the patient are usually willing to comply with family requests for treatments they judge to be futile, so long as those treatments do not inflict greater suffering on the patient.

However, in a situation involving scarce or costly medical resources, a family's demands to "do everything" for their relative when such aggressive treatments would be futile—as in the case of Kevin, the five-year-old in irreversible coma—takes on a different ethical dimension. It then becomes a question of fairness to other patients in need of those resources. It may be unrealistic to expect patients' families to be aware of problems of resource allocation in the hospital, and it is even less likely that families will readily apply principles of fairness when their emotions are tied up in their own relative's terminal illness. But the physician in charge of the intensive care unit has a responsibility to all patients, a responsibility to treat them according to a relevant principle of justice. It would be unjust to grant a patient whose medical condition did not warrant an ICU bed a place in the unit because the family is insistent or even threatening. Yet this is precisely the situation doctors sometimes face, and they are torn between taking an advocacy role on behalf of their patient's family and the greater medical needs of other patients.

Mrs. B. was eighty-two years old, with a long history of diabetes and heart disease, when she was admitted to City Hospital for a medical workup. She had been living at home with her husband, was mentally alert, and was able to do household chores and cook for them both. Like so many elderly patients, Mrs. B. began to deteriorate after her admission to the hospital. She developed pulmonary edema, an accumulation of excessive fluid in the lungs. She was transferred to the ICU, was intubated, and remained there for about ten days. Mrs. B. improved, the tube was removed, and she was sent back to a regular medical floor.

On the first day after her return, she had a seizure and was brought back to the ICU. At this point her mental status was impaired. She

couldn't converse, although she responded to her own name and recognized relatives. After improving once again, Mrs. B. was discharged
from the ICU, only to be returned in three days because of a high
fever and acute respiratory distress. A diagnosis of aspiration pneumonia was made and she was treated successfully.

But Mrs. B. continued to deteriorate. Her medical condition became unstable, she did not respond to attempts by her family and the
staff to converse with her, and consultation with a neurologist revealed
that she would not recover her former mental status. The staff had
begun to debate the wisdom of continued aggressive treatment when
Mrs. B.'s daughter, a nurse who worked in another hospital, expressed
dissatisfaction with her mother's care. She said the staff had made all
the decisions without consulting the family. The daughter perceived a
callous attitude on the part of the staff, and she insisted that everything
be done for her mother. She filed a complaint, and pestered the staff
with loud behavior.

As a nurse, Mrs. B.'s daughter had more medical knowledge and
sophistication than most family members of hospitalized patients.
When the physicians in charge of her mother's care began to discuss
whether they should do a tracheostomy on Mrs. B., disagreement
ensued. Specialists from the ear, nose, and throat service didn't want
to do the operation because they judged the patient "not recoverable."
In other words, the surgical procedure would be futile. Furthermore,
they had serious doubts about whether the tracheostomy was medically indicated for Mrs. B. But Mrs. B.'s daughter convinced them to
do the procedure anyway, and surgery was performed the next day.

Although the patient's respiratory status improved slightly, she
began to have periods in which she failed to breathe spontaneously. It
became clear that Mrs. B. would soon need a respirator. She had
already been in the ICU for several weeks and would have to remain
there indefinitely once she was placed on a breathing machine. Respirators are available only in intensive-care units of the hospital, and it
was predicted that once on the machine Mrs. B. could never be
weaned. The daughter, backed up by Mrs. B.'s husband and another
daughter, insisted that her mother be put on a respirator and kept in
the ICU.

Under other circumstances the doctors in charge of Mrs. B. might
have complied readily with the family's wishes, without being unfair
to other patients. But the ICU was full, and a twenty-six-year-old
accident victim just admitted to the emergency room was in urgent
need of a bed. Nonetheless, because of the family's insistence, espe-

cially the daughter's threat to file a lawsuit for medical negligence, the physicians caved in. Mrs. B. stayed in the ICU on a respirator until she died two weeks later.

It was clear to me that her family was a key factor in determining how limited resources were allocated. The one most affected in this situation was Clara M., the eighty-four-year-old diabetic woman who was in the ICU with a diagnosis of "rule out MI," an uncertain diagnosis that requires close monitoring and laboratory tests to determine whether a patient has suffered a myocardial infarction. A senior resident asked Clara M. if she minded being moved, and when she said she did not, she was moved to a regular floor. The young accident victim in the emergency room was rushed to the place in the ICU vacated by Clara M. She was not returned to the ICU even after test results showed that she had had a heart attack. Later that day she suffered a cardiac arrest; she was successfully resuscitated, but died two days later.

Clara M. had no family present at any time during her hospitalization, in contrast to Mrs. B. But for the strident demands of Mrs. B.'s daughter and other family members, she, rather than Clara M., might have been transferred to make room for the younger patient. Too much is unknown to draw a firm conclusion about whether this particular allocation of limited resources was unjust. Demands by patients' relatives are only one of the factors that complicate physicians' efforts to arrive at medically and ethically sound decisions about how to allocate scarce resources in the hospital. Problems in making those decisions more often stem from uncertainty and disagreement about which principle of justice is most applicable when there are not enough supplies or personnel to meet the needs of all patients.

Allocating Scarce Resources

NLIKE EXAMPLES CREATED for textbooks in bioethics, real medical cases cannot be neatly categorized. Two ethical issues that frequently overlap are the question of how aggressively to treat a patient and the problem of scarce medical resources in the hospital. Patients who might otherwise be candidates for aggressive intervention must sometimes be given less because of the scarcity of blood, beds in intensive-care units, skilled nurses, or slots in the dialysis unit.

There must be some way of determining which individuals in need of medical resources should receive them when the resources are in shorter supply than the number of individuals who could benefit from them. Decision-makers are confronted with many pressures, and the need for rapid action may preclude reflection at the time such decisions are being made. The situation calls to mind the proverbial "lifeboat ethic" story, in which some individuals must be selected to be thrown overboard lest everyone perish. On the assumption that it is better for some to be saved than for everyone to perish (an assumption not granted by all who consider the problem), the dilemma is to decide on the best scheme for dealing with this tragic situation.

The choice of one scheme over another is inescapably a moral one. Which ethical principle is chosen will depend on which values are given priority. What makes the lifeboat case appear more unsavory than the medical situation is that individuals must be selected to be thrown overboard rather than chosen to be "saved" by the life-preserving resource. But this is only an apparent difference, since if the medical resources are truly lifesaving, those who do not receive them will certainly die.

The sorts of ethical principles that apply to allocation situations are principles of distributive justice. This aspect of justice pertains to a fair scheme of distributing society's benefits and burdens to its members. In the medical context the presumed benefits are medical care and treatment (although these can also be burdens). As often as not, more patients are in need of care than there are resources to meet all of those needs.

The choice of which moral principle should govern such allocation decisions is a matter of ongoing discussion and controversy among physicians, policymakers, bioethicists, and virtually everyone who thinks about the matter. Defenders of one or another principle of distributive justice argue that their favored principle is the fairest or most just: utilitarians argue that allocation decisions should serve the greatest good for the greatest number of people who stand to be affected; meritarians support some version of a "social worth" criterion, such as the individual's past contributions to society, potential for return to a productive life, moral merit, or some other attribute of worth; egalitarians favor a scheme that treats all persons as equally deserving, with decisions based on a lottery or a first-come, first-served basis. It should be obvious why there is no clear and simple "right answer" to allocation problems in the ICU or elsewhere when medical resources are in short supply. The reason is that there are a number of competing ethical principles, principles that yield different answers to the question of who should be removed from the ICU to make room for the next patient awaiting a bed.

It is helpful to think of these principles as falling into two general categories: neutral principles and nonneutral principles.[1] Neutral principles are ones like "first come, first served" or a lottery scheme for choosing among candidates. They require no background information about the competitors for the scarce resource, and they assume no disparity except the time at which the patient comes for treatment. Nonneutral principles, on the other hand, require the decision-maker to make a comparative judgment about the conditions and circumstances of patients competing for the resource. These conditions should include medically and ethically relevant factors such as the patients' prognosis. But the relevance of other circumstances remains a matter of dispute: the relative ages of patients, their "value to others," and whether their illness is "self-inflicted." No general moral grounds exist for preferring neutral or nonneutral principles in allocation situations. A moral argument for one or the other type of principle needs to be given for each case.

W.M. was a forty-six-year-old man with a thirty-year history of excessive alcohol consumption, which doctors refer to as "ethanol abuse." He was admitted to the hospital with swelling of the abdomen and also of his legs and feet. He had signs of end-stage liver disease, as well as kidney problems. Despite the fact that he was judged to be "almost terminal" from the time he entered the hospital, quite a few procedures were performed. Two lumbar punctures, or spinal taps, were done. W.M. was given a CAT scan (three-dimensional X ray) and various drugs, including antibiotics, and was put into the ICU. Throughout all this, he protested that he wanted to leave the hospital so he could go out drinking. Despite the aggressive therapy, he died after two days in the ICU.

L.T. was a fifty-eight-year-old alcoholic with cirrhosis, a progressive disease of the liver, who had been hospitalized several times for gastrointestinal bleeding. When he entered the hospital this time, L.T. was confused and somewhat disoriented. After being treated for infection, his mental status improved. Like W.M., this patient stated his wish not to remain in the hospital. But two days later he began to bleed from multiple sites and was transferred from the medical floor to the ICU. There he received maximum doses of a number of different medications, which were administered intravenously. Efforts were made to stop his profuse bleeding, and he was intubated and placed on a respirator. Dopamine was given to raise his blood pressure, and the dosage had to be increased. His arms and legs became dark blue as a result of insufficient oxygenation of his blood.

It then became necessary to transfer L.T. to the surgical floor and to operate in an attempt to halt the bleeding. His mother, who was in her eighties, was called to give consent for her son's surgery. Although she was living upstate, she came in to the hospital to see him and to grant consent. L.T.'s blood type was O-negative—which, being relatively rare, is in short supply—yet he was given multiple blood transfusions. After he returned from the operating room, he no longer had any mental status, as he was unresponsive to all stimuli. He died two days later from liver failure.

These two cases raise the same ethical issues, which troubled the medical students and house officers caring for the patients. Both men expressed the desire to leave the hospital. Should they have been allowed to do so? Neither had any hope of recovery, and both used hospital resources that were limited in supply and costly as well. Both occupied beds in the ICU—always a scarce resource. And in the case of L.T., there was some speculation that he suffered a worse death as a result of the treatments he received in the hospital.

Alcoholic patients are often considered by interns and residents to be among the "undesirables." They are viewed as having a lower social worth than all other patients except drug addicts. Not only do they suffer the stigma of alcoholism, but they are blamed for their multiple medical problems because their condition is thought to be "self-inflicted." Overworked and stressed by the need to deliver care to many acutely ill patients, the house staff develops a prejudice against alcoholics. They question whether this class of patients deserves as large a share of medical resources as other patients. That question might be broken down into three subsidiary questions: Are alcoholics less deserving of medical supplies, time, and effort because they contribute nothing to society and, worse, are a drain on society? Do they deserve less because they knowingly caused their own physical and mental decline? Do they deserve less because all therapy is ultimately futile (either because they are too far gone when they enter the hospital, or because they will go right back out and continue uncontrolled drinking, nullifying whatever therapy had been temporarily successful)?

Although the attitude toward these patients often reveals prejudice and a tendency to "blame the victim," there is a genuine ethical worry about the expenditure of scarce resources for patients on whom it seems wasted. Wasting valuable resources is unethical, but much depends on what is to count as "waste." To attempt a liver transplant on a chronically alcoholic patient who would inevitably return to drinking and destroy his new liver is a clear example of waste. A bit less clear, but still morally troubling, is the giving of multiple transfusions of a rare blood type to an alcoholic who is bleeding uncontrollably from many sites. Futile attempts at treatment that require limited or non-renewable resources are properly construed as wasteful. Yet it is all too easy to slip into thinking that administering other medical therapies to alcoholic patients, therapies that may be costly but are not scarce, should also be considered a waste. To call aggressive therapies wasteful because the recipients are society's outcasts or "undesirables" is to cloak a social judgment in the language of scarce medical resources.

Reluctant to appear prejudiced against alcoholics on the basis of their social worth, some who claim that this group of patients deserves fewer medical resources shift their ground. They switch to the argument that alcoholics inflicted their disease on themselves, acting irresponsibly by choosing to drink to excess. According to this contention, those who contribute to their own medical illness fail to act responsibly with respect to their own health and therefore consume an unfair share of resources. Had they controlled their drinking reasonably, they would not require a disproportionate amount of resources to treat the ravages of alcoholism. It's their own fault, and society owes them nothing.

This argument has a major flaw. It begins with the uncritical assumption that alcoholics freely choose the pattern of drinking that eventually destroys them. A leading viewpoint in psychiatry and medicine sees alcoholism as a disease. Those at risk for this disease are unable to control their drinking, so their behavior pattern should not be considered voluntary or freely chosen. Others reject this argument, noting that at least the first time they take a drink individuals do freely choose, and those who discover that they are prone to alcoholism should abstain totally, seeking treatment if necessary to reinforce their willpower. This debate has its roots in an ancient philosophical controversy over whether human beings have free will or are causally determined in their every thought and action. But it is not necessary to resolve that long-standing metaphysical problem in order to rebut the claim that alcoholics deserve less in the way of medical resources because they brought on their own condition.

Suppose it is granted, at least for the sake of argument, that many alcohol abusers knowingly and deliberately continue to drink when it is in their power to refrain or to seek psychiatric help or join an organization such as Alcoholics Anonymous. What follows, regarding whether they deserve expensive or limited medical resources? If alcoholics deserve less because they contributed to their own disease, so, too, do smokers who come down with lung cancer, emphysema, heart disease, and other conditions related to tobacco consumption. And what about the many individuals whose diet contains excessive amounts of animal fats and cholesterol? Should they be denied a share of surgical and medical resources to treat clogged coronary arteries? When this line of reasoning is extended further, it results in assigning penalties even to people who fail to promote their own health through lack of exercise, poor nutritional habits, or unwillingness to relieve stress in their daily lives.

Carried to its logical extreme, a policy for allocating medical resources that reflected these considerations would not only be unworkable, practically speaking. It would have the moral consequence of rewarding people for their health-promoting behavior and punishing them for their health-risking behavior. To deliver medical services along those lines is to treat health care as a commodity rather than as a special sort of social good. To deny medical resources to those who contribute in some way to their own disease is an especially pernicious form of "blaming the victim." The argument needed to support this position must have as a premise the notion that people have an obligation to the rest of society, as well as to themselves, to make every effort to remain healthy. In an individualistic society such as the United States, which imposes so few positive duties on its members toward their fellow citizens, it is inconsistent as well as ethically suspect to hold individuals morally responsible for their own health status.

Placement in an ICU guarantees that several limited and costly resources will be expended simultaneously: the bed itself, highly skilled nurses, cardiac monitors, respirators, and medications. The director of a critical-care unit faces the awesome task of constantly making allocation decisions, usually in the form of deciding which patient should be removed to make room for the new admission waiting in the emergency room for transfer to an ICU bed. Ideally, the choice of whom to remove to make room for a new patient can go in one of two directions—a hopelessly ill patient whose death is imminent and inevitable, or a recovering patient with a good prognosis if discharged.

This is the classic situation calling for "triage"—a term used in wartime to denote a scheme for dealing with battlefront casualties. In that context three groups of wounded soldiers are identified: those whose survival depends on their receiving immediate treatment; those who need medical attention but will survive even if they do not get it immediately; and those who are hurt so badly they would not survive even with medical attention. In the triage situation the choice of who gets treatment first is based on medical need, or more accurately, greatest medical need. The goal at the front lines in wartime, however, is to return as many soldiers as possible to active combat. The analogy between this battlefield situation and the hospital ICU is imperfect, but it provides one instructive model as a basis for selection.

The example invariably offered in discussions of the ethics of resource allocation in the hospital is that of a forty-two-year-old man who has just arrived in the emergency room with a fresh heart attack, has been treated vigorously, and is in immediate need of a bed in the cardiac intensive-care unit. Everyone presently occupying beds in that unit remains in need of intensive care, but several patients are elderly.

All other things being equal, should advanced age serve as a criterion for removing a patient from an ICU bed to make room for the forty-two-year-old with the myocardial infarction?

A complicating factor is the uncertainty of predictions. There is considerable evidence that physicians' ability to estimate benefits in terms of probability of a favorable outcome is limited by the state of medical knowledge. Uncertainty stems from the fact that medicine is still an imprecise science, and the detailed course of many critical illnesses has not been fully described. There is also a lack of hard data documenting the effectiveness of many diagnostic and therapeutic procedures. Evidence about outcomes is scanty, but one recent study suggests that patients discharged from an ICU to make room for other patients in greater need of a bed did not suffer adverse consequences.[2]

Added to these problems of uncertainty in medical decision-making is a straightforward ethical concern: nonmedical values of all sorts frequently enter into the decision-making process. Criteria quite unrelated to the patient's condition or prognosis are often used. The ethical question is, then: Is it fair to employ criteria unrelated to the medical condition of patients in making allocation decisions, and if so, under what circumstances is it fair? A case that occurred in a New York hospital offers a telling illustration.

The hospital has a fifteen-bed intensive-care unit, and, as usual, on the night of the episode that unit was full. When the ICU is full and the emergency room has also reached its limit, this hospital, like others in the region, typically closes its emergency room to ambulances because it cannot treat additional patients. Ambulances that would normally bring patients to this hospital are placed "on diversion," that is, they are directed to go to the nearest hospital with an emergency room. On this night all area hospitals had closed their emergency rooms, since all were full. The consequence of closing all emergency rooms in the city's hospitals is that, practically speaking, all are open. Patients who have been picked up by Emergency Medical Service vehicles must be taken somewhere, so the hospital had to admit a patient in spite of the fact that both the emergency room and the ICU were filled to capacity.

The last patient who had been admitted to the ICU was a seventy-one-year-old chronic schizophrenic with a high fever and overwhelming infections, who was brought in from one of the city's state-operated psychiatric facilities. Another bed was occupied by a nineteen-year-old male who was brain-dead after having sustained a bullet wound while committing a robbery. The young man's parents refused to grant permission for physicians to take his organs for transplantation, and out of fear of legal liability, hospital administrators refused to remove the patient from the respirator in the ICU. (This episode not only occurred in New York State, which did not have brain-death legislation at the time; it was also before a judicial ruling in a homicide case determined that "brain death" should be the criterion for declaring a patient dead. As a result, physicians and hospital administrators were reluctant to remove life supports from patients having no encephalographic, or brain-wave, activity, except for those whose organs were about to be removed for transplantation to save another patient's life.)

A third patient in the unit was an intravenous drug abuser with a diagnosis of acquired immune deficiency syndrome (AIDS) who was suffering from pneumonia and, based on the AIDS diagnosis, was considered terminally ill. The remaining beds in the ICU were occupied by patients whose average age was seventy-five.

Now the patient just brought to the emergency room, despite the lack of an available bed in this hospital or elsewhere in the area, was a sixty-three-year-old physics professor from a prominent university who had just suffered a heart attack. The dilemma confronting the physician who had to make this allocation decision was whom to remove from the ICU—if anyone—to make room for the professor.

I PRESENTED THIS CASE as a class exercise to a group of medical students, who became embroiled in heated controversy. One student asked what should be done if two or more patients in the ICU had similar medical conditions and were equally in need of intensive care. In the discussion of how the decision should be reached, I suggested tossing a coin and asked the students what they thought of that solution.

One student protested, "That's a cop-out. You're not deciding at all when you toss a coin. It's a way of avoiding making a real decision."

Other students disagreed. "It's the only fair way," one student observed. "If there's no rational way of deciding between the patients, using a method that decides by chance is appropriate."

A debate ensued, with some students claiming that a relevant basis for choosing between the two patients could be found, if we just looked hard enough, while others maintained that a random method of choosing would be the only fair procedure. The two sides to this debate reflected the two different ways of thinking about allocation problems. One side holds that when patients' medical conditions are equivalent, justice requires that no other considerations should be morally relevant. The other side argues that a morally relevant difference can and should be determined—the age of the patients, the existence of dependents, the patients' ability to make a future contribution to society, or their past contribution, as in the case of the physics professor.

THREE LEADING PRINCIPLES can be applied to the allocation of ICU beds. The first principle is similar to the one used in battlefield triage—better prognosis. On the assumption that a choice must be made between two patients, the principle is: When both patients cannot be treated, treat the one with the better prognosis. Although the principle is attractive, it should properly be applied only where the disparity between prognoses of competitors for treatment is relatively great. The problem, then, is its limited usefulness in the ICU, where the disparity is typically not so great. All patients are presumed to be in need of close monitoring and constant, skilled nursing care, or else they would not (or should not) be there in the first place. So the prognosis principle, while perhaps of some help, does not provide an ultimate solution. It needs to be applied initially in sorting patients into appropriate treatment groups, or else medical care would be allocated so inefficiently as to be wasteful, and the scheme would be unethical. But if patients in the ICU have roughly equal prognoses, then this nonneutral principle can be of no further assistance.

The second nonneutral principle is social worth: Choose the patient who has greater value for other persons. This principle has often been attacked—and rightly so—as inviting racism, sexism, and bias against the elderly, retarded, and mentally ill. But it may be understood without that sort of bias. The principle prefers the person whose continuing life is of greater importance to others. But is this a fair criterion to use? How can rankings of greater or lesser importance to others be determined? Should the others who are affected be limited to family members? Should greater weight be given to patients whose family members are dependents or young children? Or perhaps a person's value to society at large, however that might be assessed, should be considered. Whichever characteristics are selected to denote greater social worth, they are bound to invite profound controversy, in addition to posing the difficulty of comparing incommensurable qualities.

The virtual impossibility of gaining agreement, either in general or in specific cases, is a practical reason to abandon the idea of using this nonneutral principle to select individuals to be recipients of scarce medical resources. A more compelling reason is the moral principle of justice that views every human life as equally worthwhile. Unlike the nonneutral principle based on prognosis, which is patient-centered because it makes the decision about medical treatment rest on whether it can truly benefit the patient, a nonneutral principle based on social worth evaluates patients in terms of their value to others. This is an unacceptable principle for allocating scarce medical resources at the bedside. Nonneutral principles are appropriate so long as they are patient-centered; when they are not, then a neutral principle such as "first come, first served" should be used.

The problem of which patient to remove from the ICU to make room for the sixty-three-year-old professor was only an apparent dilemma. Because the nineteen-year-old on life supports was already dead (though not "officially dead" in New York State at that time), the application of the prognosis principle yielded a clear and morally uncontroversial solution. The demands of the brain-dead patient's parents and the hospital administration's fear of legal liability constituted a practical problem, not an ethical dilemma. Physicians acted on the courage of their moral convictions and took the brain-dead youth off the respirator, making room in the ICU for the physics professor. It is rare, however, that so obvious a candidate can be found to remove from the ICU when the prognosis principle is used to make allocation decisions.

If the ICU had not had a brain-dead patient, it is reasonable to assume that one of the other patients would have been removed to open a bed for the physics professor. Even if the ICU team had wanted to be neutral, they would probably have yielded to pressure from the professor's family, possibly fearing a lawsuit. Likely candidates for transfer out of the unit might have been one of the patients over seventy-five, especially one who was severely demented, or perhaps the AIDS patient, suffering from a fatal illness in its terminal phase.

THE NEED TO ALLOCATE scarce resources is an ongoing feature of the health care system. Whether the resources in limited supply are organs for transplantation, blood for transfusions, highly trained medical and nursing personnel, or slots in a dialysis unit, the problem of selecting an appropriate means of distribution is a fundamental one. The short history of the artificial kidney provides a cautionary tale.

Technological advances around 1960 made it possible for the first time to prolong the lives of persons with kidney disease who formerly would have died. A physician at the University of Washington School of Medicine in Seattle, Dr. Belding H. Scribner, invented a device that made it possible to gain access to a patient's artery and vein, and then connect the patient to an artificial kidney machine to cleanse the blood of its waste products. The device, known as a "cannula and shunt," is inserted into the arm surgically, allowing the patient to be hooked up to a hemodialysis machine and then disconnected at the end of several hours when the treatment is completed. Individuals who have lost all function of their natural kidneys typically require dialysis three times each week for the rest of their lives.

This is an expensive technology, which could be afforded only by the well-to-do when it was first introduced. Related to its cost was the scarcity of this resource in the early days of its use. It was typically a physician, the head of the dialysis unit, who selected the patients to receive this lifesaving technology. Even when patients who were deemed "medically unsuitable" for dialysis were eliminated from the list, there still remained more patients awaiting dialysis than could be served by then-existing machines. The burden of deciding who should live and who must die fell on the physicians who directed the dialysis units, a burden they found increasingly uncomfortable.

In the early 1960s a dialysis center in Seattle introduced a novel approach. An anonymous, seven-member committee was formed, composed of members of the community, for the purpose of selecting among the medically suitable candidates for hemodialysis. It was thought that a representative group of citizens might be more appropriate for making such decisions than a single individual. Furthermore, the committee approach had the presumed benefit of diffusing responsibility for these life-and-death choices.

The move from an individual to a committee marked a procedural shift in the way the decisions were made, but there was an undeniable substantive basis for the committee's choices. The Seattle committee used a criterion of social worth to select those who would receive dialysis. Factors included age and sex, marital status and number of dependents, income, net worth, emotional stability, educational background, occupation, past performance, future potential, and personal references. The social-worth criterion for making such life-and-death choices was ethically acceptable to many people then, and is still ac-

cepted today for other allocation decisions. But the criterion was criticized by those who believe that justice requires a more egalitarian
mode of choice.[3]

My own view is that a decision-making process based on the factors
used by the Seattle committee is morally repugnant. A consistent
utilitarian would probably have to use at least some of the elements
included in the Seattle committee's criterion, but an adherent of the
respect-for-persons principle would not. That principle can be expanded to encompass "equal respect for persons."[4] In this expanded
form the principle denies the moral relevance of social worth as a basis
for choosing individuals to receive lifesaving resources.

But there is a price to be paid for adopting an egalitarian scheme,
a hefty financial price. In 1972 Congress enacted Public Law 92-603,
which extended Medicare coverage to those under sixty-five years of
age who suffered from end-stage renal disease (ESRD). In a dramatic
episode the dialysis procedure was demonstrated on an actual patient
before the eyes of the House Ways and Means Committee. With very
little debate and virtually no opposition, both houses of Congress
passed this act, enabling everyone who needs some form of renal
therapy to obtain it. The few cost estimates made at the time turned
out to be wildly inaccurate. The costs of financing this program are
now staggering, far exceeding the initial amounts. The estimated costs
under Medicare coverage for 1974, the first year of the program, were
$250 million. As of 1980, the federally sponsored ESRD program
covered about fifty thousand patients and cost over $1 billion annually
for various forms of renal therapy, primarily dialysis and kidney
transplantation. This has led many to conclude that no other life-
prolonging medical technology is likely to be made universally
available through government financing.

Unlike the United States, Great Britain has a National Health
Service through which anyone can receive medical and surgical treatment. It costs as much to perform dialysis in England as it does in
America, and the British response to the problem is both instructive
and disconcerting. Although no law or official policy prohibits dialysis
from being offered to anyone, a de facto process of rationing has been
adopted.

Two key features of the British system limit the number of patients
on dialysis. One is chronological age: virtually no patients over fifty-
five are offered dialysis under the National Health Service (wealthy
patients can "buy out" of the system and pay for treatment by physicians in private practice). The second feature is the enlargement of

criteria for deeming a patient "medically unsuitable" for dialysis. According to one description of this practice,

> a physician must change some of the attributes that, if there were
> sufficient services for all who might want them, would be con-
> sidered personal values to be weighed by the patient, into medical
> criteria to be evaluated by the doctor. For example, doctors con-
> sider certain "quality-of-life" factors such as mental and physical
> disability, family supportiveness, and ability to communicate (in
> the language of the doctor, of course) as medical factors in deter-
> mining whether dialysis is appropriate.[5]

Pressure has begun to mount in the United States for reducing health-care expenditures. It begins with the assumption that health care costs too much. At the same time there is evidence of a growing confusion between the need to allocate medical resources in a fair manner and the need to reduce the costs of medical care. This confusion begins at a conceptual level and is deepened by an uncritical acceptance of the assumption that health care generally, and hospital care in particular, cost too much. Allocation of scarce resources is being confused with rationing.

Allocation of limited hospital resources differs sharply from the rationing of hospital care, according to schemes either already adopted or proposed. An example of one economic device is the method of assigning payments according to diagnostic-related groups, known as DRGs. Government-sponsored programs such as Medicare provide a fixed sum for reimbursement to the hospital for each patient, depending on which predefined diagnostic category the patient falls within. The amount of the reimbursement remains fixed, regardless of the actual cost of delivering the medical service. This cost-cutting scheme can place a burden on the hospital, and it can also result in patients receiving inadequate care. The temptation to save money by releasing patients from the hospital prematurely, or omitting some procedures that otherwise would have been performed, is a likely consequence of this rationing scheme.

A study published by Johns Hopkins University and a report on intensive-care units from the Office of Technology Assessment both reveal that the DRG system discriminates against certain hospitals and certain patients. The Johns Hopkins study observes that "there are large and highly significant interhospital differences in the distribution of illness severity that are not accounted for by the DRG classification system."[6] And the OTA report states that DRGs encourage a form of "implicit rationing" in ICUs by pressuring physicians to alter, withhold, or withdraw expensive care and by leading hospitals to limit or reduce the number of beds in existing ICUs.[7]

A second type of rationing scheme is a reduction in the length of hospital stays allowed by insurers. This scheme virtually ignores the ethical precept of medical practice mandating that patients should be treated in accordance with their medical needs. Limiting the length of stay for which insurance will pay may succeed in eliminating some waste, but it bears the far less desirable consequence of discharging some patients who could benefit by longer hospital stays and might well suffer harm by early discharge. This policy of reducing hospital stays will most probably affect the poor more adversely than the well-to-do. Those with more money could always elect to pay for a longer hospitalization—an alternative unavailable to lower-income groups.

Rationing schemes, like principles for allocating scarce resources, can be evaluated in terms of their moral acceptability. Of course, the evaluation itself depends on which values are taken to be paramount when the overall priority is to reduce monetary costs. The least ethically acceptable rationing schemes are those that stand to harm the poorest and sickest members of our society the most. Limiting hospital care and medical services in an evenhanded manner accords with an egalitarian precept of justice. But rationing schemes that place individuals or groups already disadvantaged by poverty or incapacitated by illness at the greatest risk fail to achieve an equitable distribution of goods and services. While they may succeed in the overall utilitarian aim of reducing monetary costs, they do so by violating a leading principle of social justice.

That principle, loosely formulated, holds that any rearrangements of society's benefits and burdens should not result in greater burdens falling on those who are least advantaged.[8] An example would be the rationing device that limits hospital stays to a fixed number of days regardless of the patient's need for continued hospital care. If this scheme does, indeed, hit hardest against the sickest and the poorest, it clearly violates this principle of social justice.

A CONSEQUENCE OF a rather different sort results from rationing medical resources, a consequence that affects the doctor-patient relationship. The long-standing precept of medical ethics that physicians should be strong advocates for their patients is seriously undercut by the rationing of hospital care. Whether physicians are urged to cut costs voluntarily in treating their patients, or are required to adhere to policies instituted by others, their ability to advocate vigorously for their patients' medical needs is weakened.

When physicians are required to make rationing an aspect of their treatment decisions and their decisions about which of their patients to admit to the hospital and for how long, it creates a situation of divided loyalties. Physicians cannot at one and the same time be the advocates of their patients and also serve as society's financial watchdogs. Yet this is precisely what has begun to happen as a result of the current emphasis on cost containment within the hospital. It is already well established in Great Britain, especially for physicians who treat kidney patients. As one account observes:

> A physician knows that for each patient who receives dialysis, somebody else will not. In his role as a physician, he is obliged to explain to his marginal dialysis patient what the risks, benefits, and alternatives to dialysis would be. In his role as allocator of health services, he is obliged to see to it that the marginal patient is not provided with dialysis. Because the alternative to such treatment is usually death, it is hard to imagine how a physician who must, as the system requires, play the second role can possibly play the first adequately.[9]

When the system requires physicians to play both roles, as in England, they are probably helpless to do much about it. In the United States, however, it is likely to be the doctors' personal values that lead to their taking on a self-appointed role as protector of the taxpayer's interests. A hospital social worker reported the following episode in which she was involved.

Lori was a nineteen-year-old single woman, hospitalized for orthopedic surgery on her legs and feet to repair a birth defect. She then needed plastic surgery and a skin graft, which was successful. The patient was about to be discharged but was awaiting a brace and special shoes. The problem that confronted the social worker was providing for some sort of home care. Lori lived in an apartment with her boyfriend, who was there only some of the time. She had several siblings, but one was in jail, two were drug addicts, and one was both. Lori herself had emotional problems and her intelligence was judged to be "borderline." In the past she had not complied with her medical regimen, and the social worker was concerned that it wouldn't work to discharge Lori without any home care. To complete her recovery it was necessary to stay off her feet entirely. But with no home aide or visiting nurse, Lori would surely have to be on her feet.

The social worker obtained the proper papers that needed to be filled out before home care could be provided. The physician refused to fill out the papers. The social worker, who had been in conflict with this physician before, was not authorized to fill out the papers herself. When she asked the doctor why he was resisting, he first rebuked her, a social worker, for questioning him, a physician. Then he replied that it was "an abuse of Medicaid," and he was opposed to having "our tax dollars pay for this."

To her credit, the social worker was able to circumvent the problem by finding another physician who was willing to fill out the necessary papers. The first physician's mean-spirited behavior deserves no ethical analysis. But his appraisal of the costs that would be "saved" requires a cost-benefit analysis, which would probably show that the far higher costs of orthopedic surgery, followed by plastic surgery and a long hospitalization, would be utterly wasted if the lower-cost home care were not provided.

In case conferences devoted to ethical issues in the care and treatment of hospitalized patients, it is not uncommon for medical students, interns, residents, and even attending physicians to pose a question of this sort: "This lady is eighty-three years old and has been in this hospital for six months and on a respirator for four. Hasn't she cost society enough money already?"

Now whether this woman (for some reason, doctors always refer to women patients as "ladies") or any other patient has cost society enough money already is not the right question for her physician to be asking. There may be appropriate questions to ask about the goals of further treatment, about what the patient has requested in the way of cessation or continuation of treatment, or, in cases where patients no longer have the capacity to participate in their own treatment decisions, questions about what is in their best interests. But these are not questions motivated by the perceived need to ration hospital care or to protect society's financial interests. The rationing of medical resources has great potential for subverting the traditional role of physicians as advocates for their patients. It creates conflicting loyalties for physicians and turns them into policymakers in the clinical setting—a role for which they are ill equipped by their education and training.

Conflicting Obligations

PHYSICIANS OWE THEIR primary loyalty to their patients. It is not the proper role of doctors at the bedside to look out for society's financial interests at the expense of their patients' medical needs. But situations do arise in which physicians' duties to their patients come into direct conflict with legitimate obligations to others. This serves as a reminder of why it is a mistake to consider any duty as absolute: obligations are bound to conflict with one another.

A good example is the physician's duty to keep confidentiality, normally thought to be an overriding obligation to the patient. But if a patient poses a threat of harm to others, and if by maintaining confidentiality the doctor allows that harm to occur, then honoring one moral obligation results in a violation of another. Situations in which obligations conflict are another source of ethical dilemmas in medical practice.

Two similar cases brought up in ethics conferences posed the dilemma of whether doctor-patient confidentiality should ever be breached when not required by law. In one case the patient was a school-bus driver who was diabetic and had a history of alcohol abuse. On this occasion he had had four beers for lunch, then passed out while driving the school bus. This resulted in a minor accident, in which neither he nor any children were injured. The driver was admitted to the hospital and treated, and the question posed at the ethics conference was whether his employer, the school, should be informed of the reason for the accident.

In the second case the patient, also a diabetic and long-term alcoholic, was a switchman working for a commuter railroad. On the day of admission he had taken a double dose of insulin. He admitted drinking on the job and refused to attend meetings of Alcoholics Anonymous or to accept other help for his drinking problem. The physician in charge of this patient believed that it would violate his duty of confidentiality to notify the patient's employer, and released the man without taking any further action.

Both cases prompted some of the most impassioned arguments I have witnessed in ethics rounds and conferences. Some participants took the position that the doctor's duty to preserve confidentiality is virtually absolute, the only exceptions being legally imposed duties to disclose information about a patient. According to this position, the physician's duty to the patient takes precedence over all but a few obligations spelled out in laws.

Just as vigorously, the opposite view was put forward: the physician has a duty to disclose information about a patient when there is likelihood of harm to others. Heated debate ensued about just how likely the harm would have to be and just how severe. But some held fast to the view that in this type of situation, the physician must disclose.

The third position asserted was the intermediate view that the physician may disclose. There is neither a duty to disclose nor a duty to refrain from disclosing. One medical student described it as a "judgment call." In the language of ethics, disclosure is morally permissible, and so is nondisclosure.

The discussions at both conferences were marked by a series of moral claims invoking patients' rights, physicians' duties and obligations, the rights of innocent persons, and the good of society. When the essence of the debate was distilled, the opposing sides were reduced to a few basic propositions. Everyone agreed that physicians have a general duty to keep confidentiality. Only one person held that duty to be absolute, one that should never be breached. Everyone also believed that doctors have duties besides those owed to their patients —in particular, a duty to promote the health and safety of the populace. Disagreement began when it came to the task of drawing a line: when does the obligation to the patient give way to the obligation to others in society? Cast in this form, the dilemma of when confidentiality may or must be breached depends on which is the higher duty, or which obligation takes precedence.

The problem can also be viewed as a clash between two different moral perspectives: an ethics of duty versus an ethics of consequences. Physicians have a general duty to preserve the confidentiality of information about their patients, but that duty is not absolute. It may (and should) be overridden when consequences of serious proportions are likely to result from adhering to the duty. A train wreck or a school-bus accident in which passengers are harmed counts as a consequence of serious proportions. In this view moral duties are real but conditional. Moreover, as one medical student insisted, it is not only the magnitude of harm that must be taken into account, but also the probability that harm of a given magnitude will occur.

This way of formulating the dilemma renders the problem all but insoluble, since no one could summon the slightest evidence about the actual probability that harm would befall innocent persons if the school-bus driver and the train switchman continued in their jobs. No one could say with confidence that either man would be fired from his job if his employer were notified, or, if fired, whether he might easily find a similar job somewhere else. When the probabilities of alternative consequences are unknown or unknowable, appealing to an ethics of utility is an exercise in futility.

ETHICAL THEORIES that have the notion of duty as their central concept are known as deontological theories. (The term "deontology" comes from the Greek words *deon*, meaning "duty," and *logos*, meaning "science.") Deontological theories hold that many actions are morally obligatory, regardless of their consequences. This is in contrast to a consequentialist approach to ethics, which—theoretically, at least—enables the decision-maker to arrive at a unique solution by calculating which of several alternatives will produce the greatest happiness or benefit for the greatest number of people likely to be affected by the action.

The idea of constructing a rigid hierarchy of moral duties is entirely implausible. But if a deontological theory does not provide a predetermined hierarchy of duties, it must offer a method for deciding which obligation to follow when two or more conflict. Applying a nonconsequentialist ethical theory to a specific case is very different from making a logical deduction. Rather, it requires a balancing of values that have a potential for conflict.

Philosophers distinguish between potential duties, known as "prima facie" duties, and actual duties, those that must be performed. Only potential duties can come into conflict, and when they do, the one that is "more of a duty" becomes the actual duty. If a person is simultaneously confronted with two possible actions—saving a life and keeping a dinner engagement—the action of saving a life is the higher duty. Of course, not all choices between conflicting duties are as obvious as this one.

The chief difficulty faced by deontological theories, then, is how people are supposed to know what are their actual duties. Many deontologists hold that duties are self-evident in much the same way that the elementary truths of arithmetic are self-evident. Anyone who understands the concept of the number 1 and what it means to add two numbers can just "see" that $1 + 1 = 2$. This account of how people come to know their duties is called "intuitionism." It presumes that human beings have a distinct moral faculty (better developed in some than in others), which enables them to intuit their duties. According to intuitionism, moral judgments are objectively true or false, like statements about factual matters, but the way in which their truth is known differs. Propositions about facts can be confirmed by empirical observation, while truths apprehended by intuition cannot be confirmed or denied by experience.

Unfortunately, this method is not one that can be explained or taught. Nor does intuitionism provide a means for resolving disputes when two people have conflicting intuitions about what duty requires. One intuitionist, who claims to perceive a duty, can only accuse a second, who fails to see it, of being "morally blind." Conversely, the second intuitionist can accuse the first of "morally hallucinating" duties that simply don't exist. There is no objective means of determining which one is right, yet intuitionism does not allow for subjective moral judgments. Rather, it is supposed to afford genuine moral knowledge.

Consulting one's own "moral intuitions" provides no better guide than probing one's feelings, moral or otherwise, when ethical dilemmas arise. An appeal to sentiments or intuitions does not allow for rational argument between parties to a dispute, and disagreements over which obligation is higher, or which prima facie duty is "more of a duty," have no means of resolution. This is why the discussions in both conferences about the doctor's duty to preserve confidentiality were so heated and why the participants never moved closer to agreement. Proponents of both sides derived their positions from deeply felt sentiments or secure "intuitions" and were unmoved in the face of similarly entrenched positions held by their opponents.

It is tempting to think that dilemmas of this sort are limited to moral duties and that when it comes to legal duties, no such problems exist. But while some obligations are clearly stated by the law, this does not render them entirely free of difficulty. Legal duties requiring physicians to breach doctor-patient confidentiality fall into several categories. Physicians have a legal duty to report gunshot and stab wounds, cases of venereal disease, and instances of suspected child abuse. In these different situations the duty of confidentiality in the doctor-patient relationship is pitted against the value of preserving the life or health of innocent persons who may become victims.

Among the most troubling cases of conflicting obligations doctors experience are those that stem from simultaneous duties to two patients. A classic example, often brought up in discussions of confidentiality in the physician-patient relationship, is that of a man diagnosed in his private physician's office as having venereal disease. The man admits to an indiscretion while on a recent business trip and begs the doctor not to inform his wife. The husband is worried that his marriage will be threatened if his wife learns of his infidelity. The doctor is legally required to report the case of venereal disease to the Department of Health, which then takes responsibility for notifying persons who have had sexual contact with the diseased individual. So the man's wife will find out anyway. However, if the doctor informs the wife and begins antibiotic treatment immediately, there is greater likelihood of a quick cure, or even of preventing the disease from taking hold initially.

This proverbial story has several variations. In one the wife is also a patient of the physician. Is the doctor's obligation to the woman stronger because she is his patient than it would be if she were simply his patient's wife? Some argue that it is. According to this argument, a doctor-patient relationship is a fiduciary one, with well-defined role obligations that create a bond of trust. Duties that flow from a fiduciary relationship are special and perhaps more stringent than those that apply in ordinary interactions between people.

According to a different argument, the physician has just as strong a duty to the wife who is not his patient as he does to the wife who is. Obligations that derive from the doctor-patient relationship are special, but a physician's obligations are not limited to these. In addition to the traditional doctor-patient relationship, there is another model, the public-health model, which gives rise to duties such as preventing the spread of disease and protecting the health and safety of the population.

Under the public-health model, physicians as health professionals have obligations to persons who are not their patients. These obligations extend not only to identifiable persons such as the patient's wife who is at risk of contracting venereal disease, but also to unknown persons such as the commuter-train passengers and children on the school bus who may be endangered by an alcoholic employee. However, to point out that physicians have general obligations under a public-health model as well as within the doctor-patient relationship is not sufficient for determining which specific duties should have priority when they come into conflict.

ANOTHER SITUATION in which doctors have a legal as well as a moral duty to breach confidentiality occurs when the patient is an impaired physician. Many states now have mandatory reporting requirements for physicians who treat other physicians with evident impairment resulting from drug or alcohol abuse, a psychiatric disorder, or dementia. The widespread reluctance of professionals to reveal information that may jeopardize their colleagues' professional status or license to practice has made it difficult for many physicians to comply with this legal requirement. But in addition to their obligation to obey the law, physicians who encounter an obviously impaired colleague have an obligation deriving from the public-health model of medicine to protect potential patients.

Dr. P., a forty-eight-year-old radiologist, came to the emergency room of University Hospital after experiencing two seizures while at work in another medical institution. He had a history of heavy alcohol abuse—a quart and a half of gin a day—over the past two years. He was admitted to the hospital for withdrawal, having tried unsuccessfully to treat himself for his alcoholism. Dr. P. had also attended some meetings of Alcoholics Anonymous, with no lasting results. He admitted to the physicians now treating him that his medical colleagues at his own institution knew about his condition, but they had taken no steps either to fire him or to report his problem to the appropriate state agency.

When this case was presented at an ethics conference, it struck me that the dilemma was more apparent than real. The conflict between preserving confidentiality in the doctor-patient relationship and the duty to report an impaired physician was easily resolved in favor of the overriding legal obligation. Add to that the moral obligation to protect patients of the impaired physician who might be harmed by his errors, and the semblance of genuine moral conflict disappears. Nevertheless, the discussion at the conference proved interesting, if only to show how uncertain physicians are about where their primary obligations lie, and how hard it is for professionals to engage in whistle-blowing on their colleagues.

An intern at the conference wondered whom to notify about the fact that the patient was an alcohol abuser. Was it the patient's employer? But colleagues at the hospital where Dr. P. worked already knew that he was an alcoholic. Would it do any good to notify them about this episode? Dr. W., a more experienced physician, identified the proper agency to which a report should be made, but then the question was raised whose obligation it was to make that report. Dr. W. answered, "The treating physician," which let other doctors officially off the hook.

More subtle questions were raised. It was clear that the patient was an alcohol abuser. But what if he didn't drink on the job or at a time when patients might be endangered? Furthermore, he was a radiologist, not a surgeon. Physicians practicing that specialty often don't see patients at all but confine much of their practice to diagnostic work with X-ray films. If he were a brain surgeon, it would be a different story. But given the nature of his practice, one medical student argued, Dr. P. was unlikely to do much, if any, harm to patients.

That view created a minor uproar. Someone noted that a misdiagnosis of an X-ray or CAT scan could lead to unnecessary, even risky surgery, or, conversely, to no surgery when an operation for a brain tumor was indicated. So patients could be wronged, as well as harmed, by errors that a radiologist might make. This position calculated the possible consequences of nondisclosure and found them serious enough to warrant disclosure of Dr. P.'s alcoholism to the proper authorities.

Another participant argued that it was not a matter of weighing one set of consequences against another. This resident doctor took a deontological position, returning to the issue of obligations and duties. Quite correctly, she observed that this was a case of conflict of obligations, and the task was to decide which obligation should take priority. No one argued that the duty of confidentiality should prevail. All participants at the conference, myself included, consulted our "moral intuitions" and found that reporting the impaired physician to the proper authority was "more of a duty." Even the worry that Dr. P. might lose his license to practice medicine was not sufficient to tip the balance in favor of keeping information about his alcoholism confidential. Dr. W. said he was quite confident that loss of license was not a likely or immediate consequence, and might occur only if Dr. P. failed to seek treatment for his condition and was found on subsequent occasions to be impaired.

Still, some individuals at the conference were distressed by what seemed to be a violation of duty to the patient. That feeling was heightened by the fact that the patient was a fellow physician. Empathy for Dr. P. was affecting their ability to make a disinterested assessment.

Dr. W. pointed out that talking to the patient himself about the situation was not incompatible with fulfilling the obligation to make a report to the state agency. In fact, it would exhibit respect for the patient to hold a frank conversation with him about the existence of a statute mandating a report by the treating physician and his intention to comply with the law. The next step is to encourage Dr. P. to seek help from a professional organization that deals with problems of impaired physicians. He might well succeed in overcoming his struggle with alcoholism when confronted with these prospects, so in addition to protecting his patients from potential harm, his own career could be saved.

The analysis of this case illustrates how difficult it is to keep distinct the different ethical perspectives brought to bear on real-life situations. It is hard to keep consequences entirely out of the picture, even when an ethical analysis is conducted from a deontological point of view. And it is no easier to keep rights and duties from entering the discussion when both professional ethics and leading moral theories are couched in that language. The chief danger in using both ethical perspectives at once is the temptation to switch back and forth between them, alternating between an assessment of consequences and an appeal to rights and duties in order to make the solution finally come out in the way that "feels" right.

TATIANA TARASOFF, a student at the University of California at Berkeley, was killed by Prosenjit Poddar, a student who met Tatiana in a folk-dancing class and fell in love with her. She rebuffed Poddar, who fell into a severe depression and after six months sought psychiatric help as an outpatient at the university health service. The therapist, a clinical psychologist, found Poddar "a danger to the welfare of other people and himself" after he had disclosed his intention to kill Tatiana Tarasoff when she returned from a summer in Brazil. The psychotherapist contacted the campus police, who detained Poddar but then released him when he seemed rational and made a promise to stay away from Tatiana. However, when she returned from Brazil two months later, Poddar killed her with a butcher knife. Neither Tatiana nor her parents had been warned of the threat. The parents brought a wrongful-death action against the Board of Regents of the State of California, the campus police, and the doctors who had been involved in Poddar's treatment.[1]

The California Supreme Court ruling in this case imposes on psychotherapists a duty to warn a potential victim, or to take other preventive steps, if there is reason to believe that person is in danger from the therapist's patient.[2] The Tarasoff case gave rise to considerable concern because of the special importance of confidentiality in the psychotherapist-patient encounter. In that setting, confidentiality is more than the result of the long-standing professional ethic of loyalty to the patient or client; it is held to be vital to the success of the therapy itself.

The question of confidentiality is more difficult for psychiatrists than for physicians generally, especially when a patient openly discusses a possible future crime. If a patient tells the therapist of an intention to commit a crime, it is a sign that therapy is succeeding. It would be a therapeutic mistake as well as a moral error to expect the psychiatrist to notify the authorities whenever a patient revealed thoughts that could be considered criminal in nature. However, the obligation to keep confidentiality is not absolute. If the psychiatrist is convinced that a patient is in fact going to commit a crime that will result in injury or harm to persons or property, and if the therapist is unable to deter the patient, then there is an overriding duty to go to the authorities.[3]

This places a great deal of weight on the psychiatrist's conviction that a patient will, in fact, commit such a crime. Although skilled psychotherapists are probably better than the average person when it comes to making such assessments, they are not infallible. A combination of clinical and ethical judgment is required in such cases, treading a thin line between preserving confidentiality and the therapeutic process on the one hand, and protecting innocent persons from harm on the other. The Tarasoff case tipped that uneasy balance in the direction of breaking confidentiality to protect potential victims.

A dissenting opinion in the Tarasoff case argued on the basis of two different considerations. The first is the damage done to the therapist-patient relationship, damage that may lead fewer people to seek treatment in the first place, and will inhibit those who do from making the full disclosure necessary for effective treatment. The second consideration is the limited ability of the psychiatric profession to predict dangerousness. The dissenting opinion predicted that that inability will result in many more warnings than necessary, since therapists will tend to protect themselves by erring in favor of warning in cases of doubt.

Whether or not the psychotherapist-patient relationship has, in fact, been damaged in these ways since the Tarasoff decision was handed down, it remains a problem for the individual physician confronted with a patient who might harm another person but has not yet done so. In psychiatric cases the therapist must make some estimate of the likelihood of harm, however difficult it is to make that judgment. The physician's duty to warn overrides the patient's presumed right of confidentiality in the therapist-patient relationship. As important as that right is, other rights of more fundamental significance are upheld by the doctor's obligation to prevent harm from befalling innocent victims of a patient's violent acts.

BELINDA C. WAS A twenty-year-old woman admitted to City Hospital for complications of pregnancy in her thirtieth week. This was her third pregnancy. Both children from her previous pregnancies were now in foster care, having been taken from her because she had more than once burned them with boiling water. She was allowed to visit them, with the foster parents present during the visits. The patient told the hospital staff that she wanted a baby to replace her other children who had been taken away from her.

The staff was angry at the situation. They discussed whether this woman should be having another baby. Although many thought she should not, one resident in obstetrics phrased the question in terms of rights: "Don't individuals—at least in the United States—have the right to reproduce?" Although the answer to the question posed in this way is clearly yes, it's not so clear in answer to another query by an obstetrics nurse: "Is there an inalienable right to have children?" Few rights are inalienable, but the ethical dilemma raised by this case is when, if ever, it is permissible to prevent someone from having children.

As applied to the case at hand, the question was hypothetical, since for moral as well as legal reasons, no one even remotely considered terminating Belinda C.'s pregnancy. However, posed as a general question about reproductive rights, it addresses the scope of physicians' obligations to persons other than their patients. Doctors have a legal and moral duty to report suspected cases of child abuse. Wouldn't it be better to prevent child abuse before it occurs rather than wait until infants and children are beaten, maimed, cut, or burned? Few moral dilemmas are more disquieting than having to choose between violating an individual's right to procreate and allowing physical abuse or possibly even death to children.

Although I share the concerns of the staff that prompted their inclination to curtail the reproductive rights of people like Belinda C., I firmly oppose any policy that would sanction such actions. My opposition rests on three separate grounds: uncertainty of predictions, potential for misuse, and injustice to poor people, especially members of racial and ethnic minorities.

The fact that a parent has abused children in the past does not offer predictive certainty that the same behavior will occur in the future. It is not uncommon for only one child of several in a family to be neglected or abused. Also, the possibility exists that counseling and therapy will alter the behavior of abusing parents. And in a case like that of Belinda C., her despair at losing her children and recognition of her own responsibility for that loss could lead to very different behavior toward another child. The ability to predict the likelihood that this woman will abuse other children is too limited to justify interfering with her right to procreate.

As for the potential for misuse of policies interfering with reproductive freedom, history offers some instructive lessons. When laws and unofficial practices permitting or requiring sterilization were in force, they led to abuses of one sort or another. Either the scientific basis for embarking on sterilization programs was faulty, or the programs were motivated by ethically suspect ideologies, or individuals were mistakenly thought to have characteristics warranting sterilization when in fact they did not.

Earlier in this century, sterilization of the mentally retarded was recommended and often practiced for two different reasons. One ground for sterilizing mentally retarded persons was based on eugenics, a plan for breeding a species that is more fit, or at least for weeding out "bad genes" from the population. The second reason was to protect society, based on the belief that retarded persons suffer from a form of degeneracy and should therefore not be allowed to roam free and endanger others. Both reasons were included in a judicial decision handed down by Justice Oliver Wendell Holmes in the infamous case of *Buck* v. *Bell*, which was decided in 1927 during the height of the eugenics movement in the United States. Holmes wrote:

We have seen more than once that the public welfare may call upon its best citizens for their lives. It would be strange if it could not call upon those who already sap the strength of the State for these lesser sacrifices, often not felt to be such by those concerned, in order to prevent our being swamped with incompetence. It is better for all the world, if instead of waiting to execute degenerate offspring for crime, or to let them starve for their imbecility, society can prevent those who are manifestly unfit from continuing their kind. The principle that sustains compulsory vaccination is broad enough to cover cutting the Fallopian tubes. . . . Three generations of imbeciles are enough. [4]

Both of these beliefs are now held to rest on shaky empirical foundations. It is currently believed that mild and moderate mental retardation are forms of developmental disability, transmitted genetically only in a minority of cases. The fears of earlier eras that retarded persons pose a menace to society have also been largely dispelled, partly as a result of increased understanding of the phenomenon of retardation itself, and partly because of improvements brought about by better training and educational programs for retarded persons. Statutes in a number of states that allowed for involuntary sterilization of the mentally retarded (usually young women) have been struck down, and judicial decisions mandating sterilization have been overturned. [5]

These shifts in official policy have been brought about by a number of different factors. In addition to a better scientific understanding of mental retardation and a rejection of the ideological premises of the eugenics movement, these factors include a long-overdue recognition of the rights of mentally retarded persons and an awareness that mistaken labeling and misidentification have led to sterilization of women who were not retarded at all.

Probably the most notorious instance was that of Carrie Buck, the woman sterilized as a result of the ruling in *Buck* v. *Bell*. The "three generations of imbeciles" referred to by Justice Holmes were Carrie Buck herself, her mother Emma Buck, and her daughter Vivian. A petition to have Carrie Buck sterilized was brought by Dr. Albert Priddy, the superintendent of the Virginia Colony for Epileptics and Feebleminded, where eighteen-year-old Carrie was an inmate. Dr. Priddy, an ardent supporter of the eugenics movement, had for some time been engaged in a public campaign for sterilization legislation in Virginia, and the petition for Carrie Buck's sterilization was one of many he initiated. The question of whether Carrie Buck was "feeble-minded" was not firmly established at the trial that led to her sterilization. The majority of witnesses called to testify had no firsthand knowledge of Carrie, yet several of her teachers could have offered testimony that she was not mentally retarded, with school records to document their claims. In the five years that she attended school, she was promoted to the sixth grade.

Even more conclusive evidence can be gleaned from Carrie Buck's life story following her sterilization. She married, joined the Methodist Church, and sang in the choir. Her husband died after twenty-four years of marriage, and Carrie married again. She worked for a while assisting a local family in caring for an elderly relative. Her daughter Vivian, whose birth had led to the petition to sterilize Carrie, only lived to be eight years old. Testimony at the trial claimed that Vivian was "slow," yet she later performed quite well in her two years of schooling and actually attained a place on the school honor roll at one point.

The only one of these "three generations" who may well have been mentally retarded was Carrie's mother, Emma, about whom little is known. She was referred to in the trial that preceded Carrie's sterilization as "maritally unworthy; having been divorced from her husband on account of infidelity." Testimony at the trial described the Buck family generally as belonging "to the shiftless, ignorant, and worthless class of anti-social whites of the South. . . ."[6] Not only was the evidence that led to Justice Holmes's reference to "three generations of imbeciles" factually suspect; the entire court proceeding was marked by prejudice, moralism, and the testimony of eugenics zealots.

The story of the trial and sterilization of Carrie Buck lends support to my third reason for opposing any official policy or informal practice sanctioning the curtailment of the reproductive rights of parents like Belinda C. That reason is based on considerations of justice and fairness. Child abuse occurs in all social and economic strata, yet it is the children of the poor who are more likely to be identified as abused or neglected, and removed from their parents' homes. Lack of money, power, and opportunity to secure legal assistance makes the lower classes, which include disproportionate numbers of racial and ethnic minorities, more likely to be scrutinized and less able to protect themselves than middle- and upper-class citizens. The injustice that would result from interference with the reproductive rights of more vulnerable members of society, while more advantaged groups could escape notice or apprehension, is the final moral consideration in this argument. There may be no "inalienable right" to have children, but the overwhelming presumption in favor of reproductive freedom requires a more compelling reason for rebuttal than the one suggested in the case of Belinda C.

But if doctors do not owe a duty to potential children, individuals who do not yet exist, their obligation to a fetus soon to become an infant is more problematic. This problem arises when a cesarean section is recommended for the sake of the infant and the mother refuses the surgery, insisting on a normal vaginal delivery. A woman is placed at somewhat greater risk from a C-section than from a normal vaginal delivery. Refusal is sometimes based on the increased risks of the surgical procedure, but that is not always the case. In some instances women refuse C-sections for what doctors think are irrational reasons, or for no reason at all.

The dilemma of whether to honor such refusals or to coerce the woman into accepting the surgery differs in an important respect from the general problem of patient refusals. When it is the life or health of the patient alone (and not of the fetus) that is threatened, attempts at coercion are bound to be paternalistic. Despite the frustration and anguish physicians experience in those situations, to override a competent patient's refusal of a recommended treatment for paternalistic reasons is rarely justifiable.

However, to seek to override a pregnant woman's refusal to undergo a C-section recommended for the sake of the infant is not an act of paternalism. The principle that could be used to support interfering with the woman's autonomy is the "harm principle"—interference with an individual's freedom can be justified by the likelihood of harm to others. Whether "others" should include the unborn, in addition to the class of living human beings to which the moral principle obviously applies, is a matter of serious contention. Feminists and others who are "prochoice" in the abortion controversy fear that if legal protection is granted to the fetus in cases where cesarean sections are recommended, it will eventually erode women's hard-won right to obtain an abortion. The ethical permissibility of interfering with the autonomy of a woman in labor by forcing her to submit to a surgical delivery continues to be hotly debated.

The development of techniques that permit monitoring of the fetus has given rise to quite a number of medical indications for performing a C-section. In some urban teaching hospitals, the rate of cesarean sections is 30 percent of all deliveries, a statistic that is alarming to some and questioned by many. The decision to perform a surgical delivery while the woman is in active labor or when vaginal delivery

is already in progress is one that a woman may not be able to participate in at all. Even when she can, there is the problem of whether that
decision can be properly informed or freely arrived at.

In one case, which was brought to the hospital's ethics committee
for retrospective review, a woman had repeatedly refused to undergo
a cesarean section during the course of a long labor. The obstetrical
team was sharply divided on what to do: seek a court order to override
the patient's refusal; try to have her declared incompetent; sedate her,
tie her down, and proceed with the C-section; or allow the vaginal
delivery despite the predicted risk of death or damage to the baby.
The dilemma was resolved by time and the patient's weariness. Hours
of labor and unrelenting efforts to persuade her finally wore her down,
and she granted consent for the surgical delivery. Although she was
not literally coerced, there is no doubt that her ultimate decision was
made under extreme duress.

At least two cases of court-ordered cesarean sections are known. In
a case that occurred in Georgia in 1981, an emergency hearing was
conducted at the hospital. On the basis of a physician's testimony that
the woman about to deliver had a condition known as complete pla-
centa previa, with a 50 percent chance that she would not survive a
normal delivery and a 99 percent chance that the infant would not
survive, the court decided that the unborn child deserved legal protection and authorized "all medical procedures deemed necessary by the
attending physician to preserve the life of the defendant's unborn
child."[7] Contrary to the dire prediction, several days later the woman
give birth to a healthy baby, without any surgical procedures. Although this case serves as a reminder that medical predictions can turn
out to be totally mistaken, it should not lead us to the conclusion that
it is reasonable for patients to ignore those predictions in ordinary
situations.

In a case that occurred in Colorado, an emergency hearing was also
conducted in the hospital, and the court ordered a cesarean section on
the basis of fetal monitoring that indicated fetal distress. In this instance the surgery was performed, with no complications resulting for
the baby or the mother. Although such cases do pose problems, the
best solution is nevertheless to honor the rare case of a woman's refusal. A possible consequence is that some fetuses that might be sal-
vaged would die or be born defective. This consequence would be
tragic, but it is the price that must be paid for protecting the rights of
all competent adults, and preventing forcible physical violations of
women by coercive obstetricians and judges.[8]

Doubts and disagreements about the moral status of the fetus, even a very late-term fetus, help to resolve this conflict of obligations in favor of respecting the autonomy of the pregnant woman who refuses a C-section. As George Annas notes: "No mother has ever been legally required to undergo surgery or general anesthesia (e.g., bone marrow or kidney transplant) to save the life of her dying child. It would be ironic, to say the least, if she could be forced to submit to more invasive procedures for the sake of her fetus than for her child." Courts have ordered kidney and bone marrow donations from incompetent persons to their siblings. Since the donors in these cases were legally incompetent, their consent did not have to be sought or obtained. But whenever a person—adult or child, competent or incompetent—is considered to be a potential organ donor for a relative, a conflict of obligations is created.

A MULTIDISCIPLINARY CONFERENCE was called to discuss the case of Elena R., a four-year-old girl whose kidneys had begun to fail. Elena was born with multiple birth defects, including kidney disease, bone distortions that require her to wear long braces on both legs, anemia, and a heart murmur. She was evaluated as developmentally slow, possibly mildly mentally retarded. Elena's mother is a twenty-one-year-old woman who is separated from Elena's father. The father occasionally visits Elena when she is hospitalized but is otherwise out of the picture. Mrs. R. completed the tenth grade in the Central American country where her own mother still resides, and dropped out of school due to her pregnancy with Elena. She married Elena's father but separated after several years of being abused by him.

Mrs. R. is being considered as a candidate for a kidney donation for her daughter. She has been evaluated as a caring, loving parent who has taken excellent care of Elena and appears to deny that Elena has learning problems or shows any evidence of mild mental retardation. Mrs. R. speaks some English, but communication is somewhat limited since she is mainly Spanish-speaking. When the issue of her being a potential kidney donor for her daughter was first brought up, she became distraught and made a suicide attempt. She subsequently agreed to a psychiatric evaluation, and told the psychiatrist that she felt pressured to donate a kidney. She attributed her suicidal gesture to that pressure and her fears. In later visits to the psychiatrist, Mrs. R. revealed that her own mother (Elena's grandmother) advised her against donating her kidney.

Mrs. R. says she prefers dialysis to a transplant for Elena, but the staff is unsure if she understands fully what dialysis entails. Now they are uncertain about approaching her again to have tests to determine whether she is a medically suitable kidney donor for her daughter. One question pertains to her psychological stability: Might she make another suicide attempt or be unable to deal emotionally with her own surgery, as well as Elena's? A second question revolves around the quality of her consent: Is she capable of granting informed consent in a wholly free and voluntary manner?

A third question arises from the risk-benefit calculations. The prognosis for Elena herself, even if the transplant is successful, is poor. With bone disease, anemia, and a heart murmur, she is predicted to have a considerably shortened life span. And the chances for a successful transplant are not precisely known, but are surely less than 100 percent. As for Mrs. R., a healthy individual would be transformed into a patient. The risks of anesthesia, of the surgery itself, and of possible complications must be balanced against the benefits to her daughter. The difficulty of assessing these risks and benefits and of making an accurate, objective risk-benefit analysis is formidable.

The nephrologists (kidney specialists) in charge of Elena's care are in favor of attempting the transplant. They see it as the child's only real chance for survival. The psychiatrist who examined Mrs. R. is hesitant to judge her capable of granting fully informed, uncoerced consent and is worried about her mental stability. The psychiatrist is also concerned that there is no support system for Mrs. R. and that she lacks a proper advocate in this difficult situation.

Physicians on the home-care team, who have provided primary care to Elena over the years, are conflicted. They wrestle with trying to determine what is in the child's best interest. Refusing to define "best interest" in a narrowly medical way, they point out that Elena's best interest is intimately bound up with that of her mother. If Mrs. R.'s present and future emotional stability is open to question, it casts doubt on the wisdom of efforts to persuade her to donate a kidney. Looking at the entire constellation, the home-care team acknowledges that Mrs. R.'s mother has tried to influence her daughter but that her role is reasonable and understandable. Everyone at the conference firmly agrees that Elena's learning disabilities and possible mental retardation should not disqualify her from receiving the same medical treatments a normal child would get, all other things being equal.

Cast in my usual role of bioethicist at the conference, I was asked to sum up and draw any conclusions that seemed compelling. I did not suggest that an attempt be made to persuade Mrs. R., because the risk-benefit ratio was too tenuous. The benefits did not sufficiently outweigh the risks. Unlike the more straightforward question of whether to embark on aggressive treatment for a single patient, this case involved two patients. It required that a perfectly healthy person be turned into a patient who must undergo the risks of major surgery. Add to the uneasy balance of the risk-benefit ratio Mrs. R.'s reluctance to grant consent, and a level of anxiety that led to her suicide attempt, and a conclusion begins to emerge.

Defining the case as one of conflicting obligations made it necessary to decide which duty should prevail: the duty to prolong the life of a child, or the duty to refrain from coercing an already unstable mother into placing herself at risk. With the same reluctance and hesitation that always plagues me when I'm called upon in a conference to draw a conclusion about a moral dilemma, I said it would be wrong to put additional pressure on Mrs. R. to become a kidney donor for her child. An alternative did exist, one that held less promise of a successful transplant for Elena but that posed no risk to her mother. A cadaver organ could be obtained for transplantation. Although the chances of a successful transplant are somewhat less with a cadaver kidney than with a live, related donor who is a good tissue match, this alternative provides a means of avoiding a conflict of obligations. Finding a third option isn't always possible, but it is often the best way to resolve a moral conflict.

Experimenting on Human Subjects

OWHERE IS THE POTENTIAL for conflicting obligations more worrisome than in situations where doctors simultaneously deliver medical care to patients and use them as research subjects. Medical research on patients is usually carried out in teaching hospitals affiliated with a medical school. Patients are admitted to these hospitals by their physicians, who have appointments on the faculty and conduct studies in their medical specialty. Although most such doctors continue to comply with their primary obligation to deliver the best possible care to their patients, the demands of adhering to a strict research design can create obligations that compete with those of giving good medical care.

It is often hard for physicians to live up to the ideal of single-minded devotion to the patient when confronted with the realities of pursuing a career in an academic medical center, where higher rank and status depend on publishing the results of research. This lesson comes as a rude shock to idealistic young medical students when they learn about the clinical research going on around them.

A case presented at an ethics conference by a third-year medical student was a routine example of a typical study involving very sick patients, yet it caused great concern among the assembled group. The student who brought the case described it as "the ethics of putting patients on an experimental protocol." The patients on whom a new drug was to be tested all suffered from arrhythmias, irregular heartbeats. Some arrhythmias are life-threatening, and a number of drugs have been developed to control the condition. Like virtually any drug, these antiarrhythmics carry side effects and risks that may even be life-threatening themselves. The use of such medications can be ethically justified if patients give their voluntary, informed consent to enter the study, and if the benefits to the patient outweigh the risks. But the problem with any new drug or medical device is that the precise risks and benefits are not yet known, until a study is conducted that is large enough to yield statistically significant data.

Individuals who have recently developed an arrhythmia are the best candidates for drug treatments, since their irregular heartbeats can more easily be converted back to normal rhythms. The purpose of the study in question was to see if, once their heart rhythms are converted, the patients will maintain normal heartbeats. The medical student posed these questions: Is is fair to put patients in a study for an experimental drug when other drugs are already available to treat their condition? If the new drug is truly beneficial, is it ethical to withhold that medication from other patients not enrolled in the research who could benefit from it? Can desperately ill patients meaningfully participate in decisions to become research subjects, and how can they give a properly informed consent? Do patients in clinical trials receive the best possible care during their hospital stay? The answers to these questions, among others, are required for a moral justification of biomedical research.

The idea of experimenting on patients conjures up two quite different pictures. The first depicts persons who are sick and suffering—perhaps even dying—being subjected to the manipulations of clinical investigators who use patients in their efforts to contribute to scientific knowledge, as well as to promote their own careers. The second picture portrays untold numbers of present and future patients receiving the benefits of miraculous cures resulting from painstaking research in hospitals and laboratories. Neither of these pictures is an accurate rendering of the actual conduct of research involving human subjects, yet both contain partial truths.

Most research done on hospitalized patients consists of drug studies. As in the arrhythmia protocol, a new drug is typically compared with the standard drug for that condition. The two are compared in terms of both their risks and their potential benefits: Is the new drug less toxic than the current medication? Does it have fewer side effects? And is it more effective in curing or improving the patient's medical condition? Often the differences that emerge between the standard medication and the new drug are minute.

The actual contribution to medical knowledge gained by most clinical trials is only a pale rendering of the image of miraculous break-throughs in scientific understanding and control of disease.

The ethical dilemma created by the need to experiment on sick patients in order to advance the frontiers of biomedical science and conquer diseases is sometimes stated in the form of two unacceptable extremes. To allow unfettered experiments on human beings would open up the prospect of new abuses such as those known to have occurred in the past. The atrocities committed by the Nazis in the name of medical research are the worst example but not the only instance of unethical research conducted on human subjects. However, to prohibit research on human subjects altogether would be to close off the only avenues that could provide the scientific knowledge and technological capabilities for preventing and curing diseases.

A PARTICULAR EXPERIMENT or an entire line of research can be judged ethically acceptable or unacceptable for different reasons. These reasons rest on general moral principles, the same moral principles used to evaluate therapeutic practices in medicine. Debates in the 1970s over developing the techniques of splicing genetic material, or manipulating recombinant DNA, for example, revolved around the unknown or even unknowable risks of harm that might result. Initial worries centered on the fear that by taking genetic material from one organism and implanting it into another, a new genetic species of bacteria harmful to human beings might be created. To protect against such possibilities, new regulations required research laboratories to house genetically engineered materials in secure containment facilities. The fear that "those little bugs might escape from the laboratory" was expressed by some scientists as well as by concerned members of the public. As the research went forward and no mishaps occurred, that fear diminished and eventually disappeared. Although the early experiments with recombinant DNA did not involve human beings directly, current work on the medical applications of the technique of gene-splicing uses human subjects in the same way they are used when new drugs or devices are tested.

A similar controversy surrounded the initial attempts to fertilize a human female egg with a male sperm in a glass dish, the process technically known as in-vitro fertilization and commonly referred to as "test-tube babies." In the 1970s opponents of those research efforts claimed that they were too risky to pursue. What if a hopelessly damaged fetus were created? These skeptics held that the possible harm to human beings in the form of birth defects exceeded the likely benefits, while defenders of the research argued just the opposite, pointing to the gains to be realized and assessing a low probability of any resulting harm. The birth in England in 1978 of the first "test-tube baby," a normal healthy infant named Louise Brown, silenced this kind of objection but did not put to rest all concerns about the practice of in-vitro fertilization, such as those stemming from religious opposition to the creation of life by "artificial" means.

THE UTILITARIAN MORAL PRINCIPLE underlies the concept of the "risk-benefit equation," requiring that the beneficial consequences of research outweigh the risks of harm. The "principle of beneficence," as it has come to be known, was defined in *The Belmont Report*, one of several publications issued by the National Commission for the Protection of Human Subjects of Biomedical and Behavioral Research. The National Commission, created by the National Research Act of 1974, treated beneficence as an obligation that embraces two general rules: (1) do not harm, and (2) maximize possible benefits and minimize possible harms.

Applying a nonconsequentialist moral principle would lead to a rather different assessment of at least some research involving human subjects. Kant's categorical imperative, which states that persons are never to be treated merely as means but always as ends in themselves, might rule out all nontherapeutic research. It would surely prohibit experiments involving individuals who will receive no direct benefit and who lack the capacity to grant informed consent to participate. A plausible interpretation of the categorical imperative is that it would permit some research in which there is no direct therapeutic benefit, but only when the consenting subjects have an interest in the success of the research for a reason other than benefit to themselves—for example, if the research is investigating an illness from which a relative suffers, or if the subject wishes to participate out of altruistic motives.

A problem remains, however, when this principle is applied to research involving children and other individuals with diminished autonomy. If the research holds out no prospect of direct benefit to them, these human subjects are being used "merely as a means" to the ends of others. Does that make it unethical to conduct nontherapeutic research on individuals who cannot consent on their own behalf? The answer is yes if the governing moral principle is Kant's categorical imperative, and no if the applicable concept is the principle of beneficence. The National Commission for the Protection of Human Subjects chose the latter ethical principle as the appropriate standard for judging the acceptability of risks in human experimentation.

Another reason for judging various lines of research to be unethical is that they wrong human subjects, even if those subjects are not at risk for physical or psychological harm. This charge has been leveled against the use of deception in social science research and also against research projects in which the investigator engages in covert observations. To deceive subjects is to wrong them by failing to respect their dignity as persons. To observe people without their knowledge and consent is an invasion of their rights of privacy.

The concept of wronging the subjects of research rests on the respect-for-persons moral principle, central to the nonconsequentialist ethical perspective. *The Belmont Report* states:

> Respect for persons incorporates at least two ethical convictions: first, that individuals should be treated as autonomous agents, and second, that persons with diminished autonomy are entitled to protection. The principle of respect for persons thus divides into two separate moral requirements: the requirement to acknowledge autonomy and the requirement to protect those with diminished autonomy.[1]

The leading application of this principle is in the doctrine of informed consent. Failure to obtain voluntary, informed consent from subjects or their legally authorized representatives violates the respect-for-persons principle in the research setting as well as in the context of performing therapy on patients.

THE MECHANISM THAT has been adopted to deal with the practical problems of protecting human subjects is regulation of the research enterprise. Procedural safeguards of several kinds are in place to monitor or review the conduct of human-subjects research. Most importantly, every institution that receives funds from the U.S. Department of Health and Human Services (HHS) for biomedical and behavioral research on human beings is required to have a committee, known as an institutional review board (IRB), to review and approve research protocols before the study is actually begun.[2] Officially required only to review research conducted or funded by HHS, these committees are now in place virtually everywhere in the United States, including pharmaceutical companies that pay for and carry out their own drug research. Most IRBs—at least those in academic medical centers—are charged with reviewing all research projects conducted in their institutions, whether or not they are funded by grants from HHS.

Two federal agencies are responsible for overseeing human-subjects research. One is the Food and Drug Administration (FDA), whose regulations govern all research on new drugs and devices. The other is an office within HHS, the Office for the Protection of Research Risks (OPRR), which oversees research conducted in institutions receiving funds from the National Institutes of Health (NIH), the federal agency that sponsors most of the biomedical research in this country.

Federal regulations governing the conduct of research on human subjects charge institutional review boards with two main tasks. The first is to review the risk-benefit ratio of proposed research projects to ensure that the benefits outweigh the risks. While the risks of human experimentation are always borne by the subjects, the potential beneficiaries are calculated to include others besides the research subjects, such as future patients suffering from the same disease. I serve on my institution's IRB, and find it no easier to make these risk-benefit calculations now than when I was first appointed six years ago.

One problem stems from the nature of the comparison itself: how can risks to a relatively small group, the research population, be balanced against the potential benefits to untold numbers of future patients? If the "calculation" is to be made simply by counting or estimating the number of individuals involved, then the potential beneficiaries would always far outnumber those who are placed at risk. Calculating in that way, IRBs could never disapprove any proposed research projects because of an unfavorable risk-benefit ratio.

It is clear, then, that risk-benefit assessments must take into account qualitative as well as quantitative factors. The type and degree of risks and benefits, in addition to the numbers of people likely to receive them, must somehow be factored into the assessment. In the years I have served on the IRB, fewer than five research protocols have been rejected on the grounds of an unfavorable risk-benefit ratio. That ratio is most likely to be unsatisfactory in studies that have no prospect of direct benefit to the individual subjects. Experiments of this type, sometimes called "nontherapeutic research," are permitted by federal regulations so long as the IRB determines that the expected benefits to others outweigh the risks to the subjects.

The second task of the IRB is to determine that the requirements are met for obtaining voluntary, informed consent from research subjects. This typically involves a careful review of the proposed consent form, but rarely includes monitoring the actual process of gaining informed consent from patients. One of the tasks I regularly perform for the committee is providing an additional review of written consent forms, often helping the researcher translate the form from "medicalese" into ordinary English that patients can understand. Bilingual translators are enlisted to put consent forms into ordinary Spanish for the large number of Spanish-speaking patients who may be candidates for a clinical trial.

As important as the language of the consent form is its content. It must detail the purpose of the study, the procedures involved, the risks, benefits, and alternatives. In my six years on the IRB, only one research project has been rejected by the committee because it failed, in principle, to enable subjects to grant properly informed consent. Deception of the subjects was a major feature of the design of that study, which is not typical of research at medical centers.

However, it is not unusual for researchers in college psychology departments to design and carry out experiments that involve withholding essential information from subjects, even actively deceiving them. Some years ago, when I taught philosophy at a midwestern university, I served on an institutional review board that covered all human research conducted in the social-science departments of the university. I was surprised to see how many research protocols contained deception and manipulation of subjects, and how inadequate the consent forms were in their failure to fully disclose the purpose and procedures of the experiments. Naively, I remarked on this at a committee meeting and was rewarded with an invitation to make a brief presentation on deceptive research practices at the next meeting.

The naiveté of my remark about deception was exceeded only by that of my presentation at the subsequent meeting. I should have known better than to invoke the name of Immanuel Kant and his categorical imperative. But I was totally unprepared for the cynicism and ridicule with which several committee members responded to my critique of the use of deception in social-science research. I began with the ethical presumption that lying is wrong. Some committee members expressed the view that there's nothing wrong with lying if you can get away with it, while others were vehement in their defense of lying as a necessary, and therefore acceptable, feature of social-science research. Years later, when invited to serve on my current IRB, I was relieved to see the conscientious manner in which committee members review protocols and how careful they are in requiring full disclosure to subjects in all types of research.

A widely publicized case of violation of the respect-for-persons principle occurred in a research project conducted in 1964 at the Jewish Chronic Disease Hospital in Brooklyn, New York. Twenty-two elderly patients, nineteen suffering from some form of nonmalignant terminal illness and three cancer patients used as experimental controls, were approached by a researcher who wished to study the body's immune mechanisms. The material actually injected into these unwitting patients was tissue consisting of live cancer cells, but the patients were told only that some tissue would be injected, that a lump would form, and that it would disappear in a few days. The researcher was certain that injecting cancer cells into the subjects would not cause cancer, but he wanted to determine how quickly and in what manner the patients' immune systems would reject the cancer cells.

The main charge brought against the researcher and the director of the hospital, in a hearing conducted by the New York State Board of Regents, was that the patients had not been given sufficient, accurate information to grant properly informed consent. Probing questions were also raised about the competency of these patients to grant consent at all, since they were elderly and debilitated, some frankly senile, and others deaf or blind. The researcher told the hearing board that he saw no reason to use the word "cancer" in describing the procedures to the patients. He said the term "has a tremendous emotive value, disvalue to everybody. . . . What the ordinary patient, what the nonmedical person, and even many doctors . . . whose knowledge of the basic science behind transplantation is not great—to them the use of a cancer cell might imply a risk that it will grow and produce cancer, and the fear that this word strikes in people is very great." Acting under its responsibility for licensing the medical profession, the regents found the researcher and the medical director of the hospital guilty of "unprofessional conduct" and of "fraud and deceit in the practice of medicine." [3]

Surprising as it may seem, the charge of "unprofessional conduct" is more devastating than calling a doctor "unethical." Several years ago some questions were raised by the institutional review board on which I serve about the conduct of one physician whose research protocols are regularly reviewed by the IRB. The majority of committee members are doctors, most of whom are involved in research themselves. Despite their conscientious efforts to protect the subjects of research, they are reluctant to make trouble for one of their fellow physicians. The committee also includes nurses, social scientists, members of the hospital administration, one person drawn from the local community, and myself as ethicist. On this occasion a physician on the IRB suggested that a motion to censure the researcher was called for, and I became involved in formulating the wording of the motion. The wording included both charges—"unethical practices" and "unprofessional conduct." I was advised by a colleague to drop the second charge, as it was a "red flag," more damaging to the researcher than an accusation of unethical practices. Much less surprising was the outcome of this episode. Only one other member of the IRB was willing to vote for censuring or reprimanding the unethical investigator, and the matter was quickly dropped.

IN ORDER TO PROVIDE further protection for patients used as research subjects, institutional review boards can expand their activities beyond their main task of reviewing each research protocol and deciding whether to accept or reject it. For example, a mechanism adopted by my IRB is to appoint an ad hoc committee to study a problem that has come up and to report back to the entire IRB with its recommendations. One such committee was created to draw up guidelines for obtaining consent from special classes of patients whose ability to grant consent at the time of the research may be impaired. Eager to avoid even the appearance of impropriety in conducting research on vulnerable patients such as those who were wronged in the Jewish Chronic Disease Hospital episode, my IRB adopted the following guidelines for women in labor, patients in significant pain, and those who have been given sedatives or narcotics.

I. Women in labor
   A. Advance consent
   For research in which procedures will be carried out while a woman is in active labor or during delivery, efforts should be made to obtain informed consent in advance. If it is possible to identify in advance patients who will be candidates for the research, those women should be approached during a prenatal visit and their informed consent obtained. At the time the research procedures are to be carried out (when the patient is in active labor or during delivery), the patient should be reminded of the earlier discussion and the fact that she granted consent for the procedure. Those women who will not be selected for the study should be so in-

formed, and those who are selected should be given relevant information again, and allowed the opportunity to ask questions or to withdraw. Both the advance consent and that obtained at the time of the research should be documented in writing.

B. Consent not obtained in advance

When advance consent is not possible or has not been obtained, the following procedures should be followed for women in active labor when the research maneuver carries high risk, high potential benefit, or both.

1. The pregnant woman should be approached for her informed consent.

2. Additionally, another person close to the pregnant woman should be asked to grant consent. Such persons would typically be the pregnant woman's husband or the father of the baby, the woman's mother or other close relative. Consents granted by the pregnant woman and the other person should both be documented in writing.

3. If no family or friends accompany the pregnant woman to the hospital, the research may proceed based on her informed consent alone. In that case, it will be the responsibility of the researcher to determine the patient's capacity to grant valid, informed consent while in active labor. Consent should be documented in writing.

When the anticipated risks or benefits are moderate or lower, no one except the pregnant woman need be involved in the consent process. The degree of risk and benefit should be determined by the [IRB] when the protocol is submitted for review.

II. Patients in significant pain

A. Predictable or recurrent pain: advance consent

When possible, consent for research should be obtained in advance from patients who experience predictable or recurrent bouts of significant pain. At the time the procedure is to be carried out, such patients should be reminded of the earlier discussion and the fact that prior consent had been obtained. They should be given relevant information again and allowed the opportunity to ask questions or to withdraw. Both the advance consent and that obtained at the time of the research should be documented in writing.

B. Consent not obtained in advance

When advance consent is not possible or has not been obtained, the following procedures should be followed for patients in significant pain.

1. The patient should be approached to grant informed consent.

2. If a family member or close friend has accompanied the patient to the hospital, that person should be asked to grant consent in addition to the patient's consent. Both consents should be documented in writing.

3. If no family or friends accompany the patient to the hospital, the research may proceed only if it promises a high benefit to the patient. In that case it will be the responsibility of the researcher to determine the patient's capacity to grant valid, informed consent while in significant pain. Consent should be documented in writing.

III. Patients who have been given sedatives or narcotics

Obtaining consent from patients under sedation or to whom narcotics have been administered should be postponed until the sedatives or narcotics have worn off. Exceptions to this guideline are:

1. If the research procedure can be deemed potentially lifesaving, consent need not be postponed until the sedative or narcotic drugs have worn off.

2. This restriction need not apply in the case of patients suffering from terminal cancer.

The provisions in these guidelines for gaining consent from a relative or "significant other," as well as from the patient, are routinely followed by investigators in my institution who do research on elderly patients whose ability to grant consent may be impaired. Careful scrutiny is common for all research protocols involving children, and when the children are over seven years old, their "assent" is obtained in addition to their parents' consent. According to the Code of Federal Regulations governing research on human subjects, " 'assent' means a child's affirmative agreement to participate in research. Mere failure to object should not, without affirmative agreement, be construed as assent."[4]

One of the very few proposed research projects rejected by the IRB because of an unfavorable risk-benefit ratio was a study that required injecting hormones and other drugs into children. The subjects were preadolescent and adolescent boys who had been diagnosed as having depression and conduct disorders. At intervals over a period of weeks, the subjects were to be admitted to the hospital and have different drugs injected into them, after which their blood would be examined to see the effect of these drugs on hormones that occur naturally in the body. Each session was to last about four hours, with the boys required to undergo an overnight fast—meaning no breakfast in the morning—and to remain lying down until the session ended at 1 P.M. The stated purpose of the research was to learn more about the activity of hormones and other naturally occurring substances called neurotransmitters, and the relationship between these and the children's mood and behavior. The study promised no benefit to the children enrolled, but potential contributions to knowledge, which might benefit other children with depression and conduct disorders.

An ad hoc committee was formed, chaired by a pediatrician and including another pediatrician, a cancer specialist, a social scientist, and myself. The committee discussed the matter at length but had no trouble coming to a conclusion. We recommended that the research protocol be rejected on grounds of the poor risk-benefit ratio. Expressing the unanimous view of the group, the chair wrote:

> For many emotional, behavioral, and psychiatric disorders in children for which there has been little therapeutic breakthrough, recent attempts have been made at drug manipulation and drug intervention. This in itself is not bad, but . . . we . . . must carefully define which groups of children should be considered, what procedures can be performed on them, where they are to be performed, and under whose supervision. Children are most vulnerable to experimental research. Often their parents are desperate to find out some answer or achieve some fast result and all too unwittingly but willingly submit a child to a research protocol. At the same time, the entire area of obtaining truly informed consent from children leaves many questioning, doubtful aspects. It becomes imperative, therefore, that at least the minimal federal regulations be met when conducting research involving children.

Even though most clinical research consists of drug tests, a recent spate of surgical experiments has attracted the attention of the media and the public. The artificial-heart program begun at the University of Utah Medical Center and continued at Humana Hospital–Audubon in Louisville; the operation at Loma Linda University Medical Center in California to transplant a baboon heart into Baby Fae, an infant with a lethal birth defect, hypoplastic left heart syndrome; and the implantation of an unauthorized artificial heart known as the "Phoenix heart," by a University of Arizona surgeon—all have stirred controversies over their propriety. In those controversies, critics have not questioned the need for research in surgery, which, like biomedical research generally, stands to benefit untold numbers of future patients. Instead, concerns have been raised about the quality of informed consent granted by the patient (or the parents, in the case of Baby Fae), about the uncertainty surrounding the risks and benefits to the research subjects themselves, about the adequacy of the process by which the proposed experiments were subjected to review by an IRB, and about whether sufficient prior testing had occurred when these patients were enlisted as research subjects.

Those are the most important questions, ones that must be addressed in all research involving human subjects. But some more subtle issues have received much less attention. These questions concern all research but are especially germane to surgical experiments. They go beyond the ethical concerns raised by the dramatic episodes that have galvanized public attention.

The first question addresses the boundary between biomedical research and established therapies. Even more complex are attempts to make distinctions between experimentation, research, and innovative procedures in the practice of medicine. There is some disagreement over whether medical treatments and surgical procedures can be neatly classified as either experimental or accepted. Physicians often proclaim that all treatments have an element of experimentation, but that statement can be misleading. The fact that treatments contain some new elements, or that variations are employed for particular patients, does not make them "experiments" nor does it place them in the category of research. The essence of research is that it is an activity designed to discover generalizable knowledge. But research need not involve the manipulations or novelty characteristic of experimentation.

As vague as the boundary is between research and established therapy, the distinction is important for ethical as well as legal reasons. Although voluntary, informed consent should be sought just as scrupulously from patients about to undergo accepted treatments as from patients in a research setting, much more uncertainty exists in the latter situation. Furthermore, in delivering established therapy to patients, physicians do not have to submit to a review process, but it is by now a virtually universal requirement in the United States that experimental procedures be approved by an IRB.

Not as crucial as the boundary between research and established treatment, but useful for an understanding of the ethical issues, is the distinction between medical research and human experimentation. At a conference[5] sponsored by the Hastings Center—an internationally renowned research and educational institution founded in 1969 to study and report on ethical issues in the life sciences—conflict erupted over the meaning of the terms "research" and "human experimentation." Some argued that not all research involves experimentation, so the terms should not be used synonymously. Research can include data collection, epidemiologic studies, chart reviews, and studies comparing two or more accepted (that is, nonexperimental) treatments. It encompasses systematic observations of established procedures or practices for the purpose of studying outcomes or comparing different patient populations. In short, medical research sometimes involves experimental drugs, devices, or procedures, but it might also be devoid of experimental features.

Participants at the Hastings Center conference also disagreed about what constitutes an experiment. Some expressed the view that not everything that is novel deserves to be called an experiment, since an experiment, whether in medicine, surgery, or basic science, must adhere to the precepts of scientific method: there should be a hypothesis to be tested; procedures should be spelled out clearly, so that others can replicate the experiment; the results should make it possible to confirm, refute, or modify the initial hypothesis. Although this is an ideal model of scientific experiments, perhaps impossible to realize in many instances of human experimentation, it is still, according to its proponents, an ideal that researchers should strive for.

A quite different position was voiced by others, who maintained that the practice of medicine is itself an ongoing experiment. Since a physician or surgeon cannot predict with certainty how the individual patient will respond every time a drug is administered, an operation performed, or a treatment regimen prescribed, the doctor is always in fact experimenting on the patient. The implications of this position are troubling, since the boundary between accepted medical practice and experimentation becomes hopelessly blurred. Among other things, this view creates a problem for the review of human experimentation.

The error in the view that all medical practice is inherently experimental lies in a confusion between uncertainty and experimentation. Uncertainty pervades all of life, but we do not think of our daily lives as ongoing experiments in living. Instead, we are guided by past experiences and general knowledge of the consequences of actions. The presence of uncertainties in clinical practice does not, therefore, mean that every clinical decision or recommendation is an experiment.

What about innovative practice? Physicians or surgeons, using their clinical judgment, sometimes employ an innovative procedure on an individual patient; or they may develop an innovative intervention for a number of patients. Should that be considered research? Experimentation? And is the use of such innovations ethically acceptable? The answers to these questions require a detailed description of specific cases, but some general observations can be made.

First, it is necessary to assess the basis for the innovation and the degree of departure from accepted standards. If the proposed innovation is based on specific knowledge about a particular patient, then it falls under the heading of clinical judgment, and should need no research protocol, IRB review, or other clearance required of medical research or experimentation. For example, a doctor who has been treating a patient over the years and is familiar with idiosyncrasies of the patient's tolerance to certain drugs or a tendency to have allergic reactions is using clinical judgment in trying out new combinations or dosages. On the other hand, if a physician or surgeon undertakes an innovative procedure on a group of patients in order to see how it works, then the practice is clearly research, even if a formal protocol has not been designed or approved. As a colleague of mine puts it, "If it looks like research, smells like research, and behaves like research, then it's research!"

However, regardless of whether an innovative treatment should properly be classified as research, disclosure to the patient is ethically necessary. Just as the risks as well as the benefits of treatment must be disclosed, and just as patients should be informed of alternatives to the proposed therapy, so too should patients be told that the proposed procedure is innovative, even if it departs only slightly from the standard one. If a good physician-patient relationship has been established, the patient will have confidence in the physician and is unlikely to refuse treatment or to be made unduly anxious by such disclosure.

AFTER PROBLEMS WERE encountered following the implantation of the fifth Jarvik-7 artificial heart, the surgeon, Dr. William DeVries, was quoted as saying: "It's a learning process. This is a trial-and-error thing. This is what human experimentation is all about."[6] DeVries's remark echoes the view expressed by those at the Hastings Center conference who held that all of medical practice can be considered an experiment. While it is true that even well-studied procedures can have unplanned results, it is reasonable to question the adequacy of advance preparations for an experimental procedure.

Although even experts would need more data before venturing an informed opinion, I was struck by the circumstance that led Dr. DeVries to make his "trial-and-error" remark. The *New York Times* reported that the doctors performing the implant had difficulty in fitting the Jarvik-7 device into the chest cavity of the patient. DeVries said, "You look at this heart and it's the size of a grapefruit, and you look at the hole which is the size of an orange, and you can't get this thing in there. It's like putting a round peg in a square hole. But you realize also you can't very well stop, that's not really fair to the patient."[7]

Experts are agreed that the experience and scientific expertise of William DeVries and his associates qualify them for performing their artificial-heart experiments. There remains disagreement, however, over whether the experiments on humans are premature, whether more testing should have been done on the Jarvik-7 device itself, and whether the known risks of the device and the surgical procedure were sufficiently high to require further research and development before the present program was approved.

No such disagreement exists, however, about the Phoenix artificial heart. The Phoenix device, invented by Dr. Kevin Cheng, a dentist, was designed to be implanted into a calf, not a human. When surgeons tried to implant the Phoenix heart, which had not received FDA approval, into a desperately ill patient, they found it too large, and were unable to close the patient's chest around the device. The area was protected with sterile wrapping. It is fair to surmise that an accurate prediction could have been made about whether the Phoenix heart would fit into a human's chest, although perhaps no such prediction could have been made about the grapefruit-sized Jarvik-7 device and the orange-sized cavity.

There is little doubt that surgery, compared with other areas of medical practice, subjects fewer innovative procedures to prior review and sustained clinical investigation. An editorial in the *New York Times* following the implantation of William Schroeder's second artificial heart stated: "No one would think of letting an experimental drug on the market until it had been adequately tested for safety and efficacy. Unfortunately, no agency exists to regulate novel surgical procedures, doubtless because of an assumption that surgeons can be trusted to regulate themselves."[8] The *Times* is only partly correct, since the Office for the Protection of Research Risks (OPRR) within the Department of Health and Human Services does regulate biomedical research of all sorts, including those over which the FDA also has oversight—but only when the research is funded by the NIH. Research on human beings that does not involve new drugs or devices, and that is sponsored by private foundations, or federal agencies other than HHS, is not subject to official regulation. That leaves a great deal of research unregulated, especially if it is conducted in private, for-profit medical institutions such as the Humana Hospital chain. Medical institutions that pay for their own research activities can escape regulation by the OPRR, but not by the FDA if the research involves investigational drugs or devices.

But if surgeons and other specialists do not have to develop research protocols for their experimental or innovative procedures, they will not get the sort of detailed scrutiny given to drugs and devices before being approved by the FDA. It is incumbent on surgeons working at the frontier of their specialty to develop such research protocols and adhere to the canons of clinical investigation practiced by researchers in other areas of medical practice. That is the only sure way to protect patients from ethically unacceptable procedures. And only that way will individual surgeons be legitimately free of the sort of attacks deserved by those who implanted the Phoenix heart, the baboon heart, and maybe even the Jarvik heart.

Patients and surgeons alike would benefit from a proper scientific approach to new surgical procedures, instead of trial and error. Adherence to the canons widely used in clinical research will no doubt give rise to some ethical problems. But when medical research conforms to the highest standards of scientific inquiry, it stands a better chance of avoiding the ethical pitfalls of harming or wronging patients.

Harming and Wronging Patients

HERE ARE NO PERFECT MECHANISMS for protecting patients from inadvertent harm in a hospital. But while ethics committees and institutional review boards aren't foolproof, they do help to prevent wrongs or harms resulting from treatment or research. A case in point is the research protocol rejected by my IRB on the grounds of its unacceptable deceptive procedures.

The research project proposed to study variations in anger or aggression exhibited by the subjects. Participants were to be selected from present hospital outpatients seeking treatment for their severe mood swings. The procedures included taking blood specimens from the subjects to determine hormone levels. These physiological measures would then be correlated with the intensity of the subjects' anger or aggression brought out in a laboratory situation. The consent form for the study included this description of the procedures, risks, and benefits:

> Standard psychological tests will be administered, and to observe overt behaviors that may be associated with emotions during stress, test sessions will be videotaped. This record will allow the measurement of behaviors (handwringing or biting pencils, for example) that may correlate with subjective reports of intensity of nervousness or anxiety. These videotapes will be observed only by researchers involved in this study and will be destroyed after statistical analysis. Confidentiality is assured.
>
> There are no risks involved in this study. Because of the nature

of the psychological tests involved, you may at times feel stressed and undergo emotional changes that you normally might feel when working under time pressure.

There are no direct benefits to you for serving as a subject. However, the researchers have agreed to share the study results with you. A benefit to others, and to basic scientific knowledge, is the fuller understanding of the relationship between psychological and biological aspects of emotion.

What this consent form did not disclose was that the volunteer subjects were to be surreptitiously provoked by a trained experimental "confederate" while they were taking the paper-and-pencil tests. The full research protocol, which is always made available to IRB members, described several situations in which the subjects would be provoked to anger during the administration of the psychological tests.

In one situation a "research assistant"—a trained confederate of the researcher—was to behave in a condescending manner, criticizing the subjects' test responses in a derogatory way and alluding to their failure to attend to instructions, to their noncooperation, and to their lack of intelligence. In another, the "research assistant" would spill a vial of fake blood on the subject's test paper and then blame the subject, making an accusation of not staying still or of startling the assistant. The assistant was then to insist that the test be retaken, adding that it "was a poor job that could be dashed off by any simpleminded person." Still another called for a confederate to look over the test-taker's shoulder and make such condescending comments as "I don't know what's taking you so long; it's not that difficult" and "Hurry up or you'll never get finished." As the time limit approached, the confederate was to grab the subject's pencil and write in the correct answers, insisting that the subject would never be able to figure them out and needed help. The last "provocation situation" called for a confederate to watch and occasionally make derogatory comments as the subject was completing six simple drawings. This included laughing out loud at some of the drawings and then telling the experimenter, in a low but audible voice, that the subject was not right for the study because he was really dumb.

None of these "provocation situations" was disclosed on the consent form, since to do so would alter the results the research was seeking to explore. The protocol reviewed by the IRB described the cover story the experimenter would tell to the subjects: "To provide a plausible rationale for stimulus incidents, subjects will be informed that the experiment is testing changes in 'verbal and spatial performance.' "

The committee found this proposed project entirely unacceptable. Objecting mainly to the wrong that would be done to the patient-subjects, committee members also expressed concern about damage to the reputation of the medical center if details about the research were ever made public. I was asked to meet with the researcher to see if the project could be redesigned to avoid deception, and to acquaint him with the requirements for voluntary, informed consent. After a two-hour meeting and several telephone conversations, the investigator resubmitted the protocol. All of the original features of the research design were retained. The consent form was slightly modified, but it was still unsatisfactory in its failure to disclose what the subjects would actually undergo.

To be as fair as possible to the researcher, an ad hoc subcommittee of the IRB was formed to study the revised protocol and consent form, and report back to the board. The report addressed three issues under the heading "Deception":

a. *Deferred Debriefing.* Only after the completion of four episodes of deception will the subjects be told about the nature of the research and be debriefed. There is grave concern about the loss of self-esteem on the part of the subjects and the short- and long-term effects this may have. Subjects must deal with the reality that they have been duped and have been possibly provoked to act foolishly. The subjects' sense of self-worth may be seriously harmed. In addition to the subcommittee's assessment of an unsatisfactory risk-benefit ratio, the fact is that subjects would be wronged by blatant and repeated deceptions.

b. *Issues of Trust.* Essentially, subjects sign up for this protocol believing what the investigators tell them in terms of the nature of the experiment, its purpose, and its methods. After participating in this experiment, they find out that this is not so. The bond of trust between the investigator and the subject is broken. Taken a step further, the issue of trust between the medical-scientific community and subjects of research is seriously violated. Would it be possible for these individuals to have faith in the medical-scientific community again?

c. *Informed Consent.* Even in its revised version, the consent form still remains deceptive. It is impossible to obtain "informed" consent when material facts about the research are withheld or distorted.

Summary Opinion: Not approved.

PATIENTS ARE SOMETIMES *harmed* as a result of carelessness, negligence, ignorance, unavoidable human error, and the unforeseen consequences of properly done procedures. Rarely is the harm caused by the malevolent intent of health-care workers. Situations in which patients are *wronged* are ethically more ambiguous, except for blatant cases like the deceptive research project. Failure to obtain properly informed consent, overriding a patient's autonomy, violating a patient's privacy or confidentiality, and withholding information are sometimes inadvertent, but are more often deliberate acts on the part of physicians who singlemindedly pursue what they believe to be their patients' best interests.

One of the most common examples is that of doctors driven by therapeutic zeal. The tendency to employ overly aggressive treatments may stem from a physician's religious convictions. A sanctity-of-life morality is not uncommon among Orthodox Jews in the medical center where I work, and many Orthodox Jewish medical students experience great conflict. Most confess their inability or unwillingness to swerve from the dictates of their religion, which ranks the preservation and prolongation of life over all other values. Some have studied the field of Jewish medical ethics, which has a literature and spokesmen of its own. Yet many of these students elect to take my courses in secular bioethics and are eager to comply with what secular ethics and law require by way of informed consent and the competent patient's right to self-determination, despite the conflict with the strict mandates of Orthodox Jewish law.

One medical student, who was also an ordained rabbi, made an appointment with me to discuss his inner conflict between the demands of his religion and what he had come to accept as the moral and legal rights of patients in an enlightened age that rejects paternalism in medical practice. He was concerned that the precepts of Jewish law, which require life to be preserved and prolonged, would compel him to refuse to honor the wishes of patients who seek supportive care instead of aggressive therapy. I sympathized with his plight, and we had a long discussion. But his dilemma was a private matter of conscience, not the type of moral problem for which my professional skills could provide much help. My role in that situation was one of a teacher offering counsel, rather than a philosopher performing an ethical analysis.

Doctors who overtreat patients because of their religious convictions are in the minority. Two other reasons more often lie behind the pressure to intervene—reasons without moral motivation. The first is the fear of legal liability, either the threat of a malpractice suit or the (usually mistaken) belief that they will be found criminally liable for withholding or withdrawing treatment. The other reason is the notion that physicians are somehow obligated to "treat what's treatable," that sound medical practice requires them to be as thorough as possible in performing diagnostic tests and preventing patients from dying of curable conditions, even when they are terminally ill from another disease.

There are probably also doctors who never reflect on these issues at all, but simply act, plying their trade more like a body mechanic than like a healer treating a whole person. In the worst cases, physicians who overtreat dying patients commit both species of ethical mistake. They simultaneously harm and wrong their patients, as happened in a case I'll never forget.

Mrs. R.L. was a thirty-eight-year-old woman in the advanced stages of incurable cancer. She had been a patient at University Hospital for some months and was regularly admitted to be given chemotherapy, blood transfusions, and platelets. It was recently discovered that her cancer had become metastatic, spreading throughout her body. Earlier she had responded well to medication, but her condition had now worsened. On this occasion she came to the hospital for blood transfusions. Finding that the cancer was widespread and no longer treatable, her physician, an oncologist (cancer specialist), had decided to halt the chemotherapy.

When Mrs. R.L. was admitted to the hospital this time, her mental status was normal, although she was in extreme pain. Before the blood transfusion was given, she developed a high fever. The transfusion was administered, and Mrs. R.L. became confused and disoriented. She was given Tylenol, and her fever came down. The next day her fever again shot up, she was still in great pain, and she remained disoriented. Her physician decided she should have a CAT scan to discover the reason for her changed mental status and a spinal tap to discover whether the fever was caused by meningitis. These tests typically require the patient's informed consent, but practice differs from one hospital to another. Although formal consent is not required for every medical procedure, doctors should explain to patients what they are about to undergo. Mrs. R.L.'s pain medication had been increased, raising the question of whether her mental confusion was a result of narcotic drugs, infection due to meningitis, or metastases of her cancer to the brain.

Her husband asked: "Why do a CAT scan? My wife is dying of cancer. She's in great pain. Is this procedure necessary?" The oncologist replied: "She may have a mass on her brain, she may have an infection, or maybe it's the medication that's causing her change in mental status. We have to find out." Mr. R.L. then requested that the medication be changed, as he didn't want his wife to undergo more pain and the discomfort of being moved to another location to undergo the CAT scan. He favored the least intrusive treatment at this point.

Not wanting to disobey the orders of the oncologist, who was a senior attending physician at the hospital, the house staff and medical students had the CAT scan done on Mrs. R.L. But they did not do the spinal tap. The chief resident detected no signs of meningitis and knew that the oncologist expected the patient to live for only two more weeks at most. When the oncologist arrived the next morning and found that the spinal tap had not been done, he was enraged. He said that legally and morally, only the patient had the right to refuse the procedure. He then ordered the resident to do the tap right away.

The resident refused. Defiantly, he told the senior physician, "If you can get consent from the patient, you do the tap." The oncologist replied, "You don't need consent for this," and proceeded to attempt the procedure himself. He stuck the patient numerous times, drawing mostly blood instead of spinal fluid. The resident, highly skilled at doing spinal taps, was appalled.

Meanwhile, a neurologist was called in to do the tap, and the resident stood in his way and said no. Mrs. R.L. was not told what was being done to her, nor had she been asked for her consent. At this point, although she seemed to be having auditory hallucinations, she was oriented "times three"—to time, place, and person. At the insistence of the oncologist, a medical student finally performed the spinal tap. No meningitis was found.

The next day the oncologist seemed resigned. "No more blood, taps, IVs; we're going to let her go," he said. A medical student later reported that Mrs. R.L. had expressed the fear that if she refused any procedures, her doctor would get mad at her. She wanted to please him, worried that if he became angry at her, he might withhold medication.

The case made me frustrated and upset. It embodied multiple ethical issues: failure to obtain informed consent, making arbitrary medical judgments, inadequate assessment of the patient's competency, failure to heed the requests of the patient's next of kin, doing unnecessary procedures. But the thing that bothered me most was the inability of the majority of house staff and medical students to stand up to this physician. Only the one resident did defy him, with less than happy results. Even if the others were unwilling to defy his orders directly, I found it hard to believe that they had no further recourse in such situations. In fact, there was an option the residents and students could have taken. They could report the incident to the chief of service, either while it was happening, or afterward, in the hope of preventing similar behavior in the future. But the chance of junior doctors snitching on their senior colleagues is slim, and the likelihood of a chief of service taking definitive action even more remote.

Acts of flagrant wrongdoing by physicians and other health-care workers are rare in the hospitals where I work. But they do occur, and they create the greatest anguish for nurses, social workers, and medical students who witness them. There is rarely a structured means for addressing their concerns, which must be vented only in memos and in conversations held in hospital corridors. This is beginning to change: hospital ethics committees are being established in many medical centers, providing a forum for these discussions.

One ethics committee on which I sit—an interdisciplinary group dedicated to promoting patients' rights and interests—began to study the problem of interprofessional conflicts and their impact on patient care. At one meeting a social worker presented the case of Lori, the nineteen-year-old woman who had undergone corrective surgery on both legs and feet, whose doctor had refused to sign papers authorizing payment for a home-care attendant because, he said, it was "an abuse of Medicaid." The social worker found unanimous support for her position; no one defended the doctor who thought he was protecting society's interests by refusing to authorize the Medicaid payments.

HOSPITAL ETHICS COMMITTEES have other pressing items on their agenda, so additional opportunities must be created for a frank discussion of cases in which patients are harmed or wronged. These discussions often reveal the deep concerns of health professionals and their eagerness to deal with problems of wrongdoing in a responsible manner. Several years ago I conducted a series of informal sessions in bioethics for nurses, in which they shared these internal memos.

To: Ms. A.T., Assistant Director of Nursing
From: Ms. E.M., Nursing Supervisor
Subject: Patients' privacy
    It has been reported to me by the nurses on 3 South that the resident doctors have to be constantly reminded to protect the patient's privacy (diagnosis and treatment). Many times they will discuss a case loudly in front of the patient involved as well as other patients who may be present. This is done regardless of the diagnosis being discussed.

To: Ms. A.T., Assistant Director of Nursing
From: Ms. A.R., Nursing Supervisor
    It was reported to me this morning by Ms. L., Tour III supervisor, and Ms. S., LPN, 4 West, that M.M., a first-day post-op patient, requested pain medication at 1:30 A.M. Dr. N., the resident on call, was paged by Ms. S. Dr. N. answered but refused to come to write the order. Instead, he requested that the nurse give the medication without an order. Ms. S. explained hospital policy to Dr. N. regarding telephone orders. The Administrator on Duty was notified. Dr. N. did not come until 6:30 A.M. This is the second occurrence of this problem with Dr. N.

To: Ms. J.L., Associate Director of Nursing
From: R.A., Nursing Supervisor
Subject: Tour II—Physician coverage
    Tour II has expressed concern with the difficulties involved in getting the physician to respond to changes in the patient's condition. When spoken with, the physicians have become loud and abusive, stating that the nurses purposely make noise in the corridor to wake the physicians on call at 5:00 A.M.
    It is noted that the attitude of the chief residents is influential in establishing a positive relationship with the nursing staff. With a poor attitude the medical team does not respect nursing and nursing judgment, and does not respond to their request for patient care regarding insertion of IVs, dressing changes. Doctors then have to be nagged into seeing their patients.

It emerged in these sessions that many instances in which interns and residents neglected patients or violated their rights stemmed from interprofessional conflicts with nursing staff. Such power struggles produce bad consequences for patients, besides worsening the relationship between the doctors and nurses themselves. Although there was little I could do to improve those relationships, the nurses were grateful for the chance to air their concerns and for the ethical support I provided for their beliefs about the care of patients.

Medical students are distressed, and at the same time paralyzed into inaction, by fear of recrimination if they report incidents they have observed. Even efforts by other full-fledged physicians to find out what happened are thwarted by stonewalling and cover-ups. A physician who served as medical consultant in a hospital's patient-relations office was unable to get to the bottom of an episode described by an intern in obstetrics and gynecology.

A thirty-two-year-old woman was about to undergo a total hysterectomy. Based on the diagnostic workup, she was resigned to the removal of her female organs and consented to the surgery. However, once the woman was under anesthesia and her abdomen had been opened, the surgeon discovered that the diagnosis had been incorrect and a total hysterectomy was not called for. Nevertheless, the doctor proceeded with the planned procedure. The intern, appalled, asked the surgeon why she was continuing with the operation when it was unnecessary. The intern received no answer. Again she asked, and the resident doing the procedure replied only that the patient had given informed consent, and there was nothing wrong in going ahead with the hysterectomy.

The intern wondered: Was there any reason—medical or otherwise—that could justify proceeding with surgery in such a case? Should she have tried more vigorously to halt the surgery? What steps, if any, should she take to report the ob-gyn resident, who not only went ahead with the operation, but refused to respond to the questions of a trainee? Should the patient now be told that the surgery she consented to turned out to be unnecessary but was performed anyway?

At the ethics conference one participant, searching for a rationale for performing an operation suggested by a mistaken diagnosis, pointed out that without her female hormones, the patient would now be at less risk for developing endometrial cancer, so on risk-benefit grounds maybe it was wise to proceed with the surgery after all. Another physician replied that although there would be less risk of cancer, the patient would be more likely to develop osteoporosis. (This loss of bone mass commonly causes fractures in elderly women, and estrogen replacement is now an accepted way to prevent osteoporosis in postmenopausal women.)

The discussion continued, with medical risks and benefits hotly contested. One medical student protested, "This is all very well to debate as an issue of proper medical management. It might be an appropriate discussion for gynecologists to hold with their patients. But this lady granted consent for a hysterectomy believing it to be indicated for her condition; that turned out to be false. There can be no justification for continuing with an operation once it is found to be unnecessary." It is important to reinforce correct ethical positions in these conferences, and I seized the occasion to commend the medical student who criticized those trying to justify the wrongful surgery by appealing to risk-benefit considerations.

The question of whether the patient should be told had yet to be resolved. Again, an array of potentially bad consequences was trotted out to justify nondisclosure. What good would it do to inform the patient after the fact? The surgery couldn't be undone. The woman would probably be angry at these doctors and lose faith in the medical profession generally. Even worse, she might sue; she could even win, causing financial loss to the physicians and the hospital. Only bad consequences would result from disclosure, including possible harm to the patient, who would suffer emotional distress while recuperating from major surgery.

Several medical students objected to this consequential reasoning. One was adamant in expressing a deontological position, an appeal to moral obligation and duty: "A wrong was done to this patient. Although the act can't be undone, the only way to right the wrong is by telling her what happened. Doctors have an obligation to be truthful to their patients, even in the face of medical mistakes."

Another student tackled the malpractice issue: "It's true, no physician wants to be sued. It's always a financial loss, as well as a blow to the doctor's ego, to be hit with a malpractice suit. But a legal remedy for malpractice exists for a reason, and there's no better example of that reason than a case like this."

I was proud of the students. But I couldn't help wondering how they would behave ten years hence if they found themselves in a situation like the one we were discussing, where moral action is called for. Nevertheless, giving medical students the opportunity to voice their concerns and discuss their cases with sympathetic teachers marks a vast improvement in medical education. Acquainting young doctors with the ethical aspects of their day-to-day practice should give them some guideposts for their future professional lives. In an elective course she was taking with me, a fourth-year student who plans a career in geriatrics provided the following description of a case she had been involved in.

Mr. T. is ninety-two years old. He was brought to the hospital by his granddaughter because he complained of a swollen abdomen. On admission the patient was found to be severely jaundiced and complained of weakness and moderate abdominal pain. From the start Mr. T. repeatedly expressed the desire to go home, although he was not physically combative. It is not clear whether it was his idea or his granddaughter's to go to the hospital in the first place. He stated that he lived alone, caring for himself.

On the first day, he was put on NPO status (nothing by mouth), which involved placing a nasogastric tube through the nose down into the stomach, inserting a Foley catheter, a tube with a device for inflating a retaining balloon, into the patient's bladder to drain urine, and inserting an intravenous line into his arm. On the second day another intravenous line was placed. Mr. T. objected verbally and physically to all this, and he was kept tied to his bed to keep him from pulling out his lines and tubes—which he nonetheless managed to do a couple of times.

Diagnostic tests revealed a large mass in his pancreas. This, along with his jaundice, led to a diagnosis of pancreatic cancer. The surgical staff, taking into consideration the patient's age and his probably terminal cancer, decided to keep him in the hospital for further observation and supportive measures for his still possible intestinal obstruction. The surgical staff felt that they unfortunately could not keep the patient from eventually dying from his cancer, but that they couldn't let him die from something correctable or manageable, such as intestinal obstruction. The surgeons had not firmly decided whether to operate if the obstruction worsened, although they did say that Mr. T. was too ill and old for any major surgery.

The patient was then told he would have to stay in the hospital until his physicians could discover why his abdomen was swollen, and that he could get very sick without the hospital's supportive measures. He was not told about the diagnosis of pancreatic cancer. Mr. T. still insisted he wanted to go home. At one point he stated that he was very old, that he knew he was sick, and that it was his time soon to die; therefore, why didn't they stop sticking tubes into him and let him go home?

Throughout his hospitalization, Mr. T. was alert and oriented to person, place, and time. When questioned, he responded coherently. He was often found mumbling to himself in bed, but he was attentive to whatever was said or done to him. Although he repeatedly tried to untie himself from his bed, verbally he was subdued and always polite. No psychiatric consultant was called to assess his competency. The surgical staff kept the patient in the hospital on the wishes of his granddaughter, who felt that since he was very sick, he needed to be there.

The student who described the case had never taken a formal class in bioethics before, yet she knew Mr. T. had been wronged by those responsible for his treatment. She criticized the way the house staff treated not only this patient but many others on the basis of their age. She described the staff's tendency to infantilize elderly patients, including those who were mentally competent: it was as if they assumed aged people were incompetent until proven otherwise, rather than the other way around. The student also recounted the typical pattern of deferring to family members of elderly patients. Grown children are treated as decision-makers, even in cases where their aged parent is fully capable of participating in decisions about medical treatment, discharge from the hospital, and posthospital placement.

In Mr. T.'s case, not only did the house staff fail to disclose anything about his diagnosis; they also refused to communicate with him to discover his own wishes. The medical student had repeatedly questioned the resident in charge of the case, but he brushed aside her questions. When she insisted that Mr. T. be told about his condition and prognosis, an intern told her it wasn't her business—when she became a senior house officer, she could manage patients the way she wanted to, but for now, she was there to learn.

I was convinced that the student had tried her best. Understandably, she feared receiving a bad evaluation from the residents, who have responsibility for clinical teaching during medical students' clerkships on the wards. Reflecting on the type of role model provided by this house officer and others like him, I thought of the view expressed by doctors who resent the intrusion of ethicists into their domain. Their view is that medical ethics is best learned not in the classroom listening to a philosopher discourse on informed consent or the doctor-patient relationship, but by medical students and young physicians observing and emulating the behavior of their more senior colleagues. But clearly this method of learning can only be as good as the role models themselves.

▪ ▪ ▪

ALTHOUGH THE STORY of Mr. T. is typical of the way elderly patients are treated by the much younger house staff, Mr. T. himself was somewhat atypical in that he remained alert throughout his stay. Often, however, mental deterioration is significant, and sometimes it is rapid. Sadly, many elderly patients never regain their former mental status, either in the hospital or after discharge. This is partly because it is harder to adapt to new environments and routines as one gets older. Also, patients receive too few stimuli when they spend all day in a hospital bed, and they must be subjected to routines at the convenience of the staff.

Most causes of mental decline are probably unavoidable. But elderly patients can be both wronged and harmed if no effort is made to discover the causes of impaired intellectual function—causes that can include anything from depression to poor nutrition. Mental impairment in elderly patients can sometimes be reversed. It is critically important for physicians to try to discover the causes—not only because mental improvement is desirable in itself, but also because any major decisions affecting an elderly patient that can be postponed should wait until mental functioning is restored.

In hospitals and extended-care facilities, the most common causes of reversible impaired intellectual function are depression, metabolic or infectious disorders, and intoxication from therapeutic drugs. Most troubling are the well-documented facts about the adverse effects of medication. A 1980 task force of the National Institute on Aging reported an enormous number of implicated drugs, including diuretics, digitalis, oral antidiabetics, analgesics, anti-inflammatory agents, sedatives, and psychopharmacologic agents.[1] Add to the sheer number of drugs having this effect the fact that not only do the elderly metabolize drugs differently from younger adults, but they are often being treated with more than one drug, which leads to toxicity from drug interactions. Thus the conclusion is compelling that a significant amount of mental impairment in elderly patients is iatrogenic—that is, induced by physicians.

Several years ago I attended a lecture given to first-year medical students by a leading geriatrics specialist. The professor described making rounds and examining the charts of the older patients. One patient was getting forty-seven different medications—three for the primary medical condition, and the remaining forty-four to treat the side effects and adverse reactions caused by the drugs themselves. By the well-intentioned efforts made to help them, elderly patients are all too often harmed.

THE GREATEST ETHICAL ambiguity surrounds a group of patients likely to be both harmed and wronged, wittingly or not. They are "problem patients," as doctors refer to them: patients who are hostile, abusive, disruptive, demanding, manipulative, dishonest, or noncompliant. All possible types of problem patient are summed up in the title of an article in the medical literature: "Taking Care of the Hateful Patient."[2] With unfailing regularity, "problem patients" of a particular sort are presented at a biweekly ethics conference: individuals with sickle-cell disease who come to the hospital in crisis.

Sickle-cell disease is an incurable, inherited condition that primarily afflicts blacks; its seriousness ranges from mild to very severe. Although the disease never disappears, it is punctuated by periodic crises, characterized by acute pain in the joints, the bones, and elsewhere. The only treatment for the condition is medication, usually narcotics, to relieve the pain. The following two cases are typical of the problems sickle-cell patients pose for the medical staff.

Tiara was a nineteen-year-old with a long history of sickle-cell disease with many complications. She was periodically admitted to the hospital during crises and given Demerol for pain. She slept peacefully through the night, but when she was awake or when she was being observed, she would begin to cry. Sometimes she would scream without interruption until she was given the pain medication she demanded. A nurse and the resident in charge discussed Tiara's case. The nurse said the patient didn't need drugs for pain but was addicted; she suggested that the medication be stopped, and that Tiara would then get up and sign herself out of the hospital.

LeRoy was a twenty-seven-year-old who had had his first sickle-cell crisis at fourteen. His disease manifests itself by severe pain in his legs and abdomen. He comes to the emergency room an average of five days each week and is admitted to the hospital for a short stay as an inpatient about twice a month. Both as an outpatient and as an inpatient, he is given Demerol. LeRoy has been married and divorced, and has several children whom he sees only occasionally. No one else in his family has sickle-cell disease.

The problem occurs when he comes onto the ward twice a month. He bothers the medical staff, the nurses, and other patients. On one occasion he had to be expelled from the hospital for having sex with another patient. During a recent admission he was so abusive to a nurse that he was brought to the psychiatric emergency room. Some attempt was made to have him involuntarily committed to the psychiatric ward, but the effort was later abandoned.

Both cases prompted the same list of basic questions when presented at ethics conferences. First was the question of whether to believe these patients' claims that they are in pain. Some participants held the position that the "sicklers" were not in pain every time they appeared to be, but were addicts who had grown addicted to the narcotic medications they were given over a period of many years. As one medical student put it, "The medical profession turned this patient into a junkie!"

Others at the conference were less certain that the patients were lying about their pain and criticized the first group for their skepticism. Those who believed that LeRoy and Tiara lied in order to get drugs in the hospital saw them as manipulative and "abusing the system," and argued that patients like these should not be given narcotics in the hospital. This angered another doctor, who claimed that punitive behavior by physicians, such as withholding pain medication from patients who may be in genuine agony, is never justifiable. A senior resident contended that because physicians had caused the addiction of these patients, they were obligated to continue to give them drugs.

The unfailing suggestion is made in these discussions that an additional obligation of physicians is to try to get addicted patients into a drug-rehabilitation program. Sickle-cell patients invariably refuse, denying that they are addicted.

The discussion becomes heated. One student yells at another: "Pain is a private matter, an internal thing. No one can tell if someone else is really in pain or not. Our job as doctors is not to doubt and second-guess our patients."

An intern jumps in: "But it is our job as doctors to prevent and eradicate drug addiction. Addiction is a disease, and we're supposed to treat diseases. Whether we caused this addiction or not, we certainly have a duty not to perpetuate it."

Another medical student: "Anyone can tell by observing these patients that they're not in pain all the time they say they are. When no one is looking, they quiet down. Tiara sleeps like a baby through the night, then wakes up screaming for pain medication. LeRoy has been to every emergency room in this borough. When they refuse him at one hospital, he goes to another."

The debate takes an ugly turn: "You know what? You're a racist!

You wouldn't be making these accusations about white, Jewish, middle-class patients. It's because these sickle-cell patients are poor and black that you want to deny them the meds they're entitled to."

And so it goes. Problem patients are hardest for physicians to deal with coolly and rationally. Things go smoothest in the medical setting when patients are compliant and grateful for the care they receive, behaving like "good patients." Doctors, as human as their patients, sometimes can't control their own emotions. Working long hours, with too little sleep and not enough time for family and leisure activities, they become angry at patients who are hostile and try to manipulate the staff. Even when they are reminded of their obligations in the doctor-patient relationship, irrational forces from within make them unable to respond as the ethical ideal would prescribe. Rarely with malice, but sometimes intentionally, physicians may deal with problem patients by harming them, wronging them, or both.

Patients do have some recourse when this occurs. In the absence of a formal mechanism, a nurse or hospital social worker may step forward and act as an advocate of the patient. Many hospitals have an office of patient relations, where complaints may be brought by patients or their families. Other hospitals, lacking an entire office to deal with such matters, employ a trained individual to serve as a "patient representative." Patients or families might also bring a problem to a hospital ethics committee, although few of these committees become involved in adjudicating disputes between patients and health professionals.

A recent development in a number of hospitals is the presence of an "ethics consultant," a practicing bioethicist whose formal education may be in philosophy, law, or religion. I am frequently called on in this capacity, but only once at the request of a patient (in fact, of the husband of a patient in coma). It is usually a health-care worker who requests an ethics consultation where a patient appears to have been wronged or harmed. Although not much is known about how often patients or families receive satisfaction when they seek recourse within the hospital, the fact that help is available—from patient representatives, ethics committees, or bioethics consultants—marks an improvement over the practice in earlier times.

14

Resolving the Issues

MANY ARE STILL SKEPTICAL about the value of bioethics in resolving moral problems in medicine. The skepticism takes several forms: One focuses on the role of ethical theory, pointing out the inadequacy of theories for providing solutions to practical ethical dilemmas. Another focuses on philosophers and their methodology, arguing that analyzing a problem down to the minutest detail is no substitute for giving an answer. Still another asks why ethics is needed when we still need laws and policies to govern the behavior of doctors and hospitals and to protect the rights of patients.

Put in the most direct form, the ultimate skeptical question is, Can bioethics resolve the issues? The answer is, It all depends on how the question is interpreted. Answers like that have given philosophers a bad name. My answer seems evasive, requiring first an interpretation and analysis of the question, only then giving a conditional reply. But that is the nature of philosophical inquiry. Philosophy doesn't supply answers to multiple-choice questions. It cannot offer a "how-to" guide to ethical quandaries. The philosophical enterprise aims at providing deep understanding.

Fifteen years ago, when I first entered the new field of bioethics, I wondered whether I or my professional discipline could be of any use in helping to resolve practical problems facing doctors. Even today, when I am called for an ethics consultation or hear a case presented at a regular conference in the hospital, I have some doubts about my ability to help. Struggling to resolve the dilemma of Bunky, the disabled homeless woman who lived in a subway station and made a public nuisance of herself, I was unable to resolve the conflict between her right to liberty and her medical and social "best interest." Contemplating the case of Annabella, the mentally retarded girl visiting from a Caribbean country, whose parents refused recommended brain surgery, I couldn't achieve a definitive balance between the obligation to respect the parents' religious convictions, on the one hand, and the duty to override their refusal and perform a high-risk operation on the other. Conducting an internal debate about whether the higher obligation lay in preserving doctor-patient confidentiality or in informing the employer of the alcoholic train switchman about his impairment, I kept searching for a way to rank these conflicting obligations.

Now, however, I understand much better than when I began just what it is I am doubting. Rarely does bioethics offer "one right answer" to a moral dilemma. Almost never can a philosopher arrive on the scene and make unequivocal pronouncements about the right thing to do. But even though there is no magic wand, bioethics can go a long way toward resolving the issues, once that phrase is properly interpreted.

"Resolving the issues" can be understood in the strongest sense to mean "solving moral dilemmas" or "providing clear-cut solutions to ethical quandaries." If it is true—and I believe it is—that genuine moral dilemmas have no single right answer, then bioethics cannot "solve" them. But that interpretation not only asks too much; it also narrows the application of bioethics, since only a small percentage of the issues in medical practice and health policy are genuine moral dilemmas. This strong interpretation of "resolving the issues" is neither the only nor the best way of construing the role philosophers can play.

An altogether too weak interpretation of "resolving the issues" should also be rejected. That weak sense sees the philosopher's role only as clarifying moral problems and structuring the issues. Although that is part of what bioethicists do—both in the clinical setting and in their scholarly work—more is involved than mere clarification and structuring. Moral philosophy is not a form of "values clarification," getting people to recognize their own values and discover what they really think about perplexing ethical problems.

Instead, a philosophical approach to ethics seeks to provide understanding. Sometimes that understanding goes far enough to supply answers to moral problems. In other cases philosophical ethics shows why unequivocal answers are not forthcoming. For example, it is expecting too much of an ethical theory to settle controversial moral issues in cases where the controversies result from the two sides' holding different, often competing, ethical principles.

An important aspect of any ethical theory—at least any philosophically respectable one—is its epistemological component. Epistemology, sometimes called the theory of knowledge, is the branch of philosophy that studies the scope and limits of human knowledge and the justification of beliefs. Every area of human inquiry has roots in epistemology. Whether the subject is science or ethics, technology, law, or art, questions of what truths exist, how we come to know those truths, and how they can be justified are bound to arise.

Ethical theories embody normative principles—principles that set forth criteria for right and wrong, good and bad, just and unjust actions or policies. Normative principles are the key elements of ethical theories in their application to practical situations. But theories also contain epistemological features important for the justification of the principles themselves. Although the heart of a moral theory is the fundamental moral principle or principles it embodies, the theory itself consists of much more than its ethical content. There is at least as much controversy among philosophers over the foundations of ethics, about the theory of knowledge that lies behind an acceptance of one moral position versus another, and about the meanings of basic ethical concepts, as there is over the selection of the principles themselves.

A central aspect of "resolving the issues" in bioethics is attending to the conceptual, epistemological, and even metaphysical issues that philosophers deal with as their stock-in-trade. A good illustration is the cluster of concerns surrounding the beginning and end of human life. Many opponents in the continuing abortion controversy have maintained that if we only had an adequate account of when human life begins, or personhood, we could then decide once and for all about the morality of abortion and set public policy accordingly. This view rests on the belief that there is a strong link between being a person and being the bearer of rights, especially the right to life. One philosopher makes the equation explicit, writing, "In my usage the sentence 'X is a person' will be synonymous with the sentence 'X has a (serious) moral right to life.' "[1] The belief that there is a strong link between personhood and the right to life was further illustrated in a bill proposed in 1981 by antiabortion legislators in the United States Congress entitled "A Bill to Provide That Human Life Shall Be Deemed to Exist from Conception."[2]

However, even a cursory look at the literature in bioethics and health law reveals that there is no consensus at all on the definition of "personhood." Writers who hold a feminist bias take the stance that at no stage of development does a fetus meet the criteria of personhood. And writers from religious traditions opposed to abortion offer a standard of personhood that a zygote, a fertilized egg, can meet. My assessment of why it appears impossible for philosophers, theologians, feminists, and legal scholars to agree on the criteria for personhood is that the position they already hold about the morality of abortion is imported into the definition of "human life." This is a sophisticated form of the logical fallacy known as "begging the question": assuming what you are trying to prove. If the conclusion of a logical argument is built into the premises, it guarantees that the argument will come out the way the speaker wants it to—but at the price of engaging in fallacious reasoning. Attempts to use the concept of a person as a means of resolving the abortion debate fail for this reason.

But the situation is even more complicated. Contributors to the literature surrounding the abortion debate cannot even agree on the relevance and importance of defining "personhood." Four distinct views can be discerned.

One view argues that settling the abortion issue once and for all depends crucially on coming to some agreement about whether the fetus is a person and, if so, when in its development personhood begins.

Another side maintains that settling the abortion issue has nothing to do with when personhood begins, since abortion may be morally justified even if it is acknowledged that the fetus is a person from the moment of conception.

A third view holds that whether the fetus is a person is irrelevant to whether it should have legal protection; concerns about the health of the fetus create pressing policy issues regardless of whether or not the fetus is granted the status of a person.

The fourth position asserts that since it is impossible to agree on criteria for defining personhood, this issue must be seen as entirely irrelevant to arriving at a solution to the abortion controversy.

Defining personhood may seem to be merely a matter of semantics. Yet the question of what should count as a person, or what are the proper criteria for personhood, is a profound philosophical question belonging to metaphysics. Determining the relevance of that question to the abortion controversy is an epistemological matter. When issues of ethics and social policy are locked in perennial controversy, philosophy can illuminate those issues by showing how conceptual confusions and fallacious reasoning contribute to the problem. Although conducting a philosophical examination of these questions and issues will not succeed in resolving the debate over the morality of abortion, it does provide a deeper understanding of why the controversy remains unresolved and may even be irresolvable.

Similar problems arise for issues concerning the termination of life: euthanasia, the definition of death, and the ethics of withholding or withdrawing life supports. The leading court cases, including those of Karen Ann Quinlan, Brother Fox, Joseph Saikewicz, John Storar, William Bartling, and Claire Conroy, all revolve around the so-called "right to die." Yet conceptual confusions have added to ethical uncertainty in a number of these cases.

Initially, when the Quinlan case attracted public attention in the mid-1970s, there was a common misconception that if we only had a medically adequate and morally acceptable definition of death, then the ethical problem of removing patients from respirators would be resolved. Some believed that the answer lay in adopting the criterion of brain death, cessation of electrical activity in the brain as measured by an electroencephalograph. According to this belief, if a brain-death criterion replaced the traditional heart-lung definition of death, then moral decisions would be easier. But a look at the medical facts in the Quinlan case and those that followed reveals that Karen Ann Quinlan would not have been considered dead according to a brain-death criterion, although she was irreversibly comatose, with no hope of returning to a cognitive, sapient state. A much more radical departure from the standard heart-lung criterion would have been needed before Karen Ann Quinlan and Brother Fox could have been considered dead while in a "persistent vegetative state."

CAN BIOETHICS RESOLVE the issues? The answer is no if the question is taken to mean "Can philosophers supply unequivocal, right answers to all moral dilemmas in medicine?" But for other interpretations, the answer is yes. When there is no single, correct answer to a substantive moral question, bioethics can still make a contribution. Ethicists can analyze actual or proposed policies and laws, and address questions at the "metalevel," such as which moral problems should be candidates for laws and regulations and which are best left to informal resolution by the concerned parties. Another task at the metalevel is providing criteria of adequacy for a policy or a procedure designed to deal with ethical issues in health care.

In applied ethics, sometimes the issues are resolved by getting the disputants to agree on what are the morally relevant considerations. Doctors who come to recognize the right of patients to participate in health-care decisions no longer insist that their sole obligation as physicians is to bring about the best medical outcomes for their patients. Awareness that both the public-health model and the traditional clinical model govern medical practice leads to an acknowledgment that the physician's duty to keep confidentiality is not absolute. Coming to agree on what are the morally relevant considerations may not directly resolve a particular dilemma, but it shows with precision and clarity just what the residual disagreement is about. In this way the issues are more fully understood, if not completely resolved.

An illustration of the importance of agreeing on what considerations are morally relevant is the persistent debate over what standard of informed consent should apply to social and behavioral research. The debate begins with the fact that withholding information from research subjects, and even outright deception, have been widespread in social-science research. Some outspoken social scientists have argued that their research should be exempted from federal regulations, which were designed for biomedical experiments and have been applied to social-science research only as an afterthought. Others contend that it is all right in principle for such regulations to apply, but they should be modified to take into account the experimental design of much social and behavioral research, and the requirements for informed consent should be adjusted accordingly. Their argument is that much research could not be done without some measure of deception, or without concealing the purpose of the study or the identity of the researcher.

Opponents in this debate over the conduct of social-science research have two very different conceptions of what factors should be morally relevant. Those who argue that the usual requirements for gaining informed consent should be modified or abandoned are appealing to utilitarian considerations. They claim that more benefit than harm results from doing the research, a claim that stands in need of empirical backing if it is to be accepted as a premise in the argument. Contributions to knowledge outweigh any likely harm that could come to research subjects from their having been deceived, they say, and the overall loss to humanity would be much greater than if less-than-fully-informed consent were required, since entire lines of research would otherwise have to be abandoned. Furthermore, since all subjects are "debriefed" at the end of the experiment, deception occurs only for a short period of time, so the subjects end up being informed

—just a bit later. The only factors this side holds relevant are the benefits and risks of the research, and the only relevant moral principle is the principle of beneficence.

Their opponents, those who argue that the same requirements for informed consent should hold for social and behavioral research as for biomedical research, consider the autonomy of research subjects to be morally relevant. This side adheres to the respect-for-persons moral principle, believing in the Kantian precept that people should never be treated merely as a means to the ends of others. This side in the debate is not moved by risk-benefit calculations that purportedly show that little harm is likely to befall subjects who are deceived in an experimental setting. Kantians are never moved by an appeal to consequences (unless they are closet utilitarians). For them neither the loss of significant contributions to knowledge nor the benefits of possible future applications of the research are factors that should influence policymaking in this area. Even if no measurable physical or psychological harm is likely to befall research subjects, acts of outright deception, withholding information that might affect a subject's decision to participate, and disguised observation by researchers are all violations of trust, privacy, or autonomy. The conclusion of the argument is that the proper criterion for moral rightness is respect for persons, not a balance of benefits over harms. Deception should be ruled out in all forms of research on human subjects.

Does this exercise in applying ethical theory resolve the issues? Not under the strongest interpretation of "resolve the issues"; under the more charitable interpretation, it probably does. Although it is quite clear to philosophers who study the issue of deception in social-science research that the debate comes down to a conflict between two leading ethical principles, it is far from clear to the principal opponents in the debate. When the opponents themselves recognize that each adheres to a different moral principle, they may very well not budge an inch. But a deeper understanding of the nature of the conflict should emerge.

IF THE SKEPTICS who question the value or usefulness of bioethics still maintain that the issues are unresolved, they are demanding too much of the enterprise. When no single, rationally defensible ethical theory exists, it is misguided to expect that an appeal to theory can solve a conflict that stems from the application of incompatible theories.

As long as the debate between Kantians and utilitarians continues to rage, and as long as the Western political and philosophical tradition continues to embrace both the respect-for-persons principle and the principle of beneficence, there can be no possible resolution of dilemmas traceable to those competing theoretical approaches. But the inability to make a final determination of which theoretical approach is ultimately "right" does not rule out the prospect for making sound moral judgments in practical contexts, based on one or the other theoretical perspective.

The choice between utilitarian ethics and a deontological moral system rooted in rights and duties is not a choice between one moral and one immoral alternative. Rather, it rests on a commitment to one moral viewpoint instead of another, where both are capable of providing good reasons for acting. Both perspectives stand in opposition to egoistic or selfish approaches, or to a philosophy whose precepts are grounded in the privileges of power or wealth, or in the authority of technical experts.

When answers to substantive ethical problems are unclear or ambiguous, the natural inclination is to seek refuge in procedural solutions. One procedural mechanism that has been gaining acceptance is the use of institutional ethics committees (IECs) to address individual cases or hospital-wide issues. But a number of misconceptions exist about the functions and powers of ethics committees.

Perhaps the most widespread misconception, leading to the greatest fears about the potential for intrusion into the traditional prerogatives of the physician in the doctor-patient relationship, is the belief that once an ethics committee exists in a hospital, it will begin to make clinical decisions that supplant or supersede those of physicians. That misconception can be dispelled by the observation that committees do not define their role as decision-making in the clinical setting. Nor do they see themselves imposing a binding recommendation on the physician responsible for patient care. I'm not sure where this misconception comes from, but I've heard it voiced in hospitals and medical schools all over the country.

The most recent spur to the formation of hospital ethics committees may have been the call for establishing mechanisms for intra-institutional review of nonroutine ethical decisions in hospitals, a call issued by the President's Commission for the Study of Ethical Problems in Medicine and Biomedical and Behavioral Research. The commission outlined possible functions of institutional ethics committees in its report, *Deciding to Forego Life-Sustaining Treatment*, and stated a preference for this mechanism over judicial review of every situation in which a patient, family, or physician seeks to withhold or withdraw life-prolonging therapy.

Many requests for assistance from ethics committees by physicians and other health-care professionals focus on withholding or withdrawing life supports or determining the appropriate level of care for a patient who is terminally ill or unable to participate meaningfully in decisions. A large percentage of cases involve a decision to remove a patient from a respirator or a determination of what should or should not be withheld—fluids, antibiotics, IVs, nasogastric tubes, blood transfusions, or resuscitation for a patient whose heart has stopped. But there is a sizable group of cases that address a range of other problems common in a hospital: management of disruptive patients or patients who refuse everything the hospital has to offer but resist discharge; disagreements about proposed treatment or about full disclosure among professionals responsible for a patient's care; problems with families who refuse appropriate treatment or insist on inappropriate treatment for their relatives.

The outcome of a committee review of any such case need not be a decision binding on physicians or other health-care workers. The deliberations of ethics committees can be advisory, just as the word of a consultant called in to provide medical expertise is advisory. That is how most ethics committees describe their role.[3]

An early attempt to document the activities of hospital ethics committees appeared in the report of a study carried out for the President's Commission. Although that report noted that there were relatively few hospital ethics committees, its findings must be understood in light of how it defined "ethics committee"—as one that is in some way involved in decision-making: either the committee is itself a decision-making body, or else it engages in consultations leading to a decision by another party, usually the physician or treatment team. That rather narrow definition resulted in ignoring a considerable number of ethics committees that defined their role in some other way. Two of the committees on which I sit existed at the time but were not included in the survey because they did not fit this limited definition. This report contributed to the mistaken view that ethics committees intrude into the physician-patient relationship and erode the authority of the doctor. Once it becomes clear that committees can assume a role in clinical consultations that is not a straightforward decision-making role, then the fears arising from this misconception will evaporate.

My experience on three hospital ethics committees and one infant bioethical review committee suggests that IECs are more likely to have several overlapping roles than to have a single function. One committee's duties are described thus:

> An interdisciplinary committee, the IEC will, upon request, engage in decision review and consultation in specific cases which involve bioethical issues. It will formulate and propose general policy on issues which raise moral and ethical questions. It will engage in educational functions which assist staff in recognizing and dealing with bioethical dilemmas.

Although it is often difficult to separate the various functions of ethics committees, the modes of clinical consultation can be divided into three basic categories: retrospective case review, prospective case review, and bedside consultations.

The least problematic of these is retrospective case review, at least from the standpoint of avoiding an intrusion into the physician-patient relationship. Its value is considerable, and it may serve several purposes. One is to educate committee members themselves, both about the range of ethical issues that can arise and about the background that exists in health law and in the bioethics literature. This can be done best when one or more committee members already has expertise in bioethics or health law. But I've seen a number of committees that have quite successfully educated themselves about these background areas.

Another purpose is to enable the committee to develop a method for analyzing and discussing individual cases, a method that can then be applied to the more difficult task of prospective case review. A committee that has deliberated together about cases already completed is better able to approach cases awaiting resolution. It is more likely to achieve consistency in its recommendations than a new committee plunging into the business of deliberating on prospective cases without that experience.

The infant bioethical review committee at my institution, which reviews cases both prospectively and retrospectively, has had just that experience. One of the other hospital committees expressly limited its initial discussions to retrospective cases, before announcing its availability for consultation on ongoing cases. This also enabled committee members to learn one another's views on matters likely to produce conflicts of opinion and differing moral judgments.

One genuine worry about retrospective case review is that if it is not done with sensitivity and with some detachment from the emotional issues, it can degenerate into a forum for blaming or criticizing the caregivers involved in the case. Retrospective case review is most useful when the physicians, nurses, social workers, and others who were actually involved are present for the committee's discussion. But if the discussion is to be of value to the caregivers themselves, it is important to conduct the session in a way that won't be misconstrued as a court of ethical judgment.

In addition to the worry that case consultations will inevitably lead to interference with the doctor-patient relationship, other concerns have been expressed about prospective case review. The chief ones are, first, that committees aren't available in emergencies, when physicians most need a consultation, and, second, that committees are clumsy mechanisms for offering advice.

Obviously, it is true that an entire committee cannot be convened in minutes during an emergency. But that is when ethical advice is least likely to be needed. Most cases are not genuine emergencies, and when emergencies do arise, the proper thing to do is act first and have philosophical discussions later. That is true whether or not an ethics committee exists in the institution, and even if the only person involved in the decision is the physician responsible.

As for the second concern—that committees are clumsy mechanisms for offering advice—it is probably based on a misunderstanding of what is involved in prospective case review. Of course, it would be ridiculous to have an entire committee troop to the bedside. If bedside consultations are employed, they can only be done properly by a small subcommittee—three or at most four individuals, who can be briefed before the actual consultation and spend the minimum time required at the bedside, gathering additional evidence and speaking with physicians, nurses, and others in the unit.

An entire committee need not be a clumsy mechanism when a case is brought by a clinician seeking a consultation. An interdisciplinary committee, consisting of members having a variety of relevant areas of expertise, can provide a thorough and informed discussion of the issues, perhaps confirming what the clinician is already inclined to do, and perhaps introducing considerations the health professional had not thought of or known about.

But prospective case review, while not always clumsy, is seldom rapid. It is a time-consuming activity, and committee members must have enough time for it: each prospective review by our infant bioethics committee takes about two and a half hours. Ideally, cases are reviewed in a structured, relatively formal manner, with brief presentations by all relevant caregivers. Clinical specialists and the hospital's attorneys or risk managers are others who might have pertinent information.

A persistent ethical concern in clinical consultations of all sorts is the violation of physician-patient confidentiality inherent if consultations are not preceded by permission from patients (or their families). It is ethically proper to inform patients and families when a case is brought to an IEC for consultation, and patients or families should be given an opportunity to come before the committee themselves if the case involves a disagreement between patient or family and caregivers. However, many cases do not involve any such disagreement, and the breaching of confidentiality remains an unresolved problem.

As for bedside consultations, this mechanism is more efficient than prospective review by the entire committee, but it lacks the benefit of the many viewpoints and different experiences a larger group can bring to the discussion. If the IEC is a large one, and if requests for consultation are frequent, bedside consultations are probably the only way the committee can handle its caseload. Shifting teams of consultants ensure that the workload isn't too heavy for any one member or subgroup, but care must be taken to maintain consistency over time. This can be aided by reporting the results of consultations back to the entire committee, leaving ample time for a retrospective discussion of cases that were reviewed prospectively.

My experience has shown that the functions of ethics committees often overlap. This is best illustrated by the way in which case review leads to writing guidelines and formulating policies. One case concerned the private adoption of a child born in the hospital. We were told by the nurse and social worker who brought the case to the committee that in this instance, as in quite a few others, the adoption had been arranged by the obstetrician and the prospective adoptive parents, with the assistance of an outside attorney.

The rights of the natural mother were violated several times over. She was refused permission to see the baby by the obstetrician and by some nurses. She was not informed of all of her legal rights in the adoptive situation upon entering the hospital. Pressures were applied to get her to sign papers, although she was ambivalent about giving up the baby when she entered the hospital. The mother was confused and emotionally distraught, spoke and understood English with difficulty, and had no strong support system on the outside. No one was available in the hospital to serve as her advocate: the obstetrician who was attending her was acting as the agent of the adoptive couple; the pediatrician could properly view only the infant as her patient; and the social workers were employees of the hospital's social-service department and therefore not clearly designated to act in the role of advocate for the natural mother.

After hearing the case and discussing it fully, the IEC formed a subcommittee to draft guidelines for private adoptions conducted in the hospital. The full committee eventually voted on a final draft that became hospital policy. This illustrates how an individual case brought for retrospective review can alert the committee to a more widespread problem, leading to new institution-wide guidelines.

Another case was a second-trimester abortion resulting in an aborted fetus that was living but incapable of survival outside the mother's womb. The committee was informed that although such cases are rare, they do sometimes occur. Even less frequently, a late-second-trimester abortion results in a marginally viable infant—one that might be able to survive. The committee was virtually unanimous in agreeing that in the latter sort of case, an obligation exists to resuscitate the infant and treat it in every respect like a newborn baby rather than the product of an abortion.

Nevertheless, many questions had to be addressed—about what hospital policy should be, about what method should be used to perform the abortion, about what information should be given to a woman who comes in for a second-trimester abortion, and about what should be told her, after the fact, about a living fetus resulting from an abortion attempt. An ad hoc committee was formed, consisting of committee members, others from relevant specialties, and hospital administrators. The committee was to study the problem, to report back to the IEC periodically with its findings, and eventually to draft a policy.

In a third case, a member of the hospital administration requested a draft policy when a particular case had posed a problem. Simultaneously, the committee was conducting a retrospective case review and had begun discussions that would lead to the writing of a draft policy. The case was that of a Jehovah's Witness who refused a blood transfusion. It surprised me that such cases continue to pose ethical dilemmas and policy revisions, given the long history of confrontations between Jehovah's Witnesses and doctors and hospitals. Yet here it was again.

The patient was an emancipated minor, only sixteen years old but financially independent. This is a morally troubling situation for doctors, in spite of the law's recognition of the decision-making rights of such patients. Even when they are legally emancipated, minors are more vulnerable than adult patients and are less likely to have enough life experiences to make truly informed choices. The committee was distressed to learn of pressure exerted by family and by elders of the church on the patient to refuse the transfusion—not uncommon in Jehovah's Witness cases. This case had a happy ending: the patient did sign a consent to accept blood for lifesaving purposes, but improved and did not require the transfusion.

The committee's work was less quickly concluded, though. The draft policy had to consider many problematic special cases, such as pregnant Jehovah's Witnesses who refuse blood, thus placing both themselves and their fetuses at risk.

WORKING ON THIS DRAFT POLICY brought me full circle, back to the issue I had first grappled with years ago when I was invited to serve on a hospital panel convened to discuss a Jehovah's Witness case. While the ethical issues are the same, much has happened in the intervening years. The field of bioethics has grown to maturity, and the body of case law has grown in size and in the enlightenment of its judicial decisions.

What has not changed is the need to think clearly about moral dilemmas in medicine and elsewhere in everyday life. Although not every solution can be judged satisfactory, there is nevertheless a range of acceptable actions, practices, and policies. Ethical dilemmas are bound to exist when these come into conflict. When only one moral principle applies to a situation, there is in fact no dilemma. Trying to decide whether to act in one's own self-interest or to fulfill an obligation to someone else may be difficult, but it is not, strictly speaking, a moral dilemma.

Bioethics cannot be useful to doctors and other health-care professionals, or to patients and their families, if what they are looking for are instant answers or tailor-made solutions. Bioethics is fundamentally a philosophical enterprise, and it is likely to be helpful to almost everyone who seeks a deeper comprehension of the issues involved in today's world of medical practice. Anyone moved by the spirit of philosophical inquiry and willing to grapple with moral concepts can profit from the insights into understanding provided by the expanding field of bioethics.

Notes

1   ETHICAL DILEMMAS IN MEDICINE

1. Quoted in President's Commission for the Study of Ethical Problems in Medicine and Biomedical and Behavioral Research, *Making Health Care Decisions* (Washington, D.C.: Government Printing Office, 1982), 1:32.

2. J. Skelly Wright, "Application of President and Directors of Georgetown College," reprinted in Samuel Gorovitz et al., *Moral Problems in Medicine*, 2nd ed. (Englewood Cliffs, N.J.: Prentice-Hall, 1983), p. 61.

3. Robert C. Underwood, "*In re* Brooks Estate," reprinted in Gorovitz et al., p. 63.

4. Ibid., p. 61.

5. Ibid., p. 62.

2   APPLYING MORAL PRINCIPLES

1. Anthony M. Shaw and Iris A. Shaw, "Dilemmas of 'Informed Consent' in Children," *New England Journal of Medicine* 289 (October 25, 1973): 885–90.

2. Ibid.; and Raymond S. Duff and A. G. M. Campbell, "Moral and Ethical Dilemmas in the Special-Care Nursery," *New England Journal of Medicine* 289 (October 25, 1973): 890–94.

3. Duff and Campbell, 891.

3   GAINING INFORMED CONSENT

1. Elizabeth F. Loftus and James F. Fries, "Informed Consent May Be Hazardous to Health," *Science* 204 (April 6, 1979): 6.

2. C. H. Fellner and J. R. Marshall, "Kidney Donors—The Myth of Informed Consent," *American Journal of Psychiatry* 126 (1970): 1245–51.

3. Nicholas J. Demy, "Informed Opinion on Informed Consent," *Journal of the American Medical Association* 217 (August 2, 1971): 696–97.

4. Ibid.

5. B. R. Cassileth et al., "Informed Consent—Why Are Its Goals Imperfectly Realized?" *New England Journal of Medicine* 302 (1980): 896–900.

6. T. M. Grundner, "On the Readability of Surgical Consent Forms," *New England Journal of Medicine* 302 (1980): 900–902.

7. Natanson v. Kline, 186 Kan. 393, 409–10, 350, P.2d 1093, 1106, rehearing denied, 187 Kan. 186, 354, P.2d 670 (1960).

8. Canterbury v. Spence, 464 F.2d 772, 780 (D.C. Cir. 1972).

9. These observational studies were reported in the report of the President's Commission for the Study of Ethical Problems in Medicine and Biomedical and Behavioral Research, *Making Health Care Decisions*, 1: 80.

4 AGGRESSIVE TREATMENT

1. Joseph Fletcher, *Situation Ethics: The New Morality* (Philadelphia: Westminster Press, 1966).

2. Pope Pius XII, *Acta Apostolicae Sedis* 49 (1957): 1031–32.

3. Saul Moroff, "Ethical and Legal Issues in the Medical Management of the Terminally Ill Patient," *Einstein Quarterly: Journal of Biology and Medicine* 3 (Spring 1985): 81.

5 FORGOING LIFE-SUSTAINING THERAPY

1. In re Quinlan, 70 N.J. 10, 355 A.2d 665.

2. Superintendent of *Belchertown* v. *Saikewicz*, 370 N.E. 2d 426, n. 11.

3. Society for the Right to Die, *Handbook of 1985 Living Will Laws* (1986), p. 5.

4. This and the preceding quotations taken from the proceedings of the case *William Francis Bartling and Ruth Cheryl Bartling* v. *Superior Court of the State of California*, California Court of Appeal, filed December 27, 1984.

5. George J. Annas, "Prisoner in the ICU: The Tragedy of William Bartling," *Hastings Center Report* 14 (December 1984): 28.

6. *Ibid.*

7. Quoted in George J. Annas, "Help from the Dead: The Cases of Brother Fox and John Storar," *Hastings Center Report* 11 (June 1981): 19–20.

8. Quoted in George J. Annas, "The Incompetent's Right to Die: The Case of Joseph Saikewicz," *Hastings Center Report* 8 (February 1978): 21.

9. M. Pabst Battin, "The Least Worst Death," *Hastings Center Report* 13 (April 1983): 15.

10. All quotations and additional details of the Conroy case are taken from the opinion of the court, delivered by J. Schreiber, *In the matter of* Claire C. Conroy, Supreme Court of New Jersey, A-108, decided January 17, 1985.

6 DETERMINING INCOMPETENCY

1. James F. Drane, "Competency to Give an Informed Consent," *Journal of the American Medical Association* 252 (August 17, 1984): 925–27.

7   DECIDING FOR OTHERS

1. *In re* Clark, 185 N.E. 2d 128, 1962, p. 131.

2. Joseph Goldstein, "Medical Care for the Child at Risk," in Willard Gaylin and Ruth Macklin, eds., *Who Speaks for the Child? The Problems of Proxy Consent* (New York: Plenum Press, 1982), p. 160.

3. Details about Roman law from Barry Nicholas, *An Introduction to Roman Law* (London: Oxford University Press, 1962).

4. *In re* Quinlan, cited in Allen E. Buchanan, "The Limits of Proxy Decision-making for Incompetents," *UCLA Law Review* 29 (1981): 389–90, n. 17.

5. Cited in George J. Annas, "The Incompetent's Right to Die: The Case of Joseph Saikewicz," *Hastings Center Report* 8 (February 1978): 22.

6. President's Commission for the Study of Ethical Problems in Medicine and Biomedical and Behavioral Research, *Deciding to Forego Life-Sustaining Treatment*, pp. 133–34, n. 38.

8   THE "BEST INTEREST" OF THE CHILD

1. Joseph Goldstein, Anna Freud, and Albert J. Solnit, *Beyond the Best Interests of the Child* (New York: Free Press, 1973, 1979).

2. Ibid., p. 54.

3. 45 CFR Part 1340, *Federal Register*, April 15, 1985, pp. 14878–901.

4. Raymond S. Duff and A. G. M. Campbell, "Moral and Ethical Dilemmas in the Special-Care Nursery," *New England Journal of Medicine* 289 (October 25, 1973): 890–94.

5. George J. Annas, "Baby Doe Redux: Doctors as Child Abusers," *Hastings Center Report* 13 (October 1983): 26.

6. Bowen v. American Hospital Association, 54 LW 4579 (June 9, 1986).

7. 45 CFR Part 1340, p. 14888.

8. Quoted in Bonnie Steinbock, "Baby Jane Doe in the Courts," *Hastings Center Report* 14 (February 1984): 17.

9. Richard A. McCormick, "To Save or Let Die: The Dilemma of Modern Medicine," *Journal of the American Medical Association*, vol. 229 (July 8, 1974), reprinted in Gorovitz et al., *Moral Problems in Medicine*, 2nd ed. (Englewood Cliffs, N.J.: Prentice-Hall, 1983), pp. 396–402.

10. Ibid., p. 400.

11. Ibid., p. 401.

12. *Deciding to Forego Life-Sustaining Treatment*, p. 218.

13. Ibid., p. 219.

14. John D. Arras, "Toward an Ethic of Ambiguity," *Hastings Center Report* 14 (April 1984): 31.

10   ALLOCATING SCARCE RESOURCES

1. M. Pabst Battin, "Two Cardiac Arrests, One Medical Team," *Hastings Center Report* 12 (April 1982): 25.

2. G. E. Thibault et al., "Medical Intensive Care: Indications, Interventions, and Outcomes," *New England Journal of Medicine* 302 (1980): 938–42.

3. Details on the history of renal dialysis taken from Richard A. Rettig, "The Policy Debate on Patient Care Financing for Victims of End-Stage Renal Disease," *Law and Contemporary Problems* 40 (Autumn 1976): 201–03.

4. Amy Gutmann, "For and Against Equal Access to Health Care," *Milbank Memorial Fund Quarterly, Health and Society* 59 (1981): 542–60.

5. Robert Schwartz and Andrew Grubb, "Why Britain Can't Afford Informed Consent," *Hastings Center Report* 15 (August 1985): 24.

6. Reported in *Hastings Center Report* 15 (August 1985): 3.

7. Ibid.

8. The original principle was stated by John Rawls in his book *A Theory of Justice* (Cambridge, Mass.: Harvard University Press, Belknap Press, 1971), p. 302.

9. Schwartz and Grubb, p. 24.

11 CONFLICTING OBLIGATIONS

1. Details of the case taken from Dennis W. Daley, "*Tarasoff* and the Psychotherapist's Duty to Warn," *San Diego Law Review* 12 (July 1975): 932–51.

2. 13 Cal. 3d 177, 529 P.2d 553, 118 Cal. Rptr. 129 (1974).

3. Neil L. Chayet, "Confidentiality and Privileged Communication," *New England Journal of Medicine* 275 (November 3, 1966): 1009–10, reprinted in Gorovitz et al., pp. 233–34.

4. Oliver Wendell Holmes, Buck v. Bell, 274 U.S. 200; 47 S.Ct. 584, 71 L.Ed. 1000 (1927).

5. Ruth Macklin and Willard Gaylin, eds., *Mental Retardation and Sterilization* (New York: Plenum Press, 1981), pp. 63–79; 167–80.

6. Quotations and information about Carrie Buck and her family taken from Paul A. Lombardo, "Three Generations, No Imbeciles: New Light on *Buck* v. *Bell*," *New York University Law Review* 60 (April 1985): 30–62.

7. Cited in George J. Annas, "Forced Cesareans: The Most Unkindest Cut of All," *Hastings Center Report* 12 (June 1982): 16.

8. Ibid.

12 EXPERIMENTING ON HUMAN SUBJECTS

1. National Commission for the Protection of Human Subjects of Biomedical and Behavioral Research, *The Belmont Report: Ethical Principles and Guidelines for the Protection of Human Subjects of Research* (Washington, D.C., April 18, 1979), p. 4.

2. 45 CFR 46, *Federal Register*, January 26, 1981, pp. 8386–89.

3. Elinor Langer, "Human Experimentation: New York Verdict Affirms Patient's Rights," *Science*, vol. 151 (February 1966), reprinted in Gorovitz et al., pp. 626–32.

4. "Protection of Human Subjects," Code of Federal Regulations, 45 CFR 46, revised as of March 8, 1983, p. 16.

5. The conference, entitled "The Definition of Research and the IRB," was held September 28–29, 1983. This author was a participant in the research group and attended that meeting.

6. "Latest Heart Recipient's Bleeding Has Almost Stopped, Doctor Says," *New York Times*, April 18, 1985.

7. Ibid.

8. *New York Times*, January 7, 1985.

1 3 HARMING AND WRONGING PATIENTS

1. National Institute on Aging Task Force, "Senility Reconsidered: Treatment Possibilities for Mental Impairment in the Elderly," *Journal of the American Medical Association* 244 (1980): 259–63.

2. James E. Groves, "Taking Care of the Hateful Patient," *New England Journal of Medicine* 298 (1978): 883–87.

1 4 RESOLVING THE ISSUES

1. Michael Tooley, "Abortion and Infanticide," *Philosophy and Public Affairs*, vol. 2 (Fall 1972), reprinted in Gorovitz et al., p. 309.

2. U.S. Congress, Senate, *A Bill to Provide That Human Life Shall Be Deemed to Exist from Conception*, S. 158, 97th Cong., 1st sess., 1981.

3. Ronald Cranford and A. Edward Doudera, eds., *Institutional Ethics Committees and Health Care Decision Making* (Ann Arbor: Health Administration Press, 1985); see Section II: Descriptive Summaries of Extant Institutional Ethics Committees.

Index

RUTH MACKLIN is professor of bioethics in the Department of Epidemiology and Social Medicine at Albert Einstein College of Medicine, in New York. In 1958 she received a B.A. degree in philosophy from Cornell University with Distinction, and later was awarded a Masters and Ph.D. in philosophy from Case Western Reserve University in Cleveland, where she taught until 1976. Before being appointed to a full-time position at Einstein in 1980, Dr. Macklin was an associate for behavioral studies at the Hastings Center, an internationally renowned research institute devoted to ethics and the life sciences, located in Hastings-on-Hudson, N.Y. She lectures widely on biomedical ethics to professional and community audiences, has served as a consultant to local and federal government agencies, and has authored numerous books and articles.